HOWARD CLARK KEE

COMMUNITY OF THE NEW AGE:
STUDIES IN MARK'S GOSPEL

HOWARD CLARK KEE

COMMUNITY OF THE NEW AGE

Studies in Mark's Gospel

THE WESTMINSTER PRESS
Philadelphia

Scripture quotations from the Revised Standard Version of the Bible are copyright, 1946 and 1952, by the Division of Christian Education of the National Council of Churches, and are used by permission.

Published by The Westminster Press
®
Philadelphia, Pennsylvania

PRINTED IN THE UNITED STATES OF AMERICA

Library of Congress Cataloging in Publication Data

Kee, Howard Clark.
   Community of the new age.

   Includes index.
    1. Bible. N.T. Mark — Criticism, interpretation, etc. I. Title.
BS2585.2.K43   226'.3'06   76-49484
ISBN 0-664-20770-7

CONTENTS

FOREWORD

The New Testament theologian can approach his task with considerable freedom. He is at liberty to choose the perspective from which he will launch his inquiry from a number of New Testament possibilities. Leading theologians of the present century, for example, have chosen Paul as their norm for evaluating New Testament theology – or the Gospel of John, or the beatitudes, or the kerygma. Once a norm is established, one has a framework within which interpretation can take place.

The task of the historian of Christian origins, on the other hand, is not so clear cut. He must take into account not only the diverse perspectives within the New Testament writings themselves, but also a vast spectrum of social and cultural situations out of which these writings and related Christian literature arose. The orthodox church denounced as *docetic* the denial of the true humanity of Jesus. Yet much of what passes for historical writing about the New Testament is docetic. It fails to take account of the full range of social and cultural factors that shaped the Christian communities and their ideas, their understanding of themselves, and their place in the universe.

Fortunately, recent decades have seen the beginning of a shift in historical method as it relates to biblical studies. Social and cultural factors, in their bearing on historical reconstruction of early Christianity, are taken more seriously now than earlier. As potential aids to understanding how Christianity began, the methods of sociology and sociology of knowledge are being employed. Scholars are dealing with questions such as these: What were the potent though not explicitly acknowledged assumptions that shaped the values, the view of reality, the aspirations of the early Christians? Were those factors identical for the urban, middle-class Christians in Corinth or Rome and for the semi-literate villagers in Syria? Why are Jesus' disciples portrayed as hurrying from village to village, while Paul and his companions seek to build enduring organizations in the major cities?

The present work has at least two goals: to employ a social-cultural-historical method in New Testament study, and to do so by beginning with one of the most enigmatic books in the New Testament: the Gospel of Mark. I have written it with the primary focus on the text of Mark itself, but in full recognition that New Testament study is a collegial enterprise. Accordingly, the first part of the work seeks to assess and to shift the focus of the traditional critical approaches to the New Testament. The second part moves back and forth between historical and sociological models and the community in and for which the Gospel of Mark was produced.

As colleagues I have included both established figures and younger scholars, whose unpublished work I have been privileged to read in my capacity as Editor of the Dissertation Series of the Society of Biblical Literature. Many of the details of what I have surveyed here were worked out for articles published in journals or *Festschriften*, or for papers presented at learned societies. Some of the material was presented as Lectures in the February 1975 Convocation at Lexington (Kentucky) Theological Seminary; other ideas were developed in seminars in Berkeley, California, where I was Guest Scholar at the Graduate Theological Union for the academic year 1974–75. The sessions of the Biblical-Sociological Seminar, chaired by Norman Gottwald, and the meetings of the Center for Hermeneutical Studies, guided by Wilhelm Wuellner, were especially stimulating. For hospitality at the GTU and at the University of California, Berkeley, and for the help of the library staffs, especially at the Pacific School of Religion, I am deeply grateful. The Madge Miller Fund at Bryn Mawr College helped with the expense of typing the manuscript. Norman Gottwald and Norman Perrin read the entire manuscript at a penultimate stage, and they offered encouragement and helpful suggestions. William G. Doty gave it a critical reading in the final form; his comments will, I hope, improve its readability.

During the past decade Norman Perrin's work on Mark has developed along lines that parallel and frequently converge with my own research. This is especially evident in his treatment of Mark in his *The New Testament: An Introduction* (New York 1974), and in his *Jesus and the Language of the Kingdom* (Philadelphia and London 1976), where he stresses the function of apocalyptic language for Mark's interpretation of Jesus. The writings of Professor Perrin's students at Chicago have broadened the base of challenge and of contribution to my own study of Mark. He and I began our research quite independently, but in many respects have arrived at similar conclusions. The stimulus from his writings and that of his students has contributed significantly to the Markan Seminar of the Society of Biblical Literature in which we all participate, along with a score of other colleagues. As a sign of my respect for his learning and my gratitude for the scholarly friendship and collegiality I have enjoyed with him, it is to Norman Perrin of the University of Chicago that this book is dedicated.

Bryn Mawr, Pennsylvania   H OWARD C LARK K EE
New Year's Day, 1976

ABBREVIATIONS

ATR	*Anglican Theological Review*
BA	*The Biblical Archaeologist*
BZNW	Beiheft zur Zeitschrift für die neutestamentliche Wissenschaft
ET	English translation
FRLANT	Forschungen zur Religion und Literatur des Alten und Neuen Testaments
HTR	*Harvard Theological Review*
IB	*The Interpreter's Bible*
IDB	*The Interpreter's Dictionary of the Bible*
IEJ	*Israel Exploration Journal*
JAAR	*Journal of the American Academy of Religion*
JBL	*Journal of Biblical Literature*
JR	*Journal of Religion*
JTC	*Journal for Theology and Church*
KEK	Kritisch-exegetischer Kommentar über das NT (Meyer)
LXX	Septuagint translation of the Old Testament
MT	Massoretic text
NCB	New Century Bible
NICC	New International Critical Commentary
NovT	*Novum Testamentum*
NS	New series
NTS	*New Testament Studies*
RB	*Revue Biblique*
RHPR	*Revue d'Histoire et de Philosophie Religieuses*
SBL	Society for Biblical Literature
SBT	Studies in Biblical Theology
SUNT	Studien zur Umwelt des NT
TDNT	*Theological Dictionary of the New Testament*
VT	*Vetus Testamentum*
ZNW	*Zeitschrift für die neutestamentliche Wissenschaft*
ZPE	*Zeitschrift für Papyrologie und Epigraphik*
ZTK	*Zeitschrift für Theologie und Kirche*

I

PROBLEMS OF METHOD
IN THE STUDY OF MARK

'Ultimately a cloud remains over the question of Mark's aim . . .'[1]
Those are the disheartening but apposite words pronounced by
W. G. Kümmel towards the end of his comprehensive survey of the
hypotheses adduced in the past three-quarters of a century concerning 'The Literary Character and Theological Aim of the Gospel of
Mark'. On the specific subject of Markan christology, Kümmel is
even more explicit: 'A clear explanation that takes into account all
the facts concerning the christological aim of the evangelist has not
yet been elicited from the text.'[2] Yet, the very fact that both of these
penetrating and just observations were written with special focus on
messiahship/christology in Mark should serve as a double warning.
First, that if the christological question in Mark, on which major
interest has centred, is not settled, how much less satisfactory is the
clarification of other related issues. And secondly, perhaps an
approach to Mark which begins with almost exclusive concern for
the christological problem is not asking the right questions, and is
therefore precluding arrival at satisfactory answers. What wider
factors should be included in an investigation that might yield more
positive results in the search for the aim of Mark?

E. D. Hirsch, in his brilliant hermeneutical study, *Validity in
Interpretation*, deals primarily with the meaning of self-conscious
literary works, but much that he observes about interpretative method
in the literary realm has a direct bearing on the task of the interpreter
of such popular quasi-literary documents as Mark. Hirsch states that
the aim of interpretation is to specify the work's horizon as precisely
as possible.

> By classifying the text as belonging to a particular genre, the interpreter automa-
> tically posits a general horizon for its meaning. The genre provides a sense
> of the whole, a notion of typical meaning components . . . The probability

of an interpreter's inference may be judged by two criteria alone – the accuracy with which he has sensed the horizon of the whole and the typicality of such a meaning within such a whole.

This procedure, Hirsch declares,

simply renders explicit that which was, consciously or unconsciously, in the author's intention.

For our purposes, perhaps the most important facet of Hirsch's principles is that of the necessity to determine the author's horizon:

It is of the utmost importance to determine the horizon which defines the author's intention as a whole, for it is only with reference to this horizon, or sense of the whole, that the interpreter may distinguish those implications which are typical and proper components of the meaning from those which are not.[3]

The 'cloud' that continues to hover over past attempts to interpret Mark, and thus to determine his aim, has resulted from premature and inadequate judgments as to what Mark's horizon was. The difficulties in overcoming that problem are enormous. The task is difficult enough in analysing any work of ancient literature, but it is complicated in the case of Mark by the fact that we are dealing with an anonymous work of unknown provenance. Ancient guesses about Markan aims and origins (see below) are no more helpful than most modern conjectures. Mark's sources cannot be determined with even the limited degree of assurance that can be attained with respect to the sources of Matthew and Luke. Not only has our knowledge of the circumstances surrounding primitive Christianity prior to the end of the first century AD been limited, until recently, almost entirely to the New Testament writings, but our picture of conditions in first-century Palestine had to be derived from the anachronistic, idealized records written down in the second and subsequent centuries by the one Jewish group that survived the Roman destruction of Jerusalem in AD 70 (the Pharisees) and from the apologetic, self-serving account of that literarily prolific turncoat, Flavius Josephus. Since 1950, new evidence about Palestinian Judaism in the first and early second centuries has been made available, and more seems to be on the way, from manuscript finds and from archaeological evidence. Welcome as this new material is, however, it will not resolve the interpretative question about Mark unless new questions are asked. The 'horizon' of Mark must be extended to include not only the literary and conceptual models with which biblical scholars have been accustomed to deal, but models from the realm of social history as well, if we are to determine Mark's actual 'intention'. Without some clues as to the *cultural setting* in which the vocabulary and the literary forms found in Mark – or any other anonymous writing – were produced, we cannot avoid reading unwarranted or at least highly dubious meanings into his gospel. Without due attention to the *social dynamics* that were operative in the community by and for whom Mark was produced, we cannot reach conclusions about the cultural setting, and therefore about the writer's intention. *Sociological models* must be examined in order to try to reconstruct how such a community would have emerged. *Historical models* must be scrutinized to see how the community behind Mark was parallel to or must be differentiated from groups of the same general type.

Social philosophers have been speaking recently of a 'life-world' as the natural and social setting which provides a person with both arena and limits of action. Each step of understanding of that world is based on one's stock of experience as well as on experiences that are transmitted by one's fellows, especially parents, teachers, peers. A person's knowledge of his world is never private, but is inter-subjective, and thus a social reality, since what is given in his societal setting provides meanings and relevances and interpretations of all that he experiences. His plans, types, attitudes, and designs of action are acquired in a succession of social situations. Peter Berger has described man as 'congenitally compelled to impose a meaningful order upon reality'. The society is a human construction of externalized and objective meanings by which man seeks to establish a 'meaningful totality', or 'a shield against terror'. In interpreting a document like Mark, therefore, the horizon must include attention to the *life-world* or 'sacred canopy' in which the community that lies behind this work displays its own attempt to impose a meaningful order.[4]

Philological, literary, and conceptual modes alone or in isolation from the nature of the community will not be adequate, therefore, to remove the 'cloud' over Mark's gospel. Only when we have some precise sense of the social and cultural factors within the community that produced Mark and to which it was primarily addressed – including the life-world in which the community discovered its meaning and purpose – can we determine the horizon of the literary, conceptual, and linguistic modes that the document employs.

1. TRADITIONAL AND FORM-CRITICAL VIEWS OF MARKAN ORIGINS

Many of the ingredients essential to this undertaking have been assessed or at least considered by historians and biblical critics since the close of the nineteenth century, yet more attention has been devoted to the other gospels than to Mark. Wrede's study of the Messianic secret in Mark (considered below, pp. 167ff.) is a notable exception to the neglect of Mark, but perhaps its radical results, theologically and historically, deterred others from following his lead. Among scholars and interpreters of conservative bent, there has often been a determination to cling to the familiar claim of Papias that Mark had been the interpreter of Peter and that he had written down 'accurately all that he remembered of the things said and done by the Lord'.[5]

Even though a consensus emerged earlier in the present century, based on the analyses of the range of possible relationships and dependences among the gospels – namely, that Mark had been used by Luke and Matthew as a basic source – it was nevertheless the patristic testimony about the gospels which functioned, consciously or unconsciously, as the norm for determination of Mark's origins, with the result that in exegetical and theological practice it was St Augustine's low estimate of Mark that prevailed: Mark was a slave following in Matthew's footsteps and his abbreviator (*pedisequus et breviator*).[6] The fact that as early as the second half of the second century Matthew stood before Mark, not only in canonical sequence but in esteem as well, indicates the tacit assumption within the early church and in modern times that Mark is exceeded in glory by the larger, more systematic gospel, Matthew.

The relative neglect of Mark can be readily understood. Conservatives tended to follow the impressive leadership of H. J. Holtzmann, who in the 1860s had not only demonstrated the priority of Mark, but had found in that gospel a reliable historical account of Jesus' career, on the basis of which the development of his messianic consciousness could be traced.[7] The radical conclusions about Jesus' eschatological outlook reached independently by Johannes Weiss[8] and Albert Schweitzer[9] confirmed the impression of Mark as a mysterious, theologically intractable book. The demonstration by William Wrede that the secrecy motif had been imposed on the material by the evangelist[10] undermined confidence in the historical reliability of the gospel, while leaving unanswered the tantalizing question as to how Jesus had actually viewed his own mission.

Still more radical in its method – though potentially more constructive in its results – was the rise of *Formgeschichte*, the aims, methods, and limitations of which we must scrutinize in some detail. In offering here yet another survey of the familiar history of the form-critical method,[11] we focus attention on one aspect of that critical development: its import for the study of Mark.

The method of identifying and classifying smaller narrative, didactic and liturgical units lying behind the written text had been developed by H. Gunkel in studying the Old Testament against the background of the ancient Near East, and in his reconstruction of the development of early Christianity as well.[12] Under Gunkel's influence, Dibelius had drawn attention in his study of John the Baptist[13] to the two methodological conclusions concerning the gospels and the tradition embedded in them: that the gospel writers (whom he did not regard as authors, but as collectors, preservers of tradition) had added to the tradition such items as references to time and place, connecting links of a pragmatic sort, and summary reports; and that both sayings and narrative material existed in fixed oral forms before being incorporated by the evangelist into his gospel writing. At almost precisely the same time that Dibelius published his full-scale work on the second of these insights, *Die Formgeschichte des Evangeliums*, in 1919,[14] K. L. Schmidt produced a study in which he reconstructed and analysed the framework into which Mark had presumably incorporated the sayings and narrative tradition.[15] In his summary description of the framework of Mark, Schmidt states that Mark's specific aims are 'not immediately clear', though they are linked with 'the religious, missionary and apologetic interests' of primitive Christianity.[16] That view scarcely provides a precise picture of Mark as thinker or of the community for and to which he is writing.

Dibelius was most explicit in giving his estimate of the literary quality of the evangelists, especially of Matthew and Mark:

> Without a doubt these are unliterary writings. They should not and could not be compared with 'literary' works . . . They are collections of material. The composers are only to the smallest extent authors. They are principally collectors of tradition, editors. Before all else their labour consists in handing down, grouping, and working over the material which has come to them.[17]

He went on to observe 'how lowly' was the degree by which they 'may pass as authors', as decried the tendency to attribute to them responsibility for reshaping the tradition in terms of their own inclinations, 'just as if we were dealing with Belles Lettres'.[18] About all that Dibelius would grant to Mark was that, utilizing the passion narrative, the brief collection(s) of miracle stories, groups of sayings, and parables, he imposed on the whole his rather loose biographical interest and his theory of the secret epiphanies (Jesus was recognized as Messiah during his lifetime only by those to whom he disclosed it).[19] All this is thrice-familiar to students of the New Testament. But what has been largely overlooked, or if noted has been skewed, is that Dibelius stressed in the methodological introduction to his basic work on form criticism that *style was an essential clue to the socio-cultural setting out of which a popular document like Mark would have come.*[20] And he invoked the term *Sitz im Leben,* employed by his teacher Gunkel and others, to call attention to 'the historical and social stratum in which . . . these literary forms were developed'.[21] But the closest Dibelius came to the identification of a *Sitz im Leben* for the gospel traditions was an occasional general reference to 'the pre-Pauline Hellenistic Christianity' in Syria,[22] or simply the Palestinian church,[23] concerning which he acknowledged that we have no direct information.[24]

It is the more surprising, therefore, to turn from Dibelius to Rudolf Bultmann, the other major figure in the development of the form-critical method, whose major work in the field appeared in 1921.[25] Bultmann, in outlining the circular method according to which 'the forms of the literary tradition must be used to establish the influences operating in the life of the community, and the life of the community must be used to render the forms themselves intelligible',[26] observed that Dibelius reconstructs the history of the synoptic tradition 'from a study of the community and its needs'.[27] Yet, as we have noted, Dibelius had nearly nothing to say on the specific nature of the community. While Bultmann set up as 'the one chief problem of primitive Christianity, the relationship of the primitive Palestinian and Hellenistic Christianity', he did not begin to explore that question with the same thoroughness that he devoted to the literary and exegetical analysis of the gospel texts.[28] The negative consequence of Bultmann's simple dual classification of primitive Christianity is baldly evident in his characterization of Mark as having impressed the tradition 'with a meaning such as it needed in the Hellenistic churches of Paul's persuasion . . . Mark could well have been the normal Gospel for Pauline Hellenistic Christianity'. The purpose of the author of Mark is: '*The union of the Hellenistic kerygma about Christ,* whose essential content consists of the Christ myth as we learn of it in Paul (esp. Phil. 2.6ff.; Rom. 3.24) with *the tradition of the story of Jesus.*'[29] As we shall observe in our detailed analysis of Mark, none of the characteristic theological language of Paul appears in Mark, or if roughly similar terms occur, they are used in a significantly different conceptual framework. Bultmann's assumption that Hellenistic Christianity was a unified entity over against a unified Palestinian Christianity is a methodological lapse. If the form critics never declared this explicitly, it is assumed and implicit throughout their work. And this assumption precludes a careful posing of the question to which both Dibelius and Bultmann pointed: What was the histori-

cal, social situation implicit in and presupposed by the Gospel of Mark?
From their works and on the basis of the methodological ground rules
by which they actually function, no satisfactory answer can be forthcoming.

2. THE SEARCH FOR A *SITZ IM LEBEN* FOR MARK

In some respects, the lack of positive results from K. L. Schmidt's
study of Mark is both more surprising and more disappointing.
Schmidt drew attention to several features of Mark which had the
potential for elucidating the aims of Mark and for bringing into focus
the community aims which gave rise to the document. Thus, he
recognized the summarizing sections (*Sammelberichte*) that bind the
gospel together and give it the sense of sequence: 1.17ff.; 1.39; 2.13;
3.7–12; 5.21; 6.6b; 6.12f.; 6.30–33; 6.53–56; 10.1. Recent work on
this material has clarified and amplified awareness of the function
that this connective material served in Mark's overall literary
scheme,[30] but Schmidt's basic insight has been confirmed by subsequent study. From these summaries, however, Schmidt drew only the
largely negative conclusion that Mark did not have access to, or at
least did not employ, any geographical or chronological framework
for the career of Jesus.[31] Even the passion narrative, Schmidt asserted,
was in its chronological and topographical framework the product of
Mark. It had been preserved originally in fragments, but the arrangement of the details in their present sequence was the work of Mark.[32]
Thus Schmidt's analysis demanded an answer to the problem that he
posed: Why did Mark create this structure of Jesus' career as the
outline of his gospel?

Regrettably, his answer was general and undeveloped: worship in
the early church created the need for the gospel literature.[33] The
Jesus tradition, as preserved in the gospels, is cultically determined; it
is thus pictorial and suprahistorical. The church required such a
quasi-biographical, connected account of Jesus to meet liturgical and
apologetic needs.[34] Apart from the problem of the crucified Messiah,
Schmidt offered little by way of explanation of what these needs were
or how Mark served to meet them. An enduring basic methodological
insight was present in his work – differentiation of tradition from the
framework in which it has been placed by the evangelist – but Schmidt
could not follow through to discover concretely the purpose that Mark
as a whole served within the community by and for whom it was
created.

Within two years of each other, two works appeared that sought to locate – literally – the community that produced Mark: E. Loh-meyer's *Galiläa und Jerusalem*,[35] and R. H. Lightfoot's *Locality and Doctrine in the Gospels*.[36] Both these studies advanced the same basic thesis: that Mark was oriented towards Galilee, which he believed to be the sphere of revelation, as contrasted with Jerusalem, the sphere of rejection and judgment.[37] Without asserting that Mark was actually written in Galilee,[38] Lightfoot tried to show that for Mark the place was of paramount importance and that he expected the fulfilment of Jesus' redemptive mission to take place there.[39] But Lightfoot was able to tell us nothing further about a Galilee-oriented Christianity. Apart from the historical recollection that Jesus' activity and that of his disciples had begun there, and the dogmatic antithesis between Galilee and Jerusalem, which determined even the structure of Mark, according to Lightfoot,[40] there is no interrogation of the text of Mark with the aim of determining the nature of the community that produced the Gospel of Mark, the dogma and outline of which pivot upon Galilee.

By contrast, full-scale investigations of the literary and cultural background of Luke-Acts were carried out in the multi-volumed study, *The Beginnings of Christianity*, Part I, by F. J. Foakes-Jackson, K. Lake, and H. J. Cadbury.[41] By studies of inscriptional evidence, ancient historiography and rhetoric, source analyses, comparison between historical evidence presented in Luke-Acts and that available in pagan sources of the period, this impressive work fulfilled in a relatively effective way the assignment outlined above by E. D. Hirsch: to determine as precisely as possible the horizon of typical expectations and probabilities.[42] Yet even this impressive work did not take fully into account the 'life-world' dimensions of Luke-Acts, nor have more recent studies of the theological aims of Luke's work been wholly successful either in offering a convincing reconstruction of his theological outlook or in recreating the world-view that these documents embody.[43]

Still less successful have been the studies of Matthew.[44] Hampered by the difficulty in dating the rabbinic sources adduced as parallels, and not taking fully into account the diversity of Judaism in the period before AD 70, these learned, massive works shed effective light on a part of the possible background of Matthew's gospel, but do not succeed in reconstructing the community which lies behind the first gospel.[45]

In the case of Mark, however, nothing comparable in scope has been attempted. To be sure, there are large and learned com-mentaries.[46] And there has been a string of studies of themes in

Mark, beginning with the first to use the *redaktionsgeschichtlich* method – W. Marxsen's *Mark the Evangelist* – back in 1954, with the tide rising in recent years.[47] A useful, though one-sided, survey of some of these contributions is offered in J. Rohde, *Rediscovering the Teaching of* the Evangelists.[48] In every case, the writer has seized on a theme which he considers to be central, and in terms of which the whole gospel is to be understood.[49] The most impressive work on Mark is the huge commentary of E. Haenchen; yet, the author announces that the basic thesis of Mark is the identity of the earthly Jesus and the exalted Lord, so that he finds the organizing motif to be that enunciated more than fifty years ago by Martin Dibelius: 'the book of the secret epiphanies'.[50]

To the extent that the historical setting of Mark has been considered by its interpreters, scholars have been almost wholly content to utilize stereotypes of the situation in Judaism at the time of Jesus and in the period down to AD 70. But most interpreters of Mark have not been concerned with much beyond the theology of Mark, as though theological affirmations were formed during the early decades of the church's existence by a process of intellectual debate – the first-century equivalent of a present-day theological seminar! The crucial factors of the kind of community with which the author was identified, the social and cultural forces which shaped his existence, consciously and unconsciously, are almost wholly left out of account. In short, no serious effort is made to determine the horizon of the author of our earliest gospel.

3. Essential Elements for Interpreting Mark

What factors ought to be taken into account?

(i) *The literary genre of Mark*

There has been heated debate in recent years about the gospel as a genre, and about Mark's relationship to that genre.[51] Did he create it?[52] Or did he merely modify to his own ends an existing genre? The question is not inconsequential or trivial, since if Mark employed an existing literary model, it must also be asked whether there was a standard aim implicit in that genre and whether Mark shared the aim as well as the literary model. If, on the other hand, the genre was a literary *novum*, there must have been at least indirect influences and partial antecedents out of which Mark developed his new form. What were those ingredients? What aims did they embody? (These questions are considered in ch. II below.)

(ii) *The oral and written tradition utilized by Mark*

In addition to the problem of the overall form of Mark, the work of
form critics and that of literary critics before and since the rise of
form criticism has drawn attention to Mark's having taken over
already existing tradition into his gospel. Views on this subject range
from elaborate theories of older written sources incorporated by Mark
into his gospel[53] – or in other quarters, to the theory that Mark
represents an abridgment of another gospel[54] – through hypotheses
of very limited written sources used by Mark (the passion narrative,[55]
or a brief collection of miracle stories,[56] for example) to the conviction
that Mark worked from oral tradition only. Since this issue has
implications both for what the intention of the sources may have been
and for what Mark has done by way of adaptation of the sources to
serve his own ends, it too has important bearing on one's overall view
of Mark. (This is discussed in ch.II below.)

(iii) *The diversity of literary forms included in Mark*

Both kinds of literary analysis of Mark lead to wider questions about
the aims of Mark. Among the material incorporated into Mark are
moral teachings, wisdom sayings, interpretations of the Law, appeals
to scripture, parables, enigmatic sayings, apocalyptic pronouncements, miracle stories, instruction to the disciples, an extended account of Jesus' trial and death, as well as a briefer account of the
death of John the Baptist. Why such an agglomeration of disparate
material? And why such an abrupt, inconclusive ending (16.8) – if
indeed that is the original ending? This area of inquiry is, of course,
related to (i) above, since part of the difficulty about the question of
genre is created by the range of kinds of material brought together
within one short work such as Mark. Of course, if one adopts the
dictum of Martin Kähler that the gospel is a passion narrative with
an extended introduction,[57] the problem is eased somewhat, since
the preliminary material can be treated as relatively inconsequential. But the whole evidence must be carefully analysed before that
dictum can be responsibly adjudged to be valid for Mark. (See ch. II
below.)

(iv) *The interrelation of social, literary and conceptual modes: method in the study of Mark*

Analysis of Mark has been severely hampered by the failure to realize
that interpretation of the work of an unknown writer – unknown as to
chronological, geographical, or cultural setting – cannot be carried

out responsibly without engaging in a three-way exchange. The conceptual freight carried by the vocabulary and reinforced by the rhetorical and stylized modes of expression he employs cannot be fairly assessed in abstraction from the socio-cultural setting in which and for which the author prepared his work. Even if he is deviating from the norms of his community, he must at least have certain common meeting points which can then serve as points of departure. Without prejudging his originality, there must be some firmly established clues as to where he was when his modification or transformation of his tradition began. To the extent that he preserves set traditions, it is the more important to locate those traditions culturally.[58] The same may be said of the literary conventions that he employs. However creative and innovative he may be, there are bound to be areas of common style and structure from which the new tangents take off. And finally, however much a maverick or a rebel an author may be, he sees himself in relation to certain patterns of society, though he may repudiate or seek to transform those standards and values. For example, if Mark saw himself as the spokesman for a school tradition like that of the later rabbis, there are certain kinds of expectations or at least certain lines of inquiry to be pursued which would not be suitable if he was the paramilitary organizer of an insurrectionist movement.[59]

Obviously the main interest in the study of Mark is to discover how he understood the role of Jesus in relation to the community for which he was writing his gospel. But the theological paradigms cannot be utilized in the analysis of Mark in independence of the societal and the literary paradigms. Without the other two, the results are sterile or self-deceptive, or both. Only by means of a three-member conversation among these three modes of inquiry will it be possible to determine the horizon of Mark, and thereby to interpret his gospel.

One of the striking features of biblical studies in the past decade has been the emergence of such methodological consciousness.[60] A brilliant example of the fruitfulness of this triadic method of investigation is Martin Hengel's *Judaism and Hellenism* (London and Philadelphia 1974). A glance at the Table of Contents shows that Hengel begins his study of the period with due attention to political, economic, and cultural factors; against that background the literature is viewed. Judaism in the Hellenistic period is for him no disembodied spirit, nor is it a movement hermetically sealed off from the surrounding culture. On the contrary, the literature of the period becomes luminous when studied in its full-faceted setting. In a concentrated way, with focus on Mark alone, our aim is to locate Mark in his time and life-situation in order better to understand his gospel (see ch. IV below).

What might such a triangular method mean concretely in the analytical study of Mark? Suppose, for example, that one were to take as the decisive clue to the setting of Mark Schweitzer's proposal that the gospel is a presentation of Jesus as an apocalyptic figure who expected the kingdom of God to come very soon. If that conceptual framework were to be tested, we should expect this theological perspective to be mirrored in at least some aspects of the literary patterns of Mark; and of course that is the case for Mark 13, almost universally referred to as the 'Synoptic Apocalypse'. If, however, one were to regard Mark as basically a Hellenistic hero's life, then the focus might fall on the miracles – or so the theory runs – and elements like the apocalypse would have to recede to the periphery. But in either case – and in the case of any other working hypothesis – it would be essential to reconstruct simultaneously both the literary and conceptual models and the social dimensions of the community that might have interpreted Jesus in this way. Stated otherwise, whatever the intention of Mark may prove to be, it is not sufficient to analyse a propagandistic work like his solely as a literary form, or merely as a literary expression of a certain theological position. What is required is that the socio-cultural factors be taken fully into account, both as they are known from paradigms derivable from religious communities contemporary with Mark, and as the features may be inferred from the text of Mark itself.

It will be recalled that Bultmann asserted the interdependence of the literary forms and the 'influences operating in the life of the community'. It need not concern us whether Mark's gospel developed as a kind of cumulative or composite product, or whether it was consciously produced for the community by a single individual whose identity is lost to us. The final redactor or the author was clearly addressing himself to a community with which he identified, who shared certain values, interpretative methods, esoteric views, and for whose external welfare he had profound concerns. When we speak of 'Mark' or of the 'Markan community', we obviously do not have in mind a self-conscious man of letters or an editorial board assigned to the task of preparing a group document. Here we are not at all concerned to inquire concerning the degree to which the work is historically reliable or even the degree to which elements of the tradition may go back to Jesus. Rather, our interest is in the writer's (or writers') aim, and the dynamic factors shaping the segment of primitive Christianity which produced this remarkable document.

Accordingly, the procedure followed in this study is: initial focus on the literary questions, then on the socio-cultural features, and then on the paradigms for understanding the role of Jesus (ch. V below). In the final chapter we will come to the resulting composite picture: the nature and self-understanding of the community that is presupposed by Mark.

III

THE LITERARY ANTECEDENTS OF MARK

As an initial step towards identifying the community in which Mark was produced we have certain literary questions to raise here. Was there a gospel in existence before Mark wrote his? Did the author of the original gospel have a literary paradigm, of either Jewish or Hellenistic origin, that served him as a model for his own work? If Mark drew on existing collections of oral or written material, what were they and how did he modify them in employing them for his own purposes?

The familiar territory that his investigation must cover ought, however, to be explored afresh with more than purely literary issues in mind. Whatever the sources and paradigms that Mark may have employed, what was his aim in choosing this material and fashioning it into the literary whole that is his gospel? And what does his literary method tell us about his community?

1. DOES MARK HAVE PRIORITY AMONG THE GOSPELS?

If Mark had a predecessor as a gospel-writer, it would be instructive to see how he conformed to or diverged from his model. From the time of the ancient church down to the present, the candidate most frequently advanced as Mark's predecessor is Matthew.[1] The leading champion of the priority of Matthew at the present time, W. R. Farmer, acknowledged that Mark was the middle term between Matthew and Luke, by which he understood that Luke used Mark as one of his sources, while Mark drew his material from Matthew.[2] This interpretation of the evidence leaves unanswered a whole series of questions that were more readily answerable on the hypothesis of Markan priority. Why are Mark's versions of the narratives longer than Matthew's, and why do they contain details about Palestinian-Syrian village life not found in Matthew?[3] Why did the Markan copy contain theological difficulties[4] and stylistic infelicities[5] which were not found in the Matthean 'original'? Why does Mark reduce the more explicit theological affirmations of Matthew to vaguer statements?[6] Why are more explicit indications of fulfilment of scripture in Matthew offered in less explicit form in Mark?[7] Why does Mark change the public announcement of Jesus as Son of God at his baptism (Matt.3.17) into a private disclosure to Jesus alone (Mark 1.11)?

Turning to the matter of omissions, why — on the theory of Matthaean priority – would Mark have omitted the Sermon on the Mount and nearly all the other discourse material found in Matthew? Why does he omit the birth and infancy stories? Why does he break off the narrative with the empty tomb and the instruction to the disciples?[8] Why does Mark offer the response of Jesus to a request for a sign (Mark 8.11) in such an absolutely negative form, expressed in an awkward, probably Semitic syntax (literally, 'If a sign shall be given to this generation!') when he had available in his exemplar not one but two versions of the saying (Matt. 16.4 and 12.39), both of them in smoother Greek, both ending on the more positive note of promising 'the sign of Jonah', and one of the most explicit indications of fulfilment of scripture in the whole of the gospel tradition: 'three days and three nights in the belly of the whale/heart of the earth' (Matt.12.40)? Why, given Mark's special interest in Galilee, has he omitted Matthew's account of the appearance of Jesus to the disciples on 'a mountain in Galilee' (Matt.28.15)? The list could be extended almost indefinitely.

Recently, however, Farmer has complicated his own theory by suggesting that perhaps Luke employed Matthew directly as a source, as well as Mark, which he knew and used.[9] While this approach could account for the non-Markan material common to Matthew and Luke without resorting to the Q hypothesis,[10] it leaves unexplained why Luke and Matthew are utterly divergent in their respective accounts of Jesus until they reach the point of the earliest parallel with Mark (Mark 1.2 = Matt.3.2 = Luke 3.4) and why they go their separate ways after the best text of Mark ends (at 16.8). Nor can this theory explain why, when Matthew and Luke differ from each other in sequence of material, one of them always conforms to the Markan order. Phenomena which can be accounted for on the hypothesis of Mark as the middle term between Matthew and Luke cannot be explained on Farmer's emerging theory of Matthew as the middle term between Luke and Mark.[11] The work of Farmer, as well as that of B. Morgenthaler[12] and E. R. Sanders,[13] has had sobering, salutary results, especially in relation to challenging overly simple theories about the sayings tradition. By demonstrating the difficulties in defining the Q document and by pointing up the complexities of the tradition, these studies have irreparably undermined the neat precision of the Four Source hypothesis of B. H. Streeter,[14] with its four sharply defined sources.[15]

True, the statistical analysis offered by Morgenthaler is not conclusive. What it shows about Markan priority is, however, impressive. For example, of the 11,078 words in Mark, 8,555 have been taken over by Matthew and 6,737 by Luke.[16] Put another way, of 855 sentences in Mark, 709 are reproduced in Matthew and 565 in Luke, and of these Matthew agrees with Mark in exact words and order in 136 sentences.[17] If one were to arrange the whole of this common material in which there is word-for-word agreement, placing Mark in the centre, Matthew on the left and Luke on the right, there would be 4,000 lines of connection to Matthew and 2,500 to Luke, of which no more than half a dozen would cross.[18] Thus, in the very places where the wording of the sentences is identical, the sequence of the material is very nearly identical as well. One would have to conclude that Mark simply lopped off great sections of the sayings material to the extent of cutting the gospel in half,[19] if he had used Matthew as his source. On the other hand, these phenomena can readily be accounted for if Matthew was using Mark as his source. And that supposition receives incontrovertible support when the language of Mark and Matthew is compared: Mark's style, which is simple and vivid but also crude and awkward, does not read like an abridgment of the more sophisticated language of Matthew. And in the narrative sections, Matthew has the briefer version of the accounts, with much of the vivid detail missing[20] and some theological problems smoothed over as well.[21] Morgenthaler is right when he adds to his strictly statistical conclusions the judgment that Mark gives the impression of immediacy, originality, directness, and freshness, all of which are lacking in Matthew's and Luke's versions of the Markan material.[22] The very fact that these detailed literary features of the gospels – and in our case, of Mark – cannot be explained statistically[23] is the consequence of the gospels having been produced by human beings rather than by computers.[24] And these human beings were living and reacting in concrete historical, social settings, with the result that each evangelist's handling of the Jesus tradition differs significantly from that of his fellows. This aspect of Mark is our primary concern, and the evidence points to his having been the first of the canonical writers to undertake the task of writing a gospel.[25]

Theories on Genre

2. Did Mark have a Literary Paradigm for his Gospel?

But a prior question must be considered. Among the literary influences that might have led the author of the earliest gospel to write his account of Jesus' words and actions in the form that he chose, was there a comprehensive model that he followed or adapted? Do we have evidence for a literary model, demonstrably employed by the middle of the first century AD or earlier, that might have been used by Mark as a paradigm for his own work?

Possible model

(i) *Mark as aretalogy*

In recent years the hypothesis has been advanced, or the assumption has been made, that Mark is an adaptation of a literary genre known as *aretalogy*, and widely used in late antiquity.[26] Specifically it is assumed by proponents of this theory that there was in Hellenistic–Roman times a fixed literary form called *aretalogy* and that an (or the) outstanding feature of an aretalogy is an account of miracles attributed to a god or to a divinized man. The inference is then drawn that the Gospel of Mark, which reports the miracles of Jesus and identifies him as 'Son of God', is a Christian aretalogy.

Thesis

What is the evidence, ancient and modern, for the appropriateness of 'aretalogy' as the literary prototype of the gospel (including Mark)? The term is relatively rare in antiquity; it is used for reports of the deeds of a god, usually in connection with a cult, and does not represent a fixed literary form.[27] In recent discussion of aretalogy, the term has been defined as a biographical writing in which an impressive teacher possessed of supernatural powers encounters the hostility of the authorities and is martyred.[28] But the examples used to justify this definition do not in fact manifest these features. Several scholars who use the term are forced to assert that they mean by aretalogy no more than a collection of miracle stories, devoid of connective tissue, and that these strings of wonder stories do not resemble the canonical gospels.[29] Although Philostratus' *Life of Apollonius of Tyana* is still singled out by some as representing the best example of an aretalogy,[30] its late date (early third century AD) and the omission of details crucial to the theory have led others to turn for a model to the alleged source on which Philostratus claims to have drawn, Damis' *Memoirs of Apollonius*.[31] But this work is known solely from Philostratus' references to it; it can be reconstructed only hypothetically, and it fails to include such details as a martyrology. Furthermore, it is widely regarded by modern scholars to be a 'document' faked by Philostratus.[32] Accordingly, 'aretalogy' – for which both definitions

and exemplars are at best inadequate and at worst wholly arbitrary –
is of no use as a supposed literary antecedent for the gospel as a literary
form.[33]

(ii) *Greek tragedy as the Markan model*

The hypothesis that Mark has taken Greek tragedy as his model for
portraying Jesus has been advanced by several scholars over the past
half-century. E. W. Burch sought to prove that Mark conforms to the
Aristotelian *characteristica* for tragedy, a theory which has more recently
been revived by Curtis Beach.[34] David L. Barr,[35] in a recent study of
the genre of the gospel, has undertaken to show that: 1. the gospels
do meet Aristotle's criteria for literature, so that they are not to be
dismissed as *Kleinliteratur*, as the form critics would have it; 2. there
are striking similarities between the typical features of tragedy as set
forth in Aristotle's *Poetics* and the profile of the gospels, although Barr
also acknowledges some crucial differences. Finally, 3. Barr examines
the three early Socratic dialogues of Plato – the *Apology*, the *Crito*, the
Phaedo – in order to show common elements among the gospels,
tragedy, and these dialogues. His conclusion, however, is that the
gospels are closer in genre to the dialogues than they are to tragedy.
Even if the delineation of genres were more precise and the demonstration of links with the gospel were more convincing than they in fact
are, this approach makes possible an assessment of little more than the
passion story in Mark, which is only a fraction of the entire work.

(iii) *Mark as 'origin myth'*

Vernon Robbins, who has noted the importance of *archē* for Mark – it
is the opening word (1.1), a crucial term in the apocalyptic section
(13.8, 19), and is used elsewhere (10.6) – infers from Mark's linking
of this term with creation, that Mark is generically akin to the 'origin
myths' described by Mircea Eliade.[36] These myths narrate and justify
a new situation which did not exist from the beginning of the world.
Robbins goes on to say, however, that 'the cosmogonic myth of the
absolute *archē* and *telos* embraces the Marcan narrative in a vigorous
apocalyptic manner'.[37] But no literary structure is offered as characteristic of an 'origin myth', and even if it were, it seems unlikely
that such a myth would account for the range of material included in
Mark, so that once more we must look elsewhere for a literary paradigm for Mark.

(iv) *Mark's gospel as Hellenistic romance*

In his study of the Hellenistic romance, Martin Braun has characterized this genre as neither pure history nor pure fiction, but as a

mingling of the two 'in which historical substance is very largely interspersed with mythical or novelistic elements, and sometimes distorted by them past recognition'.[38] He finds in Artapanus' *Life of Moses* 'the oldest available version of this romance'; in it Moses combines in a single 'life' the political, military, religious, philosophical, technical, and civilizing achievements that are shared in the Egyptian–Hellenistic view by the deities Isis, Osiris, Thoth-Hermes, and the national hero, Sesostris.[39] Pseudo-Callisthenes' *Alexander Romance* draws its erudition 'from the dregs and lower strata of historiography' and has more in common with a Hellenistic–Oriental book of folk-lore than with a Hellenistic historical work.[40] Braun's description of the romance is limited to its agglutinative style and the abysmal niveau of its cultural qualities. Even if one were to agree that Mark shares with the Hellenistic romance the cultural and literary 'dregs' – which Braun does not suggest – the problem of the structure of Mark could not be resolved by appeal to such an amorphous 'form' as the romance represents. And the intention of Mark seems to be far more serious than the romance's typical delight in the bizarre and the fantastic.

(v) *The gospel as comedy*

Under the influence of structuralism in both its literary (Pouillon; Barthes) and anthropological (Lévi-Strauss) modes, D. O. Via has sought to make a case for Mark as a representative of the genre of tragicomedy.[41] Differentiating his goal from that of Lévi-Strauss, who seeks to discover the structures of the human mind that inform the various aspects of society (economics, law, art, religions, etc.), Via seeks to discern a literary model that can account for the aim and structure of Mark.[42] This he finds in comedy, or more precisely, tragicomedy:

> Mark came to be written because the/a kerygma proclaiming, and the faith in, the death and resurrection of Jesus reverberated in the mind of Mark and activated the comic genre whose nucleus is also death and resurrection. . . . The story took the shape it did because the comic genre – a deep generative structure of the human mind – generated the Gospel of Mark as a performance text,[43] a transformation of itself.

Such factors as divine man, Christian prophets, the failure of the parousia, the fall of Jerusalem, were merely the raw materials – Via calls them *bricole* or debris – lying around out of which Mark fashioned his story.[44] After tracing the essential features of the genre of tragicomedy, he concludes that they are all to be found in Mark. These features include: 1. a character fit for tragedy who contrasts with a world that belongs to comedy; 2. the illusory world of the protagonist which contrasts with the real world of the audience (in Mark, however, the real world is one of the protagonists); 3. events which victimize the protagonist himself between intention and fulfilment, appearance and reality. The genre is unified in plot, keeps a focus on itself, and therefore is a poetic work, but in the case of Mark it also has a referential dimension. Via seeks to demonstrate these elements by sketches of Mark, but especially by the development of a series of grids in which elements of the Markan narrative (syntagm) are seen to intersect with the tragicomic features (paradigm).[45] The essence of classical tragicomedy is that death is followed by resurrection,[46] and that is what Via sees as the pervasive motif in Mark; one single theme, one plot, one issue to be resolved, one climax, and one message.[47]

In the long run, Via's message is subjective and reductionist. The texts, he says, were chosen 'at random'. He might better have said 'arbitrarily', which he acknowledges to be the basis for selecting the 'one point of view' from which the analysis of the text is carried out,[48] since he proceeds on the basis of intuition. As the results of his study of Mark indicate, the outcome is highly selective in the parts of the text in which it finds the basic meaning of death-resurrection. Where the significance of passages does not suit the hypothesis in either its syntagmic sense (straightforward sequence of words) or in its synchronic sense (relationship with the contemporary culture), it is treated allegorically to force it to conform to the 'structure'. For example, the sayings of Jesus widely regarded as eschatological warnings ('Watch!') are reduced to 'Risk is the principle of life'. Jesus' saying about losing one's life in order to find it (8.34f.) is reduced to: 'To relinquish one's freedom for another is really to enhance one's own freedom.'[49]

These results will come as no surprise to the reader who has noted Via's consistently anti-contextual approach. At the outset, diachrony (conceptual and institutional change which occurs through historical development) is dismissed by Via with the announced aim of neutralizing history,[50] and the role of socio-historical factors in generating texts is explicitly denied.[51] There are repeated statements that meaning is ontologically prior to history, so that neither text nor history-as-meaning is generated by historical process.[52] And since synchrony is to be understood, not as treating of phenomena contemporary with each other but as concerned with those which have common structural relationships,[53] and since the structure of Mark is in his mind[54] rather than to be derived from his writing,[55] there is nothing to be gained from historical investigation of the epoch of Mark or from an attempt to determine inductively from the text what its genre was and thereby to discover Mark's intention in writing the book.[56]

(vi) *Martyrologies as a literary precedent for Mark*

Stories about persons regarded as remarkable for their wisdom or for their exploits, but who suffer at the hands of civil or religious authorities, appear in the popular literature of this period in the context of several religious or philosophical systems. Since the relationships between narrators and audiences vary, it is impossible to draw inferences about accounts of miracles or martyrdom without in each case reporting the larger framework of meaning in which the writer intends the reader to understand his account. Recent studies have emphasized one fact: similarity of narrative content in stories of miracles or other exploits or trials does not in itself imply anything about the overall aim of the larger works in which these details are included.

An annotated edition of the *Acts of the Pagan Martyrs* by H. A. Musurillo[57] makes this point quite well. In the course of specifying the time and the genre of these *Acts*, Musurillo expresses doubt that 'these scattered tales ever crystallized into a definite literary form'. He states that 'there is good reason to suppose that the portrait of the *vir bonus et sapiens* [the wise and virtuous man] resisting the tyrant became a stock motif in the rhetorical and philosophical schools, especially during the Roman period'.[58] Musurillo's comparative study of the martyrologies in relation to the classic contemporary forms of mime, protocol, and novel is also relevant for our analysis of Hellenistic literary paradigms. He shows that while there are in each case some similarities, especially in formal details, the overall aim of the *Acts of the Martyrs* adapts the details to the writer's special purposes, so that in no case are the parallels exact.[59] On the matter of the overall aim itself, it can be shown that in spite of similarities between the pagan Acts, and both the Christian martyrologies and the Cynic-Stoic literature of resistance to tyranny, the pagan *Acta Alexandrinorum* make material that is formally similar serve substantially different ends.[60]

After tracing the common elements – use of the dramatic protocol style, emphasis on verbal exchange and aphorisms, the display of heroic contempt for death, long speeches by the martyrs, and contempt for Roman officialdom – Musurillo states:

> But these parallels are mostly external . . . In reading the Christian martyr-Acts one cannot but be impressed by the fact that here one is in an entirely different world. And the similarities that do exist can, I feel, be explained by

. . . 'the theory of the two milieus'. For it is a fact of common experience that similar stimuli operating upon somewhat similar environments can be expected to produce somewhat similar effects; there is no need to postulate any interdependence.[61]

Additional studies could be cited to reinforce this point, but Musurillo's statement seems adequate for our purposes here. The recent revival of interest in Hellenistic literary materials that have similarities with primitive Christian literature must be tempered by a sophisticated comparative methodology that fully appreciates the independence of the social worlds of the respective literatures.

(vii) *The Hellenistic* chria *and the intention of a gospel*

Another, more recent study likewise points to the fact that in Graeco-Roman rhetoric a traditional unit may be found in two different settings with the same form and content but with a very different function. Henry Fischel, in his studies of Cynicism and its characteristic literary form, the *chria*,[62] describes the prominent part played in the Hellenistic and Roman rhetorical worlds by the figure and concept of the ideal sage, the *sophos* or *sapiens*. As the founder of a school of thought or a lawgiver or a creative statesman, this figure attracts disciples and converts them to his way of life. His wit and wisdom, his forthright actions, his closeness to nature, his courage and presence of mind, are powerful elements in his appeal. 'Socrates is often expressly named as the principal model for this type of sage, and in his image many other founder-sages make their appearance in rhetoric.'[63] The concept of the great individual in later, that is, Graeco-Roman culture, 'is thus determined not by his actual achievement – which may have been merely the catalyst – but by an *a priori* concept of the sage, and it is this concept which seems to have determined the use of *chriae* and aphorisms in the description of his wisdom and his career'.[64]

During this latter period, rhetoric was used for purposes other than mere communication; it was used to propagate virtue and to redeem society.[65] Rhetorical forms, and especially the *chria*, became an international currency, moving freely across older national and cultural boundaries. As a result, the same stories were told and the same sayings were attributed to sages in widely different settings. At times the material even appears in the same sequence, with the same similes attached in the same order to the same *chria*, in one instance linked with Hillel and Seneca respectively. Handbooks for rhetoric appear to have been used in several cultural areas.[66]

When these rhetorical forms were used at second hand, however, it was not a case of slavish imitation: to adopt meant to adapt.[67] The *chriae*, for instance, borrowed as they were from Hellenistic culture, were modified substantively to serve the needs of the rabbinic movement in the teaching of the Torah. The sarcastic element was tempered; biblical quotations were incorporated; and a transcendental element was added in order to conform to the theological views of the rabbis.[68] *Chriae* are reported concerning sages in the Jewish tradition such as Hillel, Hanina ben Dosa, and Akiba, in a manner formally close to the way Philostratus later incorporated *chriae* into his account of the sage Apollonius of Tyana. The rabbinic tradition, however, betrays none of the tendencies towards divinization that were at work in Philostratus.

There is, therefore, no guarantee that the appearance of a rhetorical form – even with similar content – in two different literatures implies that the form fulfils the same function in both cases. On the contrary, the analysis of the *chria* should lead us to expect that differing cultural contexts would adapt the form to their own distinctive theological and propagandistic ends.

(viii) *The intention of a miracle story*

Since, as we have seen, neither the larger nor the smaller rhetorical forms of the Hellenistic world offer us suitable paradigms for either the form of the gospel or its function as a whole, it is conceivable that one of the individual components of the gospel narrative will provide a conceptual link with the Hellenistic milieu of the Gospel of Mark and thus offer us clues as to the Markan aims: the miracle story.

As we noted in chapter I, the form critics observed certain similarities in form and content between the gospel miracle accounts and those preserved in both pagan and Jewish literature. But like the *chriae*, the significance of the longer miracle stories cannot be assumed automatically. Even in the case of the rabbinic miracle stories, Fiebig's classic study[69] shows that there are motifs common to both rabbinic and gospel narratives – heavenly voices, healings, feedings, raising the dead, encounters with demons, miraculous fish, warnings of impending disaster – but that the items which are so important for the gospels are missing from the rabbinic sources: exorcisms, healing the lame and the blind. Grave doubts about the relevance of even these limited parallels have been raised by critics of Fiebig's use of the Tannaitic sources.[70] But even if the parallels were more precise than they are, the miracles are offered in the rabbinic sources to demonstrate the authority of the teacher or to confirm his interpretation of the Law, while in the gospels they are manifestations of the inbreaking of God's eschatological rule.

Scholars continue to assume that miracle-working was a useful feature for propagandizing in the Hellenistic world and that the ability to perform miracles was generally regarded as a sign of a divine nature. Thus it is ironical that when H. Köster sets out to make a case for his theory that behind the gospels there lies an 'aretalogy' in which 'Jesus appears as a man endowed with divine power who performs miracles to prove his divine quality and character',[71] the only documentation that he can offer for the aretalogical model is to point to the 'typical ending' of an aretalogy in Sir.43.27–29 and I Macc.9.22. The irony lies in the fact that in neither of these texts is there the slightest hint of a divine-man concept. Sirach 43 is, in fact, a magnificent hymn of praise to God for the splendour evident in his creation. Köster might have mentioned that Sir.36.13 is one of the few places where *aretalogia* is actually used; but there, as in Sir.43, the subject is the works of *God* on behalf of his people, and there is no trace of a *theios anēr*.[72]

It is an obvious fact, though one often overlooked, that the composition of records of the deeds of the gods and the narrating of miraculous deeds of specially-endowed men did not originate in the Hellenistic period, nor was interest in these two related kinds of subject-matter indigenous to Greece or to Hellenistic culture. Indeed, both types of literature are well represented in the Old Testament canon itself, although to my knowledge scholars have not yet proposed calling them aretalogies. What is widely regarded as one of the oldest fragments of tradition in the Hebrew canon, the Song of Miriam (Ex.15.21), is a report of the miraculous deliverance of the faithful by the direct intervention of the God of Israel. Similar, though much fuller in its depiction of the wonders worked by God, is the Song of Moses (Ex.15.1–18). Other familiar examples are Deut. 26 and Josh.24; Ps.114, to mention only some of the most obvious. This motif continued to have a vital role in the religion of Israel down into the Hellenistic period, as the recital of 'the works of the Lord' in Sirach 42.15–43.33 attests. There the wisdom and power of God in sustaining the world is praised, in what we would call the realms of both nature and history. Although in the Sirach passage the emphasis is on the marvel of God's ordering the world, in Dan.6.25–27 the praise of God's acts is directly related to his miraculous intervention on behalf of Daniel:

> For he is the living God,
> enduring for ever;
> his kingdom shall never be destroyed,
> and his dominion shall be to the end.

He delivers and rescues,
he works signs and wonders
in heaven and on earth,
he who has saved Daniel
from the power of the lions.

I suspect that if a devotee of a Greek saviour-god were to come on a translation of that passage in a Greek-speaking Jewish synagogue he might well associate it formally with the aretalogies on the walls of his own shrines, in spite of the radical differences in theological assumptions.

In the biblical tradition, in addition to passages of the kind just summarized in which the miracles are simply and directly attributed to God, there is a rich tradition in which various persons are described as having been enabled by God to perform miracles in fulfilment of his purposes. In this tradition the characteristic and appropriate term for the miracles is 'sign', as the quotation from Daniel indicates. The evidential function of miracles is set forth explicitly in Ex. 4, where Moses expresses fear that no one will believe his report of the theophany and the command to lead the people out of Egypt. Yahweh then tells him about the rod that will turn into a serpent and the hand that will become leprous, miracles which Moses is to perform in order to convince all: 'that they may believe that Yahweh ... has appeared to you' (Ex. 4.5). The miracles are to be performed in the presence of Pharaoh (4.21), although Yahweh in this instance will see to it that he does not believe; the main thrust of the whole miracle cycle in Ex. 4–14 is to persuade the Egyptians that the God of Israel is behind their demand to be set free. That the miracles associated with the Exodus are a public testimony is succinctly stated in Ps. 77.14, 'Thou art the God who workest wonders, who hast manifested thy might among the peoples.' The fact that these signs were accomplished in order to demonstrate God's purpose to both faith and unfaith is evident in the closing words of the Pentateuch:

And there has not arisen a prophet since in Israel like Moses, whom the Lord knew face to face, none like him for all the signs and the wonders which the Lord sent him to do in the land of Egypt, to Pharaoh and to all his servants and to all the land, and for all the mighty power and all the great and terrible deeds which Moses wrought in the sight of all Israel (Deut. 34.11f.).

It is not the divinity of Moses that is manifested in these miracles, but the power and purpose of the God who is using him as his chosen instrument.

Elsewhere in the biblical tradition there are cycles of miracles, also evidential in function, which nevertheless *are* told in such a way as to place more emphasis on the person of the miracle worker than do the stories in Exodus. These are the Elijah/Elisha narratives in I and II Kings. The manner in which these stories focus on the identity and endowment of the miracle-working prophet is clear in II Kings 1.10, 12; there the prophet has been ordered by the king to come to him and heal him, but instead of obeying, the prophet calls down fire from heaven. In doing so, he makes the execution of the miracle a test case of his identity: 'If I am a man of God, let fire come down . . .' What we have, therefore, in these familiar stories of healing the sick, raising the dead, and invoking the fires of judgment on God's enemies, is a series of biographical narratives. The prophets are equally concerned about the purity of Israel's worship of Yahweh and the fidelity of the nation's rulers to the will of God. But the power of Yahweh resting on the prophets is seen not only in the fulfilment of their predictions but also in the miracles which they perform. As for the manner in which the stories are told, there is in these cycles a dimension of biographical, almost psychological, detail, as in the self-pity of Elijah on Horeb (I Kings 19.14) and in the peevish response of Elisha to the boys' teasing him about his baldness (II Kings 2.23ff.).

In two of the deuterocanonical books, Wisdom of Solomon and Sirach, considerable space is devoted to recounting the exploits of the leaders of Israel, and in the case of Moses, to the miracles which he performed. In Wisdom 10–12, it is personified Wisdom who was at work to accomplish the divine will in the history of the nation; Wisdom was active specifically through Moses, enabling him to perform the wonders by which the nation was led out of Egypt and preserved in the desert (10.15–21). Still more centred on persons is the famous 'Let us praise God for famous men' section of Sirach (44.1–50.21). Moses' exaltation is described: he was made equal with the holy ones; Yahweh glorified him in the presence of kings; he received the commandments face to face (45.1–5). Yet throughout the entire section, grammatically and conceptually, the subject is Yahweh; it is he who has accomplished these wonders; it is he who in 'every way does great things' (50.22). For our purposes what is most important, however, is to observe how enduring and how varied in form and intent was the practice within the biblical tradition of assembling stories of the wonders worked by the servants of God through the power he bestowed.

The same diverse aims persist in the non-canonical literature. In the *Biblical Antiquities* of Pseudo-Philo, for example, Moses is praised as God's instrument through whom were performed 'signs and wonders for my people' (9.7f.). But during the Hellenistic period in Jewish literature, a new motif begins to manifest itself, a motif which had its beginnings in the later prophetic tradition and which was to exercise a potent effect on sectarian Judaism and on early Christianity as well. This motif consists of the affirmation that just as miracles in the past accompanied and made possible the great events by which God delivered his historic people, Israel, from their enemies, so he will act *in the very near future* on the analogy of the Exodus signs and wonders to free his new covenant people in the eschatological epoch which lies ahead. In short, *miracle-working becomes a central ingredient in Jewish eschatological literature.* The roots of this development go back to the later prophetic tradition, as Paul D. Hanson's work on the origins of Jewish apocalyptic has shown.[73] The literature and the movements that produced it flourished in the period of the Maccabees and the subsequent centuries, that is, in the late Hellenistic and early Roman periods (roughly 150 BC–AD 130).

This development is apparent in the Apocalypse of Baruch, especially 71.1–75.8, where the imagery for the defeat of the powers of evil, for the deliverance of the elect and for the renewal of the earth is drawn from the Exodus tradition.[74] Similarly, when Daniel has been delivered by divine intervention (Dan. 6), and yet together with his people faces unprecedented trouble and tribulation (7.19–21; 8.24), his prayer of intercession is based on his reaffirmation of the Law, and his appeal for deliverance is based on the precedent of the Exodus (Dan. 9.11–19), ending with an appeal to God to *act*. The heavenly voice offers reassurance that evil will be overcome (10.12–14.4), and that the 'wonders' about to be performed will be the prelude to 'the end' (12.13).

Therefore, Daniel, our earliest fully-developed representative of the apocalyptic tradition, builds on two strands in the biblical tradition: the aretalogy-like *recital of the wonderful deeds of God*, and the *biography-like account* of the experiences of his servants – chiefly the prophets – through whom and on behalf of whom God performed these signs and wonders. The new feature in the apocalyptic tradition is that the signs no longer look back to the past alone, although past miracles serve as models for those yet to come; but *the signs point forward to the new act of deliverance, the eschatological end of the age.* The book of Daniel accordingly (in its present form) includes miracle stories, recitals of God's wonders, and predictions about the outworking of his purpose.

From the Qumran material we know how central for apocalyptic-ally-oriented sects of Judaism was the expectation of the coming of an eschatological prophet, in fulfilment of the prophecy of Deut. 18.

According to Deuteronomy, signs and wonders were to be performed by the prophet of the end time, but the fact that one who claimed to be a prophet performed miracles was no guarantee that he had been sent by God. Rather, he was disqualified if he called Israel to follow other gods (Deut. 13.1–3), or if his predictions failed to come to pass (Deut. 18.22). The persistence of the expectation of a liberating prophet on the analogy of Moses, the wonder-worker, is evident in Josephus. In Book XX of the *Antiquities* he describes the various insurrectionists who tried to rally the people against Rome. Theudas convinced many people that he was the divinely-appointed leader by stopping the flow of the Jordan: a second Moses. His execution by order of Fadus was that of a messianic, i.e., political pretender. Under Festus, an impostor – Josephus' euphemism for a revolutionary – promised to free from distress all those who followed him into the desert to prepare for the new age, in conscious imitation of Moses. In the desert the people were promised that they would behold the 'signs and wonders' that would show that the enterprise was in harmony with God's design. Thus, even in activist groups as late as the time of Vespasian, *the coming deliverer was expected as an eschatological, wonder-working prophet*, for which Moses was the major prototype.

Within a quietist group, such as the Dead Sea community, the expectation of the prophet was a major feature of eschatological hope, together with the confidence in a miracle of deliverance from enemies (cf. the War Scroll). It was expected that when the messiah(s) of Aaron and Israel would be revealed in the end time, the eschatological prophet would also appear (Rule of the Community 9.11; similarly in 4Q Testimonia 5–8). Although this doctrine may have gone through changes with the apparently shifting messianic views of the community,[75] it is obvious that at some point in the history of the community it awaited the appearance of the Mosaic prophet.

Parallel to that hope was the belief, attested in Sirach 48.5–10, that another prophet who had heard the word of the Lord on Sinai and had been taken up to heaven at the end of his life, and whose coming at the end of the age was likewise announced in the scriptures (Mal. 3.1–3; 4.5–6), would come at the end of the age: Elijah. The text from Sirach explicitly links his role as one who prepares for Yahweh's coming (Mal. 3) with that of Isa. 49.6 – to restore the covenant people.

Other agents whose coming at the end of days was awaited by various groups within Judaism in this period were Enoch, Michael (Dan. 12.1), or an unnamed angel (Assumption of Moses 10.2), while in the Testaments of the Twelve Patriarchs it is the eschatological figures from the tribes of Levi and Judah (Test. Dan.5.10; Test. Naphtali 8.2; Test. Judah 25.2) who are expected, although in the Test. Levi, it is the anointed priest (Levi) who seems to have the sole claim as eschatological deliverer (Test. Levi 5.2ff.; 18.1–14). In one passage (Test. Levi 8) it appears that the eschatological figure of Levi has three roles – prophet, priest, king – although in its present form, the passage goes on, somewhat inconsistently, to allot the kingship to Judah (8.14). A major function of the deliverer(s) in the Testaments of both Levi and Judah is the defeat of Satan (Beliar), which will enable the eschatological people to trample on evil spirits (Test. Levi 18.11; Test. Judah 25.3). In the defeat of evil as well as in the cleansing of the sanctuary and the renewal of the covenant people, the eschatological prophet/priest/king is endowed with divine power by the Spirit of God (Test. Levi 18.7; Test. Judah 24.3). It is significant that both these eschatological figures are described in language that makes reference to the Star from Jacob mentioned in Num. 24.17 (Test. Judah 24.1; Test. Levi 18.3); at Qumran (CD VII) the Teacher of Righteousness is apparently identified as the Star, which suggests that during his lifetime he may have been regarded as the eschatological prophet.

What we see occurring, therefore, is that while the saving acts of God continue to be celebrated by the community, *there is a growing conviction that redemption will finally be achieved by a divinely endowed agent of God*. Building on the models of the deliverers of Israel in the past (especially Moses and the early prophets), the later prophets (e.g., II Isa., in Isa.61) and the extra-canonical writers testify to the conviction that God is about to act decisively in the miraculous deliverance of his people. An entire book at Qumran, the War Scroll (IQM), is devoted to a description of the preparation for and the final outcome of the eschatological war between the Sons of Light and the Sons of Darkness. The literary traditions of Judaism were adapted in the period of the second Temple to serve the eschatological aims of those groups within the covenant community who looked not to human armies as in the days of Joshua and David, or even in Maccabean times, but to God's wonder-working agents to accomplish his purpose in the world.

The result of our survey is to show that Hellenistic models which have been appealed to as having served Mark as a paradigm for his representation of Jesus are either too formless to have functioned as a genre model or are merely modern constructs, lacking either precise definitions or ancient exemplars. The features that Mark does share with Hellenistic rhetorical forms serve only to make the general and obvious point that Mark was influenced by the predominant Hellenistic culture of his time, but they tell us nothing about Mark's specific and distinctive aims. The closest analogies to the miracle tradition, both in form and theocentric outlook, are in the eschatological literature of post-exilic Judaism. Although this apocalyptic literature shares with Mark such common features as the necessity of suffering, the defeat of Satan through exorcisms, the promise of divine deliverance and the eschatological visions of vindication, there is no real analogy to his gospel as a literary whole. Accordingly, we must agree with the judgment of Amos Wilder: '[The gospel] is the only wholly new genre created by the Church and the author of Mark receives the credit for it.'[76]

3. The Literary Components of Mark

After our survey of literary forms which have been proposed by various scholars as having provided Mark with the paradigm for writing his gospel, we turn to the question of smaller cycles or clusters of tradition that may have served as sources for Mark. These possibilities range from the extended narrative complex of the passion story and the elaborate discourse in Mark 13 to briefer groupings of narrative or sayings material.

(i) *The passion narrative in Mark: source or literary product?*

In an offhand remark, tucked away in a footnote, Martin Kähler observed that the gospels might be described 'somewhat provocatively' as passion narratives with extended introductions.[77] The form critics adopted this suggestion,[78] so that Bultmann considers the passion kerygma to be the organizing centre around which Mark developed his gospel.[79] More recently, H. Köster has reaffirmed Kähler's dictum, though with a small but significant variant. The Gospel of Mark 'is nothing but a passion narrative with a *biographical* introduction' (italics mine).[80] Paul's gospel provided the norm for Mark, so that the inclusion of sayings and other narratives 'are actually an extension of the kerygma of Jesus' passion and resurrection'.

If the pericope dealing with the plot to kill Jesus is taken as the beginning of the passion narrative (14.1ff.), then about one-sixth of the whole of Mark is devoted to this theme. Foreshadowings of Jesus' death appear as early as 2.20, and indications of the plot to destroy him are found at 3.6, so that the passion story offers the reader no basic surprise. But does the pre-passion material serve no other function than that of introduction (so Kähler) or extension of the kerygma (Köster)? On the face of it, would one expect a writer to occupy five-sixths of his space with preliminary or merely introductory matters? A satisfactory answer to that question can be offered only when we have examined more fully the structure, method, aim, and life-situation of the Markan community, as we propose to do below. For the moment, however, we may ask: how unified a work was this alleged kernel, the passion narrative? Dissection of the account leaves us with very little that is clear about the content or extent of the alleged pre-Markan passion report.[81]

Bultmann's analysis of the passion section is detailed, but the results are neither positive nor definitive. He differentiates the units of the passion material as follows:

Pre-Markan tradition	*Markan or independent additions*
Conspiracy and Judas' Betrayal	Anointing at Bethany
Preparation of the Passover	Foretelling of Betrayal
Institution of the Lord's Supper	Jesus in Gethsemane
Road to Gethsemane and Foretelling of Peter's Denial	Trial by Sanhedrin
	Ill-treatment of Jesus
Arrest	
Peter's Denial	Crucifixion and Mocking of Jesus
Burial	Women as Witnesses

Throughout the entire section,[82] Bultmann draws attention to 'legendary' embellishments, without indicating whether these occurred at the pre-Markan stage, whether they were part of the original document, or whether they were added by Mark. He finds genuine historical reminiscences only in the accounts of the arrest, condemnation and execution of Jesus.[83] Although he attributes to the kerygma the power to have created 'a coherent narrative', and in spite of his positing the existence of 'a primitive narrative which told very briefly of the arrest, the condemnation by the Sanhedrin and Pilate, the journey to the cross, the crucifixion and death',[84] he goes on to acknowledge that if all the suspected secondary additions are removed and 'we ask *whether what remains constitutes a narrative complete within itself*, the answer is strictly negative'.[85]

A careful examination of the passion narrative indicates that a whole series of motives is at work, and some of them show clearly the hand of Mark himself: 1. There is an evident desire to link up the Last Supper with the Passover, even though the details of the Passover are imperfectly grasped. 2. The intention to show that all that happened to Jesus was in fulfilment of the divine will and therefore

in accord with scripture has almost certainly led to the introduction
of narrative details (see below, 45–49). 3. The concern to show the
fulfilment of Jesus' own prophecies is also a powerful factor, in
relation to his own arrest (cf. 8.31 and 14.41) and in his having been
both betrayed and denied by his own disciples (cf. 14.30 and 14.71).

4. The determination to dissociate Jesus from any revolutionary
messianic movement[86] pervades the passion story: Jesus is seized 'as a
λῃστής'[87] (14.48) and yet declines to make any effort at defence
(14.65; 15.5); ironically, a real revolutionary is released (15.7), while
Jesus is executed as a political leader (15.12, 18, 26) in the company
of two insurrectionists (15.27). Although Bultmann accurately observed the disorder of the narrative in its present form at 15.37–39,
the disorder is not so much a result of legendary formulation as of
diverse and complex traditions which Mark has imperfectly sorted
out while adapting them to his own purposes. On purely stylistic
grounds, it is worth noting that the peculiarities of Mark noted by
J. C. Hawkins occur with the same relative frequency in the passion
section as they do in the rest of the gospel,[88] and so do the characteristics listed by Vincent Taylor.[89] In sum, there is no interpretative
advantage in speaking of a pre-Markan passion narrative and no
unambiguous evidence pointing to its existence. The pervasiveness of
the theme of Jesus' death throughout Mark is so apparent that there
can be no question of its paramount significance for Mark,[90] but the
existence of a sequential account of the passion before Mark's cannot
be demonstrated.

(ii) Cycles of miracle stories utilized by Mark

For the past two centuries scholars have been proposing theories
about written sources for the gospels, including Mark.[91] In the present
century the hypotheses concerning the sources of Mark range from
the compilation of groups of tracts,[92] to the combination of Jesus
traditions with proof-texts from the Old Testament,[93] the postulating
of a common Palestinian document used by all three synoptists,[94] and
of course, to the Gospel of Matthew itself.[95] Recent proposals for
Markan sources have ranged from the general (a collection of
parables, a miracle source)[96] to the specific: controversy stories
(2.1–3.6); parables (4.1–34); a cycle of *Novellen* (4.35f., 52); instruction about discipleship (10.2–45); apocalypse (13); and, of course,
the passion narrative.[97] Our concern here is solely with the possible
cycles of miracle stories, so that only the *Novellen* group comes under
consideration from among these categories. Since, however, several
of the so-called controversy stories are in fact accounts of miracles, it

would seem unwarranted to exclude them from consideration on arbitrary terminological grounds. Furthermore, Mark uses the term 'teaching' (1.21, 22, 27) with reference to Jesus' exorcistic and healing activity, so that the term occurs both in Markan editorial connective material, and as an element that Mark has introduced within the narrative tradition (e.g., 6.30, 34). Our investigation, therefore, will look at narrative material of which miracles constitute a part, rather than arbitrarily limiting itself to pericopes which fall within the modern critical category of 'miracle stories'.

Perhaps the most substantial study yet offered on the subject of sources behind Mark's miracle tradition is that of Paul J. Achtemeier.[98] By means of a method which differentiates (i) Markan editorial material, (ii) the content of what is likely to have been the original narratives, and (iii) the Markan pattern of interpolations,[99] Achtemeier has made a strong case for Mark's having used two parallel miracle cycles in 4.35–8.26:

Stilling of the Storm 4.35–41	Jesus walks on the Sea 6.45–51
The Gerasene Demoniac 5.1–20	Blind Man of Bethsaida 8.22–26
Woman with Haemorrhage 5.25–34	Syrophoenician Woman 7.24b–30
Jairus' Daughter 5.21–23, 35–43	The Deaf Mute 7.32–37
Feeding of Five Thousand 6.34–44, 53	Feeding of Four Thousand 8.1–10.

The detailed justification offered for this reconstruction by Achtemeier is persuasive,[100] and the analytical method seems to be sound and productive. While the evidence is not beyond dispute that Mark found this material in sources rather than as scattered narrative tradition, the degree of probability in favour of written collections is high. And the fact that the interpolation technique (see below, 54–56) is evident in the inserting of the story of the healing of the woman with the haemorrhage in the middle of the story of Jairus' daughter (5.21–24 + 25–34 + 35–43) strongly suggests that Mark was working with a written source. Achtemeier has wisely chosen the neutral term *catena* to designate these groups of narrative.[101] It is probably part of Mark's intention that four of these five stories are explicitly located in non-Galilean – i.e., Gentile – territory: The Walking on the Sea is en route to Bethsaida, by which Mark intends Bethsaida Julias, located to the east of the point where the Jordan enters the Sea of Galilee, rebuilt by Herod Philip in the Hellenistic style,[102] and lying with the district of Gaulanitis. It is in that city that the blind man is healed, as well. The stories of the Syrophoenician Woman and the Deaf-Mute are both depicted by Mark as taking place in the district of Tyre (7.24, 31). Although there is no locale given within the story of Feeding the Four Thousand, the last place-name given in Mark's report is the Decapolis (7.31), and he probably intends the reader to understand the feeding as occurring in this region. Thus, the whole of the second series of miracles is localized in Gentile territory, most certainly as Markan editorial balance to the first cycle, which includes a miracle in Gentile territory (5.1–20), but which concentrates on dealings with Jews (the synagogue ruler, 5.22) and builds on familiar Jewish images, such as God's power overcoming the waters of chaos,[103] the commanding word which brings under control the God-opposing powers,[104] and the miraculous feeding in the desert – features which are lacking in the parallel accounts.[105] The evidence thus points to separate, parallel cycles of material, reworked by Mark and incorporated by him into his overall scheme.[106] Using the same method and criteria, is it possible to discern other miracle cycles that Mark used?

The search for a possible additional miracle cycle in Mark narrows down rapidly when it is noted that the only miracles described after the close of the second cycle (8.26) are the Healing of the Epileptic Boy (9.14–29), the Healing of Blind Bartimaeus (10.46–52), and possibly the Cursing of the Fig Tree (11.12–14). All these have been so overlaid with symbolic meaning for Mark (faith is essential for the healer to be able to effect cures; only a blind man can recognize who Jesus is; the old covenant people is about to fall under the judgment of God) that it is impossible to recover an original form or to establish links with other miracle stories within the tradition. In the chapters preceding those where the dual cycles are incorporated by Mark (1.1–4.34), however, there are four miracle stories which require attention, and a series of sayings which bear on Mark's understanding of the significance of Jesus' exorcisms. Do these represent a pre-Markan cycle as well?

In 1.23–26 we have the core of a compact story of a demoniac cured by Jesus.[107] Verses 21f. and 27f. with their distinctive Markan vocabulary about his 'teaching', their concern for his authority over against that of the scribes, and for the spread of the mission, have surely achieved their present form at the hand of Mark. In the nucleus of the story, however, the technical language of Jewish exorcists is employed,[108] and the title assigned by the demon to Jesus ('the Holy One of God') is in continuity with the Old Testament 'man of God' tradition, both in the designation itself (II Kings 4.9, where it is used for Elisha) and in the sense of threat that the holy man constitutes (I Kings 17; 18, where it is used for Elijah)[109] in the prophetic tradition. In the apocalyptic tradition the term appears in the plural (the saints or the holy ones) as a designation for the eschatologically vindicated people of God (Dan. 7.18, 22, 25, 27; Sim. Enoch 48.7; 51.2; 62.8; 71.1) while God is called 'the Holy One' (Enoch 1.2; 9.4; 14.1; 92.2, 6; 93.11; 98.6). Yet this vision of the throne of the Holy and Great One (especially in Enoch 14) is one which foretells the defeat of the demonic powers. Since this title is assigned to Jesus only here in Mark and therefore does not seem to have been of major importance for Mark among the titles of Jesus that he reports, it probably stood in the tradition on which Mark is drawing for these opening, paradigmatic miracle narratives.

The pericope describing the cleansing of a leper (1.40–45) was probably preserved in the tradition as it stands in Mark, with the exception of the generalizing comment in v. 45. Confusion in the interpretation of ἐμβριμησάμενος made the story appear more awkward than it actually is: once it is recognized that the word in question is another way of rendering the technical Semitic term for exorcizing demons, גער,[110] the flow of the narrative is smoother and plausible. What is 'thrown out' (v. 43) is not the leper but the demon. The injunction to silence (v. 44) may well come from Mark as part of his complex scheme of secrecy,[111] but the original setting is presumably Palestine where there are priests available to determine ritual cleanliness and where the ritual laws are taken seriously. Since Mark does not seem to have been written in a locale where these factors were operative, it is unlikely that Mark has created this scene. Rather, he seems to have incorporated it into his overall structure.

The briefest of all Mark's miracle stories concerns Peter's mother-in-law (1.29–31). With a minimum of editorial addition (29a ?) we learn of the woman's fever, Jesus' approach and raising her by the hand, the departure of the fever, and her resumption of household duties. It is perhaps significant that in his parallel account of this incident (Luke 5.39), Luke uses the technical term ἐπιτιμᾶν for Jesus' expulsion of the fever.

The fourth of these stories exhibits one of Mark's favourite rhetorical devices: the interpolation technique (Mark 2.1–12). Again, there is a minimum of introductory editorial material (1a), identifiable by syntax[112] and vocabulary.[113] Other Markanisms are apparent in λόγος (2.2), but even more clearly in the portion of the narrative dealing with the scribes: participles with εἰμί (2.6), εὐθύς,[114] historical present (λέγει, 8), a parenthetical clause (10a).

The introduction of the term 'Son of Man' for the first time in the gospel and without clear logical links to the context calls for explanation as well. It is almost universally acknowledged that Mark has taken a miracle story, which consisted originally of 2.1–5 and 11–12a.

The phrase in 10b, λέγει τῷ παραλυτικῷ, echoes the end of 5a, and constitutes a literary seam. Mark has related the section from 5b to the end of 10 to the healing theologically, but the logical connections are by no means clear and the literary seams are obvious. We shall consider below what role forgiveness had in the Markan community, and why it was connected with the Son of Man, as it is here. But for present purposes it is enough to recognize that what remains when the theological interpolation is removed is a fairly straightforward miracle story. The setting is a simple one-room house with a beaten earth roof, through which the determined friends lower the paralytic when the single entrance and the room to which it led were hopelessly crowded by the able-bodied hearers and suppliants of Jesus. Luke's unfamiliarity with houses and construction methods of this type led him to write of removing the tiles – a much too elegant circumstance for a village home in Palestine or Syria (Luke 5.19).

The four stories are unified in their cultural setting, their use of language suggesting a Semitic background,[115] by vividness of detail and succinctness of narrative. The very fact that what was originally a miracle story (the Healing of the Paralytic) has been transformed into a controversy story about Jesus' authority to forgive sins and placed in the literary context of a series of controversies (of which more below) indicates that Mark is here adapting an existing account rather than inventing it or fashioning it freely from loosely structured oral tradition. When further account is taken of the presence in Mark of an extended summarizing section (1.31–39), then the four pericopes we have examined may be seen in sequence, whether or not their original order can be determined. If one seeks for a *Sitz im Leben* for such a collection, the first in the series gives us a clue: it is a community in which Jesus is regarded as an agent who has come in the end time to defeat the powers of Satan.

Just before the next summarizing section in Mark (3.7–12) and at the end of the series of controversy stories the story of the man with the withered hand (3.1–6) is told. In its present form its main focus is on the issue of sabbath observance, and its function in the overall framework of Mark is to serve as the occasion for the initial formation of the coalition of Pharisees and collaborationists (Herodians) who plot to destroy Jesus (3.6). But if we apply the same literary technique to this story that we have applied to 2.1–12, it becomes apparent immediately that here too we have a repeated phrase of address (λέγει τῷ ἀνθρώπῳ) and that if the phrase is treated as a seam, one can read in unbroken logical sequence from 3.1 to 3.3 to 3.5b, beginning with ἔκτεινον and continuing to the end of the verse. What we then have is a miracle in anecdotal form, comparable to the others we have examined above. If that reconstruction is valid, then here as in 2.1ff. we have an example of Mark's having transformed an anecdotal miracle narrative into a controversy story.[116] Whether this story was part of the cycle now embedded in Mark 1–2 is impossible to determine, but the suggestion is not implausible.

It is in another interpolated sequence (3.20–35) that we have from Mark our best clue to his understanding of the significance of Jesus' exorcisms. Sandwiched between the originally connected account of the opposition to Jesus on the part of his family (3.20–21, 31–34) is a series of sayings in response to a charge attributed to scribes from Jerusalem (3.22). The passage is sprinkled with typical Markan words and expressions[117] and assumes the explanation of the central meaning of Jesus to the disciples in private sessions (3.23).[118] The concluding verses of the passage (3.28f.) treat the same theme as does Mark's interpolation in 2.1–12, namely, forgiveness, which must have been an important and perhaps controversial issue in the Markan community. The sayings in 3.23b–27, however, share an element in common with each other and with the exorcism stories we examined earlier: the defeat of the enemy (Satan). All are rhetorically balanced statements:

Satan/Satan	3.23b
Kingdom/Kingdom	3.24
House/House	3.25
Satan/Satan	3.26
Strong Man's House/Strong Man	3.27

The details of the image change, but the basic point remains throughout: Satan's hold on the present order is being successfully challenged by the exorcisms which Jesus is performing. The importance of the theme for the gospel tradition as a whole is evident in that a similar complex is found in the Q material (Matt. 12.25–30 = Luke 11.17–23). Bultmann notes that 'the discussion presupposes an exorcism preceding it', and then goes on to assume that Mark has linked it with the generalized description of healings and exorcisms in 3.9–12).[119] He may be correct about the Markan origin of the context, although the passage occurs at an important transition point in Mark – following a summarizing section (3.7–12) and a Call pericope[120] and just prior to the first main section on private instruction to the disciples (Mark 4.1–34). But the exorcism account to which the sayings may have been earlier attached is likely to have been the miracle cycle which may be reconstructed from Mark 1–3.

What sort of setting should be supposed for a collection of materials such as this reconstructed cycle – in which healings and exorcisms are not merely present, but are seén as contributions to a larger enterprise? Would the setting be the overcoming of the powers of evil? The answer is obviously to be found in some group informed by Jewish apocalyptic views. The theme of conflict with the hostile powers is featured in Daniel (for example, 10.13) and in other apocalyptic writings, especially the Testaments of the Twelve Patriarchs (Test. Simeon 6.6; Test. Levi 3.3 (arm 'B' text); 18.11f.; Test. Issachar 7.7; Test. Dan. 5.6; 6.1, 4; Test. Naphthali 8.4; Test. Asher 7.3; Test. Benjamin 3.3.[121] While adapting these narratives to his own more immediate purposes, Mark has retained the features which these stories possessed in the cycles in which they were preserved.

(iii) *Controversy stories as modification of pre-Markan tradition*

Ignoring the rather arbitrary distinction between sayings and narrative material, which as we have seen cannot be carried through in any case, the following sections of Mark might be classified as controversy stories:[122]

Jesus' Authority to forgive Sins	2.1–10 ⎫	Adapted from miracle stories
Healing on the Sabbath	3.1–6 ⎭	
Jesus, Friend of Outcasts	2.13–17	
Fasting	2.18–20	
Work on the Sabbath	2.23–28	
Jesus in League with Satan	3.22 ⎫	Linked in the Marcan structure
Jesus pronounces Forgiveness	3.28–30 ⎭	
Defilement	7.1–23	
Demand for a Sign from Heaven	8.11–13	
Divorce	10.1–12	
How to gain Eternal Life	10.17–31	
Source of Jesus' Authority	11.27–33	
Obligation to Caesar	12.13–17	
Resurrection	12.18–27	
The Greatest Commandment	12.28–34	
Messiah, Son of David?	12.35–37a	
Woes against the Scribes	12.37b–40	

Is there evidence of a controversy-story source lying behind Mark? We have already seen that Mark has reworked the tradition in at least two cases to convert miracle stories into controversy situations (2.1–10; 3.1–6). Bultmann notes 'the increasing tendency of the church to clothe its dominical sayings, its views and its fundamental beliefs in the form of controversy dialogue'.[123] In ensuing chapters we shall be concerned with the evidence for Mark's aims in structuring and expanding the tradition he has drawn upon. But is there further evidence of such a process here in the controversy material? Or did Mark have a controversy cycle already in the tradition he drew upon?

We leave out of consideration those pericopes which Mark seems to have refashioned from miracle stories (2.1ff.; 3.1ff.) and the creation of a controversy situation from what were probably isolated sayings (3.22, 28–30). Bearing in mind that all the material has been placed by Mark in the service of the needs of his community of Christians, the following categories may be discerned: (a) material which is clearly composite, evidencing Markan editorial touches throughout; (b) material in which the needs of the church have permeated the whole, so that it is difficult to differentiate Markan from pre-Markan stages of development; (c) material preserved in a relatively pure form, with the editorial impact extrinsic to the pericope.

In group (a) are the section on defilement (7.1–23) and the story of the rich young man (10.17–31). Unmistakable are the explanatory observations in 7.3f., 11, and 19b, the Markan linking devices (καὶ ἔλεγεν αὐτοῖς, 7.9, 14 and καὶ λέγει αὐτοῖς, 20), the drawing aside of the disciples (7.14) and the private explanation offered to them (7.17) in response to his esoteric statement (παραβολή, 17). Here, too, there is a private comment to the disciples after the main event (10.23 and 24), there are Markan favourite words (πάλιν), repetitions (cf. 10.23 and 24), the attachment of what were probably isolated sayings (10.25), typical Markan locutions (ἄρχομαι as a helping verb, 10.28) and then a radical change of subject from possession to family obligations. Thus, the passage is composed of two pericopes (10.17–22 and 28–31), with editorial material and detached sayings stitched together by Markan editorial technique.

In group (b) are the sections on fasting, sabbath work, the source of Jesus' authority, and the woes. At the root of 2.18–20 was probably a parabolic saying about joy at a wedding feast, offered as justification for the joy and freedom that characterized the messengers of the good news. But in its present form, and even in the form in which it is likely to have been taken over by Mark, the absence of the bridegroom becomes the more important reality (2.19b), which in turn provides the ground for the adoption of fasting in the community. What follows in 2.21f. is a string of sayings about the incompatibility of the old order and the new, with no clear connection with the image or significance of the bridegroom. The discussion about the sabbath (2.23–28) seems to have little relation to work on the sabbath, since the disciples are represented as helping themselves to a bit of food, not working in defiance of the commandment. The Markan style permeates the section (ἄρχομαι, καὶ . . . ἔλεγεν αὐτῷ, καὶ λέγει αὐτοῖς), and the final saying is unmistakably – conceptually and stylistically – an appendage, in which Jesus (= Son of Man) is declared to be the Lord of the sabbath. The terms used to refer to David's followers are those that Mark uses of the disciples: οἱ μετ' αὐτοῦ (1.36; 2.25), τοῖς σὺν αὐτῷ (2.26).[124] But most significant is the ground of justification offered for violation of the sabbath law: it was essential to support David and his men in their urgent mission (I Sam. 21.1–7), even if to do so required using consecrated bread. Accordingly, Mark's point is that it is essential that Jesus and his followers be supported in their mission on behalf of the coming kingdom, even if breaking the sabbath law is necessary in order for them to be sustained.[125] Although it is conceivable that there is a core of this account which is pre-Markan, it would appear that in its present form it is offered by Mark to authorize flexibility in observance of the Law in view of the urgency of the Christian mission.

Similarly, the woes as they stand in Mark have been thoroughly modified by him, by the use of characteristic vocabulary and style both in the introductory phrases (διδαχή, καὶ . . . ἔλεγεν, 12.38), and in the term which introduces the general admonition, βλέπετε. Of the fourteen times that word occurs in Mark, eight have the special meaning of 'be on the lookout', two have a technical meaning, 'discern the meaning of scripture', i.e., from a Christian point of view (4.11; 8.18), and two mean 'see', but in the sense of 'recognize who Jesus really is' (8.23f.).

In the case of the saying about a request for a 'sign from heaven', 8.11 and 8.13 are strewn with Markan expressions,[126] so that only the saying in 8.12 – with its Semitic turns (ἀμήν the dangling protasis, εἰ δοθήσεται . . .) is almost certainly pre-Markan, but it is not connected with the narrative tradition and thus cannot be even provisionally assigned to a cycle.

The remaining pericopes are preserved in relatively pure form, and do indeed appear in direct sequence: Taxes to Caesar (12.13–17); Resurrection (12.18–27);[127] the Great Commandment (12.28–34);[128] Messiah Son of David (12.35–37a).[129] Thus it is conceivable that in Mark 12, a cycle of stories has been included which presented the Christian side in debates with Jews (or even perhaps with other Christian groups) over major points in the interpretation of the scriptural and legal tradition. The rest of the controversy material has been so thoroughly imbued with Markan locutions and notions that it is no longer possible to separate out what the tradition might have looked like when Mark received it. And in several instances, what we now have has clearly been structured by Mark himself. More significant than the question of prior existence of controversy cycles is the range of issues within the Markan church that this material has been made to address.[130]

Type of Issues	Specific Problem
Legal/ethical	Divorce; Greatest Commandment
Authority	Relation to the State; Source of Jesus' Authority; Divine Sign
Cultic	Defilement; Sabbath Observance; Fasting
Doctrinal	Resurrection
Christological	Messiah, Son of David

To address these issues Mark has drawn freely and widely on what was largely oral tradition, though the possibility of a written cycle cannot be excluded.

(iv) Mark's use of wisdom and eschatological sayings, including parables

While on formal, theoretical grounds it is obviously possible to differentiate in most cases between parables and metaphorical sayings, in function and intent they are often so close as to warrant treating them together. Scrutiny of Mark shows that he has brought together isolated sayings and placed them in a variety of contexts: as the culminating word in a 'pronouncement story' (1.17; 2.20; 2.27f.; 6.4, etc.); as material to supplement a parable (4.21–25); to serve as the core of a controversy story (3.33–35); or as an addendum to a controversy story (2.21f.). Others stand in relative isolation, as do the words about salt and fire (9.49f.). Naturally, there is no indication that these scattered sayings were preserved in a pre-Markan document, so that we may assume they have been taken over from the oral tradition.

On the other hand, the string of parables included by Mark in 4.1–34 (with evidence of Markan editorial links and additions alternating with traditions that are likely to predate Mark) give us our best case for a pre-Markan sayings source. Mark's editorial hand is seen in 4.1–2, 10–11a, 13–21a, 23, 24a, 33–34; what remains – which is the essence of the parables and the related sayings – may well come from a parable source. Below we shall consider how Mark has interpreted these parables for his community.[131] But here our focus is primarily on the literary phenomenon: with the exception of the seemingly inappropriate explanation as to why Jesus uses parables (4.11f.),[132] a collection may be assumed to underlie Mark's present literary arrangement.

The only other extended parable (or allegory) in Mark is 12.1–12.

There the imagery drawn from Isa. 5, together with other prophetic motifs about the eschatological judgment and the rebuilding of the new community, have been so thoroughly interwoven with specifically Christian and historical concerns (especially the fall of Jerusalem) that the earlier form of the 'parable' is impossible to recover. The same may be said of a series of wisdom/eschatological sayings throughout Mark, beginning with Jesus' summary statement of his mission in 1.15. And that is surely the case with the sayings about Elijah (9.9–13) also. No firm conclusions can be drawn from this passage about the original form of the sayings or, conversely, about the extent to which polemics between the followers of the Baptist and the early Christians has reshaped the material. 9.9f. clearly represent a post-Easter outlook, and 9.11 implies a scribal debate; but what the scripture is that is referred to in 9.13 as the prediction of Elijah's suffering remains a mystery. The tradition received its present form, in all likelihood, in the setting of formulation and defence of the community's view of Jesus' christological role.

The remaining wisdom/eschatological sayings tradition has been almost completely adapted to the community's needs, and therefore is of no value in the effort to reconstruct a pre-Markan document or cycle. The passion predictions (8.31–33; 9.30–32; 10.33f.), the sayings about forgiveness (3.28f.), the enigmatic remarks about bread and leaven (8.14–21), the disputes about greatness (9.33–37), about the admission of children (10.13–16), about exercising authority in the name of Jesus (9.41), about temptations and self-discipline (9.42–48), and about discipleship and martyrdom (8.34–9.1) have all been worked over so thoroughly in the interests of the Markan community that it is perilous and unproductive to try to sort out what Mark may have found in his sources, much less to try to reconstruct a sayings cycle that he may have used. What we learn from the wisdom/eschatological sayings, therefore, is highly instructive about the uses that have been made of the Jesus tradition in the community of Mark. But we are probably justified in assuming that this material reached him primarily in free-floating form from the oral tradition.[133]

(v) The Markan community as mirrored in the disciples' cycle

Although in the first half of Mark considerable space is devoted to the call and commissioning of the disciples, much of the material occurs in passages which seem clearly to be Markan constructs (1.35–39; 3.7a, 13–19; 6.30–32), and the rest has been thoroughly worked over in the interests of Mark. Thus, as L. E. Keck has pointed out, 3.7–12 serves as the conclusion of the first main section of Mark, and 3.13–19 introduces the next section, with the stress on Jesus' miracles and the prominence of the sea as the locale of Jesus' activities.[134] And 6.6b–13; 6.30–32 similarly serve as both summarizing and transitional statements.[135] In the second half of Mark, the admonitions to the disciples about their role have to do with the issue of ambition/humility, as in the disputes about who is the greatest (9.33–37; 10.35–45), or with the use of Jesus' name (9.38–41), or with true generosity (12.41–44). Both the subject matter and the terminology employed (ἐν ὀνόματι μου, ἐκωλύομεν,[136] which in 9.38f.; 10.14; Acts 8.36 is a technical term for admission to the community), as well as in vocabulary (e.g., προσκαλεσάμενος in 10.42 and 12.43, as in 6.7) point to the early Christian community. Characteristic of the instructions to the disciples in the second half of Mark are the ὡς ἄν declarations about responsibility and judgment (8.35; 8.38; 9.37; 9.41; 10.15; 10.43f.; 11.23).[137] Thus, the Markan strand treating of the disciples seems to be based on the needs of the Markan community rather than on a definable cycle or source which Mark has simply edited for merely literary purposes.

(vi) *The apocalyptic discourse: Mark's major sayings component*

The one sayings section widely viewed as representing a pre-Markan document is the apocalypse of Mark 13, yet the original extent of this source is widely disputed.[138] Bultmann considers the apocalypse to be an edited version of a Jewish document (13.5–27, or possibly vv. 30 and 32 are the original end of the Jewish apocalypse).[139] Haenchen, on the other hand, regards the extent of the original document as unimportant compared with Mark's use of the material, and suggests that Mark may have compiled the whole from scattered sayings tradition.[140] Lohmeyer, however, sees in Mark 13 an elaborate poetic structure, the main part of which consists of six strophes: 13.5–8, 9–12, 14–16, 17–20, 21–23, 14–27.[141] Beginning with v.14, Lohmeyer thinks Mark has used 'a kind of apocalyptic flysheet' circulated in the early church, since 'let the reader understand' implies an existing written document before Mark.[142] He thinks that the composition as a whole is to be attributed to Mark, who has composed it out of scattered – mostly oral – tradition.[143]

In general terms, that latter judgment is confirmed by a careful examination of the chapter. The opening section probably reflects the charge brought against Jesus about the destruction of the Temple (14.58; 15.29), and is followed by the private explanation to the disciples that is characteristic of Mark throughout (13.3, κατ' ἰδίαν). The speech and its editorial framework are alike filled with Markan expressions: βλέπετε (5, 9, 23, 33); ἤρξατο +inf.; δεῖ γενέσθαι (13.7; cf. 8.31; 9.11), the name of Jesus (13.6, 13).

Two studies devoted primarily to analysis of Mark 13 have, in fact, made an overwhelming case for the composite origin of Mark 13. Jan Lamprecht[144] has shown that the whole setting in which Mark has placed this discourse is a literary arrangement: time, place, preceding conflicts with authorities, the listeners, the schedule of the entire day on which it was putatively uttered – all is 'kunstlich geschaffen'.[145] He perceives redactional elements in the individual verses as well, although they have not been created by Mark, but adapted by him for his own purposes.[146] Redactional, however, are 1, 2a, 3f., 5a, 7f., 10, 13, 14, 17, 20, 23, 27. Lamprecht rejects the 'fly-sheet'[147] theory as well as the neat strophes of Lohmeyer.[148] His theory is that Mark has fashioned this speech of thirty verses, structuring it himself by means of temporal indications, recurrent words and constructions,[149] and rhetorical patterns.[150] As a consequence, it is not possible to trace any parts of the speech back to Jesus with certainty.[151]

The other crucial study, developed along quite different lines but confirmatory of Lamprecht's conclusions on the whole, is that of Lars Hartmann, who has analysed Mark 13 against the background of Jewish apocalyptic.[152] He sees the basis of Mark 13 in a 'coherent exposition of or meditation on' the book of Daniel, especially Dan. 7; 11; 12; with passages borrowed from other Old Testament apocalyptic-type prophetic utterances.[152] Even the parenetic elements interspersed throughout the discourse are based on Daniel, so that 'midrash and parenesis are one'.[154] We shall discuss Mark's use of scripture in the final section of this chapter, but there has been general acknowledgment among commentators that the basic perspective of Mark 13 resembles that of Dan. 9, from which there is, of course, an unmistakable quotation at one of the two crucial points in the apocalypse: the desecration of the Holy Place (Mark 13.14 = Dan. 9.27). The same theme appears in Dan. 11.31 and 12.11 as well as in I Macc. 1.54. The fact that Dan. 9 is itself a meditation on and a transmutation of Jeremiah's seventy years (Jer. 25 and 29) is good precedent for what Mark has done with the visions of Daniel in Mark 13. The climax of the apocalypse, which comes with the parousia of the Son of Man, is described by means of a pastiche of prophetic quotations, culminating in a passage from the LXX of Dan. 7.13f., which is alluded to again in the response to the high priest (Mark 14.62). Similarly, the transfiguration narrative (9.2–8) and the enigmatic ending of the book (16.8) both contain allusions to Daniel 10 (see below). Even if one were not to go so far as to say with Hartmann that Mark 13 is a midrash on Daniel, there can be no doubt that it was that first, great apocalyptic writing which informed in method, structure, and detail the apocalypse that Mark created out of the tradition to bring to a close his portrait of the teaching ministry of Jesus. There is, of course, an obvious candidate for the historical event that called forth this reshaping of the Jesus tradition: the fall of Jerusalem. Since the concrete details of Mark 13 seem to be closely associated with the events of AD 67–70, there is no reason to accept Hartmann's subordinate thesis that this document was prepared as early as the year 50, a proposal which is not rendered more credible by his acknowledgement that the text received its final form at the hand of Mark.[155]

(vii) *Mark's interpretation of scripture*

Theories that the early church had available collections of testimonies or proof-texts[156] have understandably not found wide support. But the discovery of the Dead Sea Scrolls, with their non-rabbinic interpretative methods, has stimulated interest in the whole question of Jewish and early Christian use of scripture. Attention to that question is essential in the study of Mark because of the hundreds of allusions to and quotations from scripture that this little book contains.[157]

For example, in Mark 11–16 alone there are more than 57 quotations.[158] Of these, only eight are from the Torah, and all but one of those appear in the context of the controversy stories in ch. 12. Two are from the historical writings, 12 from the Psalms, 12 from Daniel, and the remaining 21 are from the other prophetic writings. An analysis of the allusions to scripture and related sacred writings gives the same general picture: of 160 such allusions, half are from the prophets (excluding Daniel), and about an eighth each from Daniel, the Psalms, the Torah, and from non-canonical writings. The same disproportionate interest in Daniel prevails throughout the book, as A. C. Sundberg has noted: Daniel alone among all the Old Testament books is quoted from every chapter;[159] it is of the highest level of significance for the New Testament as a whole as a result of its overwhelming importance for Mark.[160] Not only in the synoptic apocalypse of Mark 13, but also in his portrayal of the career of Jesus, beginning – as Daniel does – with miracle stories, and moving through the issue of martyrdom (Mark 8.31ff.) to personal (Mark 9.2ff.; cf. Dan. 10) and cosmic revelations (Mark 13 = Dan. 7; 9), Mark has been influenced directly by Daniel in his representation of the career and intention of Jesus.

This general observation is confirmed in the details, some of which were referred to above (p. 33). Both the narrative detail and the

vocabulary of the Transfiguration story and the enigmatic ending of
Mark (16.8) are closely related to the vision granted to Daniel alone
in Dan. 10.[161] The coming of false prophets (13.22) is dealt with by
reference to the Deut.13 passage concerning validation of the true
prophet and to Dan.11.36–45. The high point of the apocalypse
comes in the parousia of the Son of Man, whose appearance is linked
with Dan.7.13f. The confession before the high priest is composed of
quotations from scripture, of which Dan.7.13 is a central element.

In addition to Mark's preference for the prophetic tradition in
general and for Daniel in particular, a noteworthy feature of Mark's
use of scripture is his dependence on the LXX.[162] In the following
list of Markan scriptural quotations and allusions, the argument in
each case turns on the details of the LXX reading:

11.9	Ps.118.25a
11.17a	Isa.56.7
11.17b	Jer.7.11
12.10f.	Ps.118.22f.
12.29	Deut.6.4f.
12.31	Lev.19.18
12.33c	Hos.6.6
12.36	Ps.110.1
13.4a	Dan.12.7
13.7b	Dan.2.29,45
13.19	Dan.12.1
13.22	Deut.13.1–3 (cf. Dan.11.36–45)
14.27	Zech.13.7
14.34	Jonah 4.9
14.38	Dan.12.10
14.62	Ps.110.1; Dan.7.13
15.32	Ps.69.8 (=LXX Ps.68.10)
16.8	Dan.10.12.

When to the extent of this list is added the factor of the centrality of
these texts for the developing picture in Mark, it is evident that the
LXX tradition is a fundamental pillar in the thought of the evangelist,
and that when he uses the phrase 'as it is written', the writings are
known to him in their LXX form. The cultural and theological
conclusions implicit in that observation will be drawn in ch. IV below.
But yet another feature of Mark's handling of scripture is to be taken
into account.

This feature is his practice of merging or blending scriptures, rather
than quoting them in isolated units. As E. E. Ellis has noted, in the
pesher quotations found in abundance among the Dead Sea Scrolls,
'the interpretation or exposition is incorporated into the body of the
text itself, thereby determining its text form'. Not only does Mark not

hold to a single authoritative version of the text or scripture, but he is not concerned at all about the literal details or the original import of the text which he finds fulfilled in Jesus.[163] J.A. Fitzmyer has observed that in what he calls 'accommodated texts' the original meaning has been 'modified to meet the new situation' in the interpreter's own time, and the version of the text employed is chosen so freely that the critic cannot ascertain whether the quotation is based on the Hebrew or Greek recensions, or on some deviant or corrupt text.[164] Examples of these merged or synthetic quotations and divinatory interpretations are evident from the beginning to the end of Mark, and occur at some of the crucial points:

1.1	(= Mal. 3.1 + Isa. 40.3)
11.1–11	(builds on Zech. 9–10 + Ps. 118)
12.1–12	(builds on Isa. 5 + Ps. 118)
13.24f.	(= Isa. 13.10; 34.4; Ezek. 32.7f.; Joel 2.10 + Dan. 7.13)
14.62	(= Dan. 7 + Ps. 110)

Not only are these texts synthesized by Mark as a kind of literary splicing exercise, however, but the meaning which is derived from them is far more than a simple addition of the meanings of their components. In describing the scriptural interpretation at Qumran, Dupont-Sommer has remarked that the *pesharim*

> are interpretations of biblical texts based, not on their natural or historical meaning, but on their secret or mystical significance. The biblical books were thought to refer essentially to the end time and to be full of instruction concerning the events of that period; it was the task of the commentator to discover, or rather to divine, all these superior meanings by means of his superior intuition.[165]

This view of the interpreter as divinely endowed recalls to the reader of Mark the familiar words of 4.4, 'To you has been given the mystery of the Kingdom of God, but to those outside all things are in παραβολαῖς (= enigmas).'[166] Here the mystery (*raz*) and its interpretation (*pesher*) stand in precisely the same relationship as that noted by F. F. Bruce in comparing IQpHab VII.1–5 with Dan. 2.30; 4.9; 7.15; 12.4ff., where the secret contained in the visions is perceived only by divinely granted interpretation.[167] The force of this in Mark 4.11 is heightened by the scriptural quotation from Isa. 6.12, where the form of the text (akin to the Targum, rather than LXX or MT)[168] was chosen in order to make the point that only those within the community can perceive the meaning of Jesus' teaching about the coming kingdom.

In spite of efforts to read Isa. 53 into Mark, especially at 10.45,[169] the controlling factor in Mark's portrayal of the events leading to Jesus' death and his portrayal of the struggles within himself reflected in the scenes in Gethsemane and on the cross is not a theory or even an image of atonement, but the Psalms, especially the psalms of lament. Here again we have a parallel in the Qumran material, where the Hodayoth seem to express the inner conflicts and ultimate submission to the divine will that was experienced by or attributed to the founder of that community. To draw this parallel is not to suggest dependence, but rather to point to an analogous development in the inner struggles of the leaders of eschatological movements that were roughly contemporary in Palestinian Judaism. The most relevant passages in the Hodayoth are IQH 5.20–39; 6.23f.; 7.1–5, of which the following is a representative sample:

> And I, I was the butt of the insults of my enemies,
> an object of quarrelling and dispute to my companions,
> an object of jealousy and wrath to those who had entered my covenant,
> an object of murmuring and contention to those I had gathered together.
> And all who ate my bread lifted up the heel against me.
> And all who joined my assembly
> spoke evil of me with a perverse tongue.
> And men of my council rebelled and murmured round about.
>
> And to (my) distress they added still more.
> They shut me up in the darkness
> and I ate the bread of groaning
> and my drink was in tears without end.
> For my eyes were darkened because of sorrow
> and my soul was (plunged) in bitterness every day.
> Fear and sadness encompassed me
> and shame covered (my) face,
> and my bread was changed into quarrelling
> and my drink into an enemy that entered my bones,
> causing the spirit to stagger
> and consuming strength.
> They changed the works of God by their transgression
> according to the Mysteries of sin. (IQH 5.22–24, 33–36)[170]

In these lines and elsewhere in the Hodayoth are parallels to the treachery of Jesus' followers, the spiritual struggle and the acknowledgement of weakness, the conflict with Satan (Beliar), the diabolical nature of human opposition, and then the confidence in ultimate vindication (IQH 5.25; 6.15ff.; 7.18ff.). The suffering of Jesus is portrayed in Mark, therefore, in keeping with the biblical and extra-biblical tradition of the faithful messenger of God. The Psalms alluded to or quoted in Mark include 31; 41; 69, and, of course, 22. But the prophets are represented as well: Mic. 5.1; Isa. 50.6; Amos 8.9; Zech. 13.7; Amos 2.16; Ezek. 23.31–34; Isa. 13.9f.; Lam. 2.15 – to mention only some of the more obvious allusions. Thus it is Christian reading of scripture that has shaped, or brought into sharp relief, the way in which the suffering and death of Jesus was in accord with the divine plan.

4. CONCLUSIONS

The components from which Mark has created his gospel are, therefore, of three types: units of oral tradition, small collections of narratives and/or sayings, and the Jewish prophetic-apocalyptic practices of eschatological exegesis, which include reworking prophetic tradition *in the light of the immediate, critical needs of his community*. The first two provide much of the substance of the Markan material; the third provides the approach to scripture and reinforces the self-understanding of the community and its place in the purpose of God. Out of this convergence of tradition, exegetical method, and community-consciousness, Mark shaped his gospel.

III

THE STYLE AND STRUCTURE OF MARK

Consciously or unconsciously, any writer reveals aspects of his own background by the language he employs, quite as much as he discloses the aims of his writing by the style in which he presents it. These dimensions of a work are as important as the content, especially since they provide evidence of the social level, the common assumptions that the writer shares with his reader concerning the meaning of life and the structure of their world. Approached in this way, Mark's language, style and structure are revealing as to the situation that he is addressing. After surveying a range of proposals for defining the structure of Mark, we offer our own solution, which combines the structure of history as perceived by Mark with the literary structure of this document.

1. SOME DISTINCTIVE FEATURES OF MARKAN VOCABULARY AND LOCUTION

By his list of 'harsh constructions' in Mark (19 examples of asyndeton; 151 historical presents, as contrasted with 4 in Luke; 88 sections or subsections[1] that begin with καί) and of 'rude, harsh, obscure or unusual words or expressions',[2] Hawkins made clear that Mark is not written in elegant Greek. Taylor and Hawkins have drawn up lists of Latinisms, the diminutives,[3] and the distinctive vocabulary,[4] although even the unusual words are found in the papyri, as Taylor notes.[5] The language is literate, however, and with a few exceptions,[6] offers no evidence of translation from Aramaic. As we have already observed,[7] the frequent biblical quotations and allusions are from the LXX or a related Greek text rather than from the Hebrew of the MT, so that there is no reason to suppose either that Mark has been translated from a Semitic original or that any language other than Greek was the *lingua franca* of the community for which he was writing.

The atmosphere of urgency is heightened by the frequency of use of ἐνθύς and ἐνθέως, while the sense of power and efficacy is increased by the use of superlatives and expressions of astonishment throughout. Other noteworthy stylistic features are the frequency of double negatives (1.44; 2.2; 3.20, 27; 5.3; 5.37; 6.5; 7.12; 9.8; 11.14; 12.14; 14.25, 60, 61; 15.4, 5; 16.8) and of the use of ἄρχομαι as a helping verb (1.45; 2.23; 4.1; 5.17, 20; 6.2, 7, 34, 55; 8.11, 31, 32; 10.28, 32, 41, 47; 11.15; 12.1; 13.5; 14.19, 33, 65, 69, 71; 15.8, 18). Other less common, but nonetheless unusual linguistic features are parataxis, anacoloutha, impersonal plurals, multiplication of participles, ἄν with the indicative, and pleonasms.[8] These linguistic usages are not out of place in *koine* Greek, and lend to the account a kind of simple, direct vividness which has been lost in the polishing and editing of the material carried out by Matthew and Luke. Where Mark says that the heavens were split (σχιζομένους) at Jesus' baptism (1.10), Matthew and Luke report simply that they were opened (ἠνεῴχθησαν, Matt. 3.16; Luke 3.21). Where Mark has Jesus thrown out (ἐκβάλλει, 1.12) into the desert prior to his testing there, in Matthew (4.1, ἀνήχθη) and in Luke (4.1, ἤγετο) he was merely led out into the desert. Thus the harsh expressions have been smoothed over by the other two evangelists who used Mark as their basic source.

More significant than vocabulary or style, however, are the distinctive Markan phrases which provide evidence for the evangelist's editorial activity in bringing the older tradition into the sequential form which he created in his gospel. One such feature which has often been noted by scholars is the introductory phrase frequently used by Mark, especially to introduce sayings material: καὶ ἔλεγεν αὐτοῖς.[9] The phrase occurs in 2.27; 3.23*; 4.2, 11, 21, 24; 6.4; 6.10; 7.9, 14*; 8.21; 9.1; 9.31; 11.17. (In the case of the two starred references, a phrase separates the copula from the verb and the pronoun, but we shall see below that in each instance the phrase is itself an important clue to Markan editorial activity.) The phrase is regularly used as a connective, most frequently in the interests of linking sayings material with a context which seems suitable for Mark but which he did not derive from the tradition itself.[10] Three of these instances are apparent exceptions to the norm, in that in each case the phrase occurs in the context of a narrative: the Rejection of Jesus in Nazareth (6.1–6), the Mission Charge to the Twelve (6.6b–13), and the Cleansing of the Temple (11.17). In all three places, however, it is likely that the 'narrative' has been constructed on the basis of sayings. As Bultmann observes, the 'biographical apophthegm' in 6.1–6 is 'an imaginary situation . . . built up out of an independent saying'.[11] The same may be said of the mission discourse in its present form.[12] Although the story of the cleansing of the Temple has an independent narrative core which Mark has incorporated, the attachment of the saying in 11.17 is the work of Mark – an impression which is confirmed by the use in the same sentence of another favourite Markan term, ἐδίδασκεν (cf. 4.2).[13]

The function of the phrase as an editorial link is unmistakable in the setting of the collections of sayings in which it is found. Some of these groupings are simple, as in the loosely associated sayings of 4.21–25, with καὶ ἔλεγεν αὐτοῖς functioning as a connective only. A more emphatic role is assigned to the phrase in the first part of Mark (4, however: it serves as an introduction to the parable (4.2); it prefaces the explanation as to why Jesus teaches in parables (= riddles, 4.11); it leads into the interpretation of the parable of the sower (4.13). In a majority of the occurrences, the phrase introduces private information for the disciples, a feature which we shall see below is of great significance for Mark.

A study of related expressions shows much the same picture, however, so that καὶ ἔλεγεν αὐτοῖς cannot in itself be considered a tip-off for esoteric teaching. καὶ λέγει αὐτοῖς too is used in connection with esoteric arrangements that the disciples are to make (11.2), with a private disclosure of his supernatural powers (4.35) and of his mission (1.18), and elsewhere in private instruction (4.13; 6.31, 50; 7.18; 10.11; 14.34). At the same time it is used in the context of controversy (2.25; 3.4; 12.16). A phrase similarly used in a controversy setting is καὶ εἶπεν αὐτοῖς (2.19),[14] although it occurs also in the context of private instruction (4.40). Other variants include private advice to the cleansed leper (1.44 καὶ λέγει αὐτῷ) and private instruction to the disciples (8.1, with καὶ omitted).

Closely akin to these phrases which so often depict Jesus as offering private explanations to the disciples are terms which explicitly state that Jesus took his followers aside or away from the crowds to give them special instruction or interpretation. One prominent term in this connection is προσκαλεῖν, which occurs nine times in Mark. In only two of the texts where it appears is it used as an address by Jesus to the crowds or opponents (7.14; 3.23), and in the latter case the passage is ambiguous, so that it could mean that, following the public attack on Jesus by those who accused him of being in league with Beelzebul, he explained to his disciples (αὐτοῖς) why that could not in fact be the case. The confidential force of the word is implied in 15.44, where Pilate is reported as having conferred privately with the centurion in charge of the crucifixion. Elsewhere the word occurs in contexts which describe Jesus as taking the disciples aside for esoteric instruction (3.13; 6.7; 8.1; 8.34; 10.42; 12.43). Significantly, the term is used in these last six instances in editorial passages which provide the setting for what Jesus is about to say or do.

Another Markan term which functions in an even more explicitly esoteric way is the phrase κατ' ἰδίαν, with its synonym, κατὰ μόνας. These are found in Mark eight times; in each instance there is a private instruction or a private act involved. Mark 4.10, 34, and 13.3 describe explanation in private of public teaching (parables; announcement of the destruction of Jerusalem). 7.33 and 9.28 represent healings performed out of the sight of the crowd, while 6.31f. describes an unsuccessful attempt at withdrawal and rest which culminates in the feeding of the multitude by the lake. 9.2 introduces the story of the special vision of Jesus exalted with Moses and Elijah. The fact that in every instance this expression of privacy occurs in the editorial framework of the narratives or teachings is important for our immediate purposes.

Although Jesus is addressed as teacher by friend and foe in Mark, and within the main body of the pericopes included in Mark,[15] it is in the editorial framework that his teaching (both noun and verb) is referred to with great frequency: διδαχή 5 times; διδάσκω 17 times. In one case, the term occurs in a quotation from the LXX – quoted in a controversy story when Jesus' opponents are trying to trap him with the question about obligations to Caesar (12.14). But in all the other texts the term is purely editorial, serving to introduce or provide the setting for the narratives or sayings material that follows. It is enough for a moment to note the phenomenon; in ch.5 we shall consider the implications of this choice of language for describing Jesus and his work.

In the opening paragraphs of this chapter we noted that Mark has a fondness for using ἄρχομαι as a helping verb. Indeed the usage appears 26 times in the gospel, and is distributed throughout the work, with only four chapters lacking at least one occurrence. The majority of the occurrences are in Mark 6; 8; 10; 14 – mostly in texts which are of major significance for Mark's understanding of Jesus and the gospel, and frequently in conjunction with such other Markanisms as διδάσκειν. Every one of the 26 occurrences of the word in Mark represents the helping-verb usage. In 15 of these, the word appears in the editorial or introductory framework of the particular pericope: 1.45; 2.23; 4.1; 5.20; 6.2; 6.7, 34, 55; 8.11, 31, 32; 10.32; 11.15; 12.1; 13.5. In the other instances the term is found within the body of the pericope: 5.17; 10.18, 41, 47; 14.19, 33, 65, 69, 71; 15.8, 18. In each of these instances the intent seems to be to heighten the dramatic qualities of the incident, as when the Gerasenes urge Jesus to leave their district, or when Peter rebukes Jesus, or the young maid insists that Peter was indeed a follower of Jesus, or Jesus' struggles begin in Gethsemane, or his tormentors attack him. In short, ἄρχομαι[16] as a helping verb is clearly a stylistic favourite of Mark. Its presence in the editorial frames of pericopes and in the body of longer narrative sections (which is the case with all the references in our second grouping above) suggests that both of these have undergone Markan adaptation, just as the connective tissue has been fashioned by him and bears the impress of his vocabulary and style.

2. THE SIGNIFICANCE OF MARK'S INTERPOLATION TECHNIQUE

One of the striking stylistic features of Mark, mentioned earlier and long noted by commentators,[17] is the way Mark has inserted material as a unit in the middle of another unit. In some cases the result is an interruption of a narrative, while in others it effects a transformation of the narrative. Of the eight most obvious instances of this interpolation technique, four include a word or phrase when resuming the interrupted unit, which recalls the earlier half. In tabular form the interpolation phenomenon looks like this:

INTERPOLATION TECHNIQUE IN MARK

Original Unit	Interpolated Unit	Repeated Term
2.1–5a + 2.10b–12 Healing of Paralytic	2.5b–10a Authority to Forgive	λέγει τῷ παραλυτικῷ
3.1–3 + 3.5b–6 Healing of Man with Withered Arm	3.4–5a Healing on Sabbath	λέγει τῷ ἀνθρώπῳ
3.20–21 + 3.31–35 Jesus' Family in Opposition	3.22–29 Beelzebul Controversy and Forgiveness	καὶ ἔρχεται
5.21–24a + 5.35–43 Healing of Daughter of Synagogue Ruler	5.25b–34 Healing of Haemorrhaging Woman	
6.6b–13 + 6.30 Sending and Return of Twelve	6.14–29 Death of John	παρήγγειλεν αὐτοῖς ἀπήγγειλαν αὐτῷ
11.12–14 + 11.20–25(?) Cursing Fig Tree	11.15–18 Cleansing the Temple	
14.53f. + 14.66–72 Peter's Denial	14.55–65 Sanhedrin Hearing	
15.6–15 + 15.21–32 Sentencing and Execution of Jesus	15.16–20 Mocking by Soldiers	

The interpolation technique functions in a variety of ways in Mark: in the first two cases (2.1ff.; 3.1ff.) it serves to convert a wonder story into a controversy story; the third (3.20ff.) eases the otherwise embarrassing account of opposition towards Jesus from his own family by shifting the onus to 'the scribes from Jerusalem' (3.22). The fourth adds to the suspense of the first healing by inserting the second (5.21ff.), while in the fifth example, mention of John the Baptist in connection with mounting public notice of Jesus' activities opens the way for the vivid digression about John's death – in a manner reminiscent of the famous recognition scene in the *Odyssey*, when the reader must wait through a detailed description of how Odysseus received his scar before learning whether his former nurse will identify him by it. This literary technique, described illuminatingly by Erich Auerbach in relation to the Homeric passage,[18] serves here to occupy the attention of the reader while two open-ended factors are in view: the outcome of the disciples' missionary circuit, and the ultimate response of the civil authorities to Jesus.

This interpolation embodies a marked departure for Mark on several counts. Nowhere else in the gospel is there such a story without any direct connection with Jesus.[19] The language of the pericope is more cultivated than is usual for Mark; it lacks historical presents, and includes several Markan ἅπαξ λεγόμενα, as Lohmeyer noted.[20] Thus, the narrative seems to represent a somewhat higher cultural level than is normal for Mark, and may embody a report from a previously existing document. The neutrality of attitude towards both John and Herod would tell in favour of a non-Markan origin for the pericope, but it has been incorporated into the narrative in a wholly Markan fashion with a notably different tradition serving as its literary frame.

In the three remaining interpolated sections (11.15–18; 14.55–65; 15.16–20) the fulfilment of scripture plays a central role. In 11.17, a verse introduced by typical Markan editorial terms, the meaning of the cleansing of the Temple turns on the combination of passages quoted from Isa. 56.7 and Jer. 7.11: the Temple is disqualified as the place where mankind approaches God to honour him. In the hearing before the Sanhedrin the climax is reached in the confession of Jesus which consists of a combination of scriptural texts (Ps. 110.1 and Dan. 7.13) and asserts God's ultimate vindication of Jesus. In the last of the interpolations there is an ironical recollection of the kingly tradition of Judaism, derived from the Hellenistic tradition (I Macc. 1.9; 11.13) and aped by the later Maccabean rulers (I Macc. 10.20, 62), with their golden crowns and purple robes.

In this section of Mark, however, the theme of fulfilment of scripture comes in the representation of the crucifixion itself, where Mark points to the correspondence between its details and the psalms of lament (Pss.69.21; 22.18; 109.25). *Thus the interpolation procedure serves in some cases to alter the tradition in order to make it more directly useful or acceptable to the community of Mark, or to heighten its dramatic impact, or to demonstrate the conformity of the trial and death of Jesus to what God had ordained in scripture.* Literary means are employed to serve dogmatic and pragmatic ends.

3. The Function of Mark's Framework and Transitions

The first scholar to focus attention on the framework of Mark and its significance for interpreting the gospel as a whole was K. L. Schmidt.[21] After identifying editorial language, Schmidt proposed that the following are summarizing passages produced by Mark to serve as connectives for the tradition which he was arranging and organizing:[22]

1.21ff.; 1.39; 2.13; 3.7–12; 5.21; 6.6b; 6.12f.; 6.30–33; 6.53–56. In addition, Schmidt asserted that the passion narrative in its chronological and topographical framework was the product of Mark. The church required such an account for apologetic and liturgical needs. The material had been preserved in fragments; Mark put it together.[23] On the primitive nature of the basic tradition, however, Schmidt's outlook was generally conservative and confident. Schmidt was primarily sceptical about the sequence; he attributed nearly the whole of it to Mark.

In retrospect, however, one wonders why Schmidt limited himself to such a short list of connective passages.[24] A more useful distinction, which for reasons discussed below cannot be sharply maintained in every case, is that between summarizing passages and transitional passages. They may be grouped as follows:

Summarizing Passages: 1.32–34; 3.7–12; 6.12f.; 6.53–56; *Transitional Passages*: 1.21f.; 1.39; 2.13; 4.1; 5.1; 6.6b; 6.30; 7.1; 9.14; 9.30; 10.1.

Closer examination of the summarizing sections shows that they have been carefully positioned by Mark to draw attention to the nature of the mission of Jesus and his followers. 1.32–34 describes what Jesus' ministry includes – especially healings and exorcisms – and then turns to a compact account of the outreach into other villages of his work of preaching and healing (1.35–39). 3.7–12 again summarizes the activity of Jesus, but this time we are led into the report of his choosing the Twelve to extend his own activity (7.13–19). The third summary (6.12f.) is immediately preceded by another account of the dispatch of the disciples on their mission and of the specific instructions given to them for carrying out their assignment (6.6b–11). In the last of these more extensive summaries we have once more a description of Jesus' own activity (6.53–56), but it is preceded by the solemn note that the disciples did not yet comprehend the significance of Jesus or his intentions (6.52).

The first summary marks the end of Mark's initial series of anecdotes in which the healings and exorcisms of Jesus are succinctly depicted; it was probably those anecdotes contained in the collection noted in ch.II that served as one of Mark's sources. Between the first and second summary is a group of controversy stories, shaped from various traditional sources by the special interests of Mark's community. The material between the second and third summaries is miscellaneous, including as it does parables, accounts of conflicts, and the most extensive wonder stories in Mark (5.1–43). The two last summaries bracket the stories of the Feeding of Five Thousand and the Walking on the Sea.

Before examining the passages we have labelled transitional, we must ask, Why are there not summaries in the rest of Mark comparable to those found in the first six chapters? It is almost universally recognized by interpreters of Mark that two major transition points in the later parts of the gospel appear: 1. when Jesus begins to ask the disciples directly about his identity, in the vicinity of Caesarea Philippi (8.27–30), an incident followed by the first direct prediction of his death, and 2. when Jesus takes his disciples with him towards Jerusalem (11.1).[25] Preceding each of them in Mark is the story of the restoration of sight to a blind man (8.22–26 and 10.46–52). And prior to each of these healing stories is an extended pericope in which the inability of the disciples to understand who Jesus is is presented – precisely the note that was sounded in connection with the fourth of the stylized summaries referred to above. In 8.14–21 the disciples are challenged and implicitly rebuked by him for their failure to understand what Jesus has been trying to communicate to them. The immediate problem is a dispute over 'the breads' (8.16), but it is clear that this term is a symbolic reference to something far more profound than a temporary food shortage. Their inability to comprehend is attributed to hardened hearts, a failing which is itself in accord with scripture (8.18 = Jer. 5.21 or Ezek. 12.2 in LXX).

Without entering into the question here of the symbolic reference, it is evident that there is an intended link between the inability of the disciples to 'see' and the story of the blind man who receives sight – in two stages! – in what follows. Similarly, the faith of blind Bartimaeus (a factor underscored in 10.52) stands in contrast to the self-seeking bid for power and position on the part of James and John in the story that precedes it (10.35–45). The full meaning and the ultimate demand of discipleship are explained to the disciples, even though the subsequent events portray them as unable to comprehend that truth, much less to accept it. Thus, *both* stories of the blind who see throw in sharp relief the portraits of the disciples who cannot understand even when an explanation is offered to them: ὀφθαλμοὺς ἔχοντες οὐ βλέπετε. Accordingly, these stories fulfil the same transitional role in Mark as did the earlier summaries, in that they sum up what has gone before (the great miracles of feeding in 6–8; the necessity of suffering in 8.27–10.45) and yet point ahead to the inability of the disciples to perceive the reality to which Jesus' actions and instructions correspond. What is most important about these stories is not the substance of the miracles but the implicit epistemology: for Mark *understanding of reality is not achieved by availability of evidence but by revelatory insight.* The stories stand, therefore, as illustrations of the dictum set forth in Mark 4.11, which might be paraphrased, 'God has graciously given to you, the members of the chosen community, to comprehend the secret of his eschatological kingdom; but to outsiders everything remains enigmatic.'

The connection with the sight-to-the-blind stories is confirmed by the quotation here of a related text (Isa.6.9f.): βλέποντες βλέπωσιν καὶ μὴ ἴδωσιν. That the inability to perceive is the intended outcome rather than merely a chance result is clear from the final line of the quotation, μήποτε ἐπιστρέψωσιν καὶ ἀφεθῇ αὐτοῖς. Thus, the two strategically located stories of healing look ahead to the events in 14–15, which will simultaneously demonstrate how Jesus' own unconditional commitment to the divine will leads to his suffering and death (as he had predicted) and how the disciples' lack of comprehension of what had been explicitly told them led to their betrayal and abandonment of Jesus.

The first of the transitional passages listed above includes several features of Mark's view of Jesus and the gospel which are of central importance for the Markan scheme (1.21f.). Since the story proper begins clearly with 1.23, there is no mistaking that these verses are introductory material, and a comparison with other introductory material throughout Mark has shown that the language and perspective are Mark's own. First, Jesus is presented primarily as a teacher, although his 'teaching' includes powerful acts, such as the exorcism which is about to be described (1.23–28). That is made explicit in the repetition of διδαχή and ἐξουσία in v.27 (cf.22). Second, at this stage in Mark's narrative, Jesus' activity is focused on the Jews and its locale is the synagogues. His antagonists are the scribes, and his work is differentiated from them by virtue of the authority (ἐξουσία) which his teaching evidences. 1.21f. serves, therefore, as a transition from the preparatory events in the public career of Jesus - baptism, testing, thematic statement of his gospel, initial summoning of the core of the community of his followers – by specifying the locus, the mode, the quality, and the nature of the opposition to the work of Jesus as the herald of the kingdom of God.

1.39 has been indicated in our list as a transitional passage, and such it surely is. In form and wording it recalls 1.21ff.; it is a briefer summary of the summary that precedes it (1.32–34) and an anticipation of the summary in 3.7–12. But in fact that whole section, 1.35–39, is a transitional passage, [26] and adds nothing to the picture of Jesus' public activity. The one new element is the link between his activity and the implied divine mission, εἰς τοῦτο γὰρ ἐξῆλθον (1.38),[27] but that is already disclosed to the reader by the voice at Jesus' baptism (1.11). And the factor of prayer which is introduced here appears throughout Mark in contexts where either Jesus withdraws to commit himself to the will of God in preparation for his mission (6.46; 14.32, 35, 38, 39) or the disciples are urged to resort to prayer to meet their obligations and challenges (11.24, 25; 13.18; similarly, the noun, προσευχή, in 9.29).[28]

Thus 1.35–39 serves as a transition into the next set of miracle/controversy stories in Mark, even while looking beyond them to the passion events and the wider mission. There is probably some schematic significance in the further mention here of Galilee, which was noted in 1.14 as the place of the launching of Jesus' mission, and again in the rounding-off comment at the end of the first miracle story (1.28), where it is emphatically asserted that the report of Jesus' exorcisms went out *everywhere*, *immediately*, throughout the *whole* of the territory *surrounding* Galilee. Again (1.39) it is the *whole* of Galilee that benefits from Jesus' preaching and exorcisms.

Two vocabulary features of 1.38 may be noted: κωμοπόλεις is found nowhere else in the New Testament, and is likely to be Mark's own term, since elsewhere he uses the more common πόλις and κώμη; the phrase τὰς ἐχομένας is uncommon in the New Testament, and probably is used nowhere else in the New Testament with this connotation of 'nearby'.[29] Both the editorial origin of the whole passage (1.35–39) and the familiarity of the editor with Greek are indicated by these terms.

2.13; 4.1, and 5.1 are editorial, transitional passages that have in common the locus of Jesus' activity: the sea. Teaching is mentioned as the central feature of his activity in 2.13; 4.1, and 6.6b, as it is in 6.30. Mention of the crowds that thronged about him appears in 2.13; 4.1; 9.14; 10.1, while an indication of the encompassing scope of his activity is given in 6.6b, and in 6.31 the size of the crowds forces Jesus and his followers to withdraw. Only in 9.30 is there specific mention of Jesus' desire to be concealed from the crowds, although in 5.1 his initial contact in Gerasa is with the single person, the demoniac (5.2, ἄνθρωπος ἐν πνεύματι ἀκαθάρτῳ). In short, *the transitional passages* – with the possible exception of 7.1 – *are highly stylized in form, content, and function.* Not all elements are present in them all, but there is a remarkable and significant commonality about them. They all not only serve to move from section to section of Mark's account of Jesus, but also *underline the picture of him as an itinerant teacher, whose interpretation of the will of God is manifest in his powerful actions, especially the exorcisms and healings, as well as in his interpretations of the Law.*

The function of these transitional passages is not really different, therefore, from the function served by the more elaborate *Sammelberichte*. Indeed, in several instances critics have been hard put to make a sharp differentiation between the two types of editorial material. A closer look at 3.7–12 and 6.53–56 will indicate the reason for this difficulty, or to put it positively, analysis of the two extended passages will show why shorter and longer summarizing sections serve much the same purpose in the intention of Mark. The following common factors may be noted:

1. The disciples. In 3.7, Jesus, together with his disciples, withdraws to escape the pressure of the crowds. In 6.53–56 the disciples are not mentioned, but the end of the preceding pericope concerning the walking on the water treats explicitly of the incomprehension of the disciples (51b, 52).

2. The sea. The destination of Jesus and the disciples in 3.7 is the sea, just as it is in 6.53. In both cases they then retreat into a boat (3.9; 6.54).

3. The occasion for the retreat in both cases is the size of the crowds attracted by Jesus (3.7; implicit in 6.54bff.).

4. Although in 6.53ff. there is no indication of the places from which the crowds originate, in 3.7f. they are said to be from Galilee, Judea, Jerusalem, Idumea, beyond the Jordan, and from the vicinity of Tyre and Sidon. Thus Mark wants clearly to imply that already during his lifetime Jesus was evoking a response of faith from among Gentiles. In 6.56, on the other hand, attention is given to the kinds of

places where Jesus was active: fields and public market-places, cities and villages.

In spite of these similarities, the two summary passages have significant differences as well. In 3.11 the unclean spirits acknowledge Jesus to be 'son of God', and must be commanded to keep this silent (3.12). In 6.56 faith in him has reached the level that it is sufficient for the person in need merely to touch him, presumably without his speaking a commanding word, as in the earlier Markan accounts of exorcisms (e.g., 1.25). What is probably at work here, however, is the summarizing function of the 6.53–56 passage whereby Mark recalls for the reader that the woman with the haemorrhage had been healed by her touching Jesus rather than by his word (5.28–30).

On the other hand, μάστιξ (3.10) is found elsewhere in Mark only in the story of the haemorrhaging woman, and thus probably is intended by Mark to anticipate that narrative in 5.25ff. Exorcisms are mentioned in the earlier summary, which is located in close proximity to a series of exorcistic stories and which leads into a discussion of the source of Jesus' authority in performing exorcisms (3.22ff.). Although the summaries differ in detail, they are alike in that both contain words not found elsewhere in Mark, as well as typical Markan expressions.[30] On the grounds of both style and content, *these summaries as we have them are clearly the work of Mark*, and have been developed by him with considerable literary skill to give balance and movement to the whole first part of Mark.

But how do they function in relation to the overall structure of Mark? If our observation is correct that they are more nearly transitional elements than summaries of what has gone before, how are they to be understood in relation to the outline of Mark's gospel? A specific proposal in that connection has been made by L. E. Keck.[31] He sees a kind of chiasmic structure in the first half of Mark in the following pattern:

3.7–12	leads to	4.35–5.43
(Summary)		(Novellen)
6.31–52	summarized in	6.53–56
(Novellen)		(Summary).

The material is found in its present scattered form because Mark has interspersed it with other material and thereby distributed it.[32] Keck's attempt to separate out from the summaries the Markan material fails fully to persuade since he does not take into account the favourite Markan words and expressions which appear in both summaries. In any event, the present form of these passages is what we have to account for in Mark, and the Janus-like quality of them has already been demonstrated. Thus Keck's reconstruction is of limited service in bringing into focus the outline of Mark.

4. Has Mark used an Outline?

The unsatisfactory nature of the outlines proposed for Mark becomes apparent once they are examined in some detail. E. Lohmeyer's proposal is a mixture of geographical and topical designations:

I	1.1–3.6	The Beginnings
II	3.7–6.16	By the Lake of Gennesareth
	6.17–29	John the Baptist
III	6.30–8.26	The Miracle of the Bread
IV	8.27–10.52	The Road to Suffering
V	11.1–13.37	Jesus' Message to Jerusalem
VI	14.1–16.8	The Passion

Ending (shorter and longer forms).

The strength of this proposed outline lies in the fact that it quite rightly marks out as important turning points in the Markan story the confession of Peter (8.27–30) and the entry into Jerusalem (11.1ff.). It also takes into account the significance of the summary in 3.7–12, with which Mark begins a new section, according to Lohmeyer. Its weaknesses outweigh the strengths, however, since the material about the death of John has to be treated as an unattached insertion, and what is more serious, the outline gives no hint of the degree of attention and space allotted to questions about interpretations of the Jewish Law in Sections II, III, IV, V.

Lohmeyer's theory about Galilee as the place where the gospel is to be demonstrated[33] and where eschatological fulfilment is to occur, and Jerusalem as the place of judgment, leads him to emphasize *place* in his outline, although considerations of locale recede in the two central sections. Furthermore, his Galilean hypothesis forces him to assume that the gospel originally ended with an account of an appearance of the Risen Lord to the disciples in Galilee.[34] Certainly Mark 14.28 and 16.7 can be interpreted as pointing to Galilee as the place of resurrection or parousia, but that Mark therefore requires an account of this appearance as the conclusion to his gospel is by no means self-evident.[35] Thus, while the titles Lohmeyer assigned to the various sections of his outline are not wholly inappropriate to the text, they are by no means an adequate indication of the diversity of the material or the complexity with which the story unfolds.

The outline offered by Vincent Taylor in his massive commentary on Mark has the aesthetic merit of symmetry: except for the Introduction (1.1–13) and the Passion and Resurrection (14.1–16.8), every section bears a geographical reference.

1.14–3.6	Galilean Ministry
3.7–6.13	Height of Galilean Ministry
6.14–8.26	Ministry beyond Galilee
8.27–10.52	Caesarea Philippi. Journey to Jerusalem
11.1–13.37	Ministry in Jerusalem.

Taylor is correct that all of Jesus' activity in his Galilean ministry section presumably takes place there, although, as we have seen, Mark takes care to point out from what a wide territory the crowd came to share in the benefits of that ministry – from far beyond Galilee (3.7f.). And a large part of the 'Height of the Galilean Ministry' takes place in the Decapolis and elsewhere east of the lake of Galilee (5.1ff.; 5.21ff.). The Ministry beyond Galilee begins with the death of John the Baptist, and includes activity apparently within Galilee (6.53, although the identification of Gennesaret is debated).[36]

The most serious deficiency in Taylor's outline is that it fails to take into account the thematic shifts in Mark, preferring instead to concentrate on change of locale. One suspects that this may have been done, consciously or unconsciously, to heighten the sense of the historicity of the narrative, of which Taylor was convinced.[37] Not by a tracing of the progress of the gospel from Galilee to Jerusalem, however, but by an analysis of the skill with which Mark has interpreted the career and teaching of Jesus in order to demonstrate its significance for his own time and his own community, can we appreciate Mark's achievement in writing this gospel.

These factors have been taken more fully into account by Norman Perrin in his outline of Mark,[38] especially since he is sensitive to the transitional function of certain passages in Mark:[39]

1.1–13	Introduction
1.14–15	Transitional Markan Summary
1.16–36	Authority of Jesus in Word and Deed
3.7–12	Transitional Markan Summary
3.13–6.6a	Jesus as Son of God and rejected by his people
6.6b	Transitional Markan Summary
6.7–8.21	Jesus as Son of God: misunderstood by his Disciples
8.22–26	Transitional Gaining of Sight Story
8.27–10.45	Christology and Discipleship in Light of the Passion
11.1–12.44	Days in Jerusalem Prior to the Passion
13.1–5a	Introduction to the Apocalyptic Discourse
13.5b–37	Apocalyptic Discourse
14.1–12	Introduction to the Passion Narrative
14.13–16.8	Passion Narrative

Once again the outline gives no hint as to the diversity of material in each section, nor does it suggest the way in which issues with the Jewish leaders over the interpretation of the Law are to be found in every part, even in the passion section.

No recognition is given to the lengthy treatment of parables in the section 3.13–6.6a, which is described in the outline as though it dealt solely with christological issues. Indeed, three of Perrin's titles for sections include christological references, while much more than christology is presented in those passages. If a geographical structuring of Mark is inadequate for pointing up the intention of the gospel, so is an outline that is primarily christological.

It would appear that Mark no more lends itself to analysis by means of a detailed outline developed by simple addition of components than does a major contrapuntal work of music. In spite of illuminating and ingenious attempts to discover *the* one theme which provides the unity of meaning for the structure of Mark, none has been found. The failure, as we noted above,[40] has been compounded by widespread acceptance of the neat dictum that Mark is a passion narrative with an extended introduction. What is required in analysing Mark is to recognize from the outset the multiple themes that are sounded throughout this document. Its simplicity of language must not lead the interpreter to infer a simplicity of thought patterns. At the same time, the search for a master key to Mark must not lead to coercion of texts by over-subtle exegesis. The abandonment of an outline approach based on a process of addition may be a useful first step in discovering the aims of Mark.

5. The Thematic Structure of Mark: Beginning, Middle, and End – Literary and Redemptive-historical Aspects

Viewed externally and as simple narrative, Mark could be considered a tragedy, especially if the seemingly inconclusive end at 16.8 is taken to be the end intended by the author.[41] Following the literary canons of Aristotle, Mark considered as tragedy should exhibit wholeness, evident in a clearly delineated beginning, middle, and end. Quite apart from the inadequacy of this approach for dealing with the whole of the gospel – it is precisely the wholeness that Aristotle insisted must be evident[42] – the attempt to deal with Mark on exclusively or even largely literary terms is doomed to failure, whether that approach be from the standpoint of aesthetics or historiography.

Erich Auerbach brought into focus some of the reasons for this failure when he wrote that the gospels evoke 'the most serious and most significant sympathy' within us because they portray

> something which neither the poets nor the historians of antiquity ever set out to portray: the birth of a spiritual movement in the depths of the common people, from within the everyday occurrences of contemporary life, which thus assumes an importance it could never have assumed in antique literature.[43]

Commenting on the gospel account of Peter's denial of Jesus, he observes that this literary material 'cannot be fitted into a system of judgment which operates within static categories', rather, it 'fits into no antique genre', is

> too serious for comedy, too everyday for tragedy, politically too insignificant for history – and the form which was given it is one of such immediacy that its like does not exist in the literature of antiquity.[44]

Beyond Auerbach's perceptive and accurate observations about the impossibility of fitting the gospels into the genres of antiquity, another important dimension of the Gospel of Mark which differentiates it from biography and historiography of its time, and yet manifests kinship in certain respects with familiar forms of Jewish literature of that period, is the view of history which it embodies and the resultant mode of 'historical' narrative that this view leads the writer to produce. This type of writing is Jewish apocalyptic.

In Chapter IV we shall turn our attention to the historical development of that movement, to other details of its literary features than those to be considered here, and above all, to the social structures in which this literature was produced. Here, however, we confine ourselves to the interrelation between historical outlook and literary mode, as it has bearing on the structure of Mark, viewed as a product of an apocalyptic community.

The classic document produced in the apocalyptic category is, of course, the book of Daniel.[45] Three features of that work concern us: 1. The work is given the form of historical description, in which, by the use of both literal and symbolic modes, the meaning of the crisis in which the writer finds himself and his community is represented as providing the clue to the whole course and the culmination of human history. 2. The literary sequence of Daniel is such that, although the work includes detailed depictions of the events of the end time, 'Daniel' represents himself as expecting to live on in the present crisis, pending the ultimate denouement. After learning through visions about the end of the age when 'all these things would be accomplished' (Dan.12.7), he is told, ' "Go your way, Daniel, for the words are shut up and sealed until the time of the end . . . None of the

wicked shall understand, but the wise shall understand"' (Dan.
12.10). The work ends on a note of expectancy rather than of fulfilment. 3. The immediate concern of the writer is with the response of
his addressees to the present crisis – rather than with either a factual
recounting of the past or a detailed portrayal of their vindication in
the future. Thus, the stories at the beginning of Daniel serve as advice
to the community addressed by Daniel as to how it is to respond to
paganizing pressures in matters of diet (Dan. 1), divine honours to the
ruler (Dan. 3), and personal piety (Dan. 6).[46] The stories of God's
deliverance of his faithful from the wicked schemes of pagan rulers is
a guarantee that he will vindicate his people and fulfil his purpose in
the end time. Meanwhile, they must trustingly and courageously
endure.

The apocalyptic literature, therefore, embodies *simultaneously two
different conceptions of beginning-middle-end*. The first is the *literary mode*,
which begins with the rise of the present crisis, even while sketching in
the historical antecedents and precedents, points ahead to the eschatological denouement, but concentrates primarily on the present penultimate critical moment in which is required endurance of the
faithful, even to the point of martyrdom (Dan. 4). The second is *the
eschatological-historical mode*, according to which the purpose of God for
his creation has been thwarted by diabolical powers, whose rage is
being poured out in an especially venomous way upon the writer's
contemporary community of the saints. They are called upon to
persevere and have been given the wisdom and insight to do so
through the revelation given to them of the ultimate fate of the
wicked and vindication of the faithful. Can Mark be appropriately
understood on the basis of these dual modes, with what might be
called an apocalyptic philosophy of history as its presupposition and
with the literary strategy of apocalypse as providing its structure?
Both parts of this question must be answered in the affirmative.

Mark indeed presupposes an age-long purpose of God, which he
traces back to the beginning of creation (10.6; 13.19), a phrase which
– not incidentally – Mark shares with Dan. 12.1! Both passages are
highly significant. The 10.6 reference is to the purpose of God in
creation, as evident in his having made human beings with sexual
differentiation, so that marriage has been a part of the divine order
since creation. In 13.19 the whole sweep of human history is represented as beginning with the creation and coming to its climax in the
pangs through which creation passes before the new age dawns.
These 'days' are further differentiated from ἕως τοῦ νῦν (19b) in which
Mark is addressing (or portrays Jesus as addressing) his readers. The

epoch of Mark is represented by the opening phrase of his writing: 'The beginning of the gospel of Jesus Christ' (1.1). By metaphor (13.28) as well as by direct statement (13.30, 'this generation will not pass away before all these things take place'), but with due caution nevertheless (13.32, no one except the Father knows the day), the end is expected within the lifetime of Mark's readers, as the instructions to be ready and watchful clearly imply. Only those to whom the 'mystery' has been given – i.e., by God – are able to perceive what is taking place (4.11). When the final violent acts of the evil powers (13.14) take place just prior to the end (13.13), it is only the divinely enlightened 'reader' who will be able to 'understand' (13.14).

We shall see in the next chapter how Mark regards the saints as a redefined community, but it should be noted here that the crisis calls for a re-examination of the tradition embodied in the Torah, a re-assessment of obligations to established authorities, and a heightened sense of mutual responsibilities within the covenant community. It is on account of these factors that the controversy stories and the discussions about the Law are neither mere anti-Jewish polemics, nor are they extraneous to the main concerns of Mark. While the Markan community differs from scribal Judaism on specifics in its interpretation of the Law, the Law provides it with its basic orientation as well as with the images and models – social and historical – in terms of which it regards itself in the purpose of God.

As this view of God, of the world and its history, and of the community of faith informs the thought of Mark, it manifests itself in literary ways as well. Mark begins his writing, not with the 'beginning of creation' but with the 'beginning of the gospel', the event that provides him and his community with a perspective on the whole of the purpose of God from creation to consummation. He writes with the clear conviction that the recent past in which Jesus came from God with his words and acts is constitutive for both the present life of the community and for its vindication in the future. But the 'present' of the Markan account is (ostensibly, as in Daniel) not the time of the Markan community but the time of Jesus, the καιρός fulfilled, the nearness of the kingdom of God (1.15), the time for repentance and faith in the good news of what God is beginning to do in preparation of the creation for the consummation of his purpose. Side by side, therefore, there must run several themes: revelation and lack of understanding; minor triumphs and the major tragedy; proximate defeat and ultimate vindication; changing rules and binding obligations; ancient images and their contemporary transformation. Only the 'reader' who 'understands' will perceive in this the meaning of the past of Jesus, its significance for him and his community, not only in its critical present but in its glorious future as well. Thus, the story ends without a conclusion – outwardly terminating in the seeming defeat of Jesus and his mission, an inference which is complicated, however, by the mysterious business about an empty tomb and a promise of resumption of relationship between Jesus and his followers in Galilee. Like Daniel's vision of the last days (Dan. 10.6–11 [Theodotion]), those who receive the heavenly message are overcome with fear, ecstasy, and trembling.

In structuring his gospel, Mark has bracketed it with the beginning of Jesus' public mission as the opening, and the awestruck response of the faithful women to the message (addressed to the disciples) at the end (16.8). The final outcome of the redemptive enterprise has been made clear throughout, however, especially in Mark 13. But the overall aim of Mark is not to offer a complete, sequential report of the career of Jesus nor to depict in detail what the end of the age will be like. He includes elements of both to the extent that they have direct significance for the religious community of his own time. It is with the community's present that he is mainly concerned, although the details of the story of Jesus that he reports are of fundamental importance for that community's self-understanding.

The literary device of speaking to the crises of the religious community in the present under the guise of an account from the past is a characteristic feature of the apocalypticists. 'Historical backdating'[48] was used in Daniel to safeguard the community from alerting the Seleucid rulers to the document's political implications. Similarly in I Enoch and Jubilees, the backdating technique is employed at least in part for protective purposes, although other documents written as though they came from earlier periods (such as the Testaments of the Twelve Patriarchs,[49] II Baruch, the Ezra Apocalypse and Testament of Abraham) either reflect no known political crisis or deal with the aspiration towards eschatological fulfilment in more personal terms.[50] Rather than intending primarily to conceal the group's secrets from outsiders, the backdating of the apocalypses seeks to place the community and its destiny in the framework of a larger, longer-range context of divine purpose, and to lend to the anonymous or pseudonymous writer the weight of authority of a worthy man of God from Israel's past. As the Revelation of John shows, the factor of distancing the document from the writer's situation by the literary device of backdating was not always operative in Christian apocalypses, even though the basic pattern of seeing the present crisis within the community in the context of the past and future disclosures of God's purpose is evident in Revelation, as it is in all apocalyptic writings, including Mark.

One of the most important literary devices of the apocalypticists is their biographical or autobiographical stance. In all its parts, the Book of Enoch is told in the first person, the writer representing himself as describing scenes and visions that have been granted to him. Jubilees surveys the past and future history of Israel; the work is described as having been conveyed through an experience of Moses himself on Sinai (Jub.1.4ff.). Although the situation of the writer is clearly the Maccabean period (Jub.32.1, where the priests are given a title used only in Maccabean times), he illumines his time by tracing the history of the nation from creation onward, placing it in the rigid, deterministic framework of Qumran chronology. The Testaments of the Twelve Patriarchs all include an autobiographical sketch, ostensibly by the progenitors of each of the twelve tribes. The foundational document of the Qumran community CD, or to give it its full title, The Document of the New Covenant in the Land of Damascus, begins with a biographical account of the origins of the sect: after describing briefly how God's providence had preserved the remnant following the destruction of the Temple and the exile of his people, the writer declares:

> But they were like blind men,
> and like men who groping seek their way
> for twenty years.
> And God considered their works,
> for they had sought him with a perfect heart;
> and he raised up for them a Teacher of Righteousness
> to lead them in the way of his heart
> and to make known to the last generations
> what he would do to the last generation,
> the congregation of traitors.

(CD 1, 9–12)

Similarly, the Hodayoth in their entirety are confessions – presumably by the Teacher – of the oppression he experienced and of God's sustaining grace, both aspects of which are to serve as paradigms for the community as a whole. Thus the apocalyptic writers do not develop their ideas in the abstract, nor are they presented in terms of broad generalizations about the course of history. The authors adopt the stance within history as it is known to the community, and focus upon a central figure as the one through whom God has graciously supplied insight by revelatory means into his purpose, his expectations of his people, and the destiny of those who ignore or oppose his will. The narrative and biographical dimensions of this literature are integral to its objectives, and are not merely an allegorical device for conveying theological ideas or principles. Apocalypticism must be seen, therefore, not only as a literary form or a pattern of history, but as a life-structure as well.

However, it is possible to derive certain conceptual presuppositions from these documents, and an awareness of these is obviously an important facet of the apocalyptic world-view. The aims of apocalyptic, theologically perceived, may be grouped as follows:[51]

1. Assert the Triumph of the Rule of God.
2. Assert the Defeat of the Hostile Powers.
3. Redefine the Community of Faith.
4. Demonstrate the Certainty of the Outcome.
5. Present the Message to the Community: Stand Firm!

(i) *The rule of God and its triumph*[52]

Under the influence of Persian dualism, with its angels and demons, its personification of evil,[53] post-exilic Judaism came to stress not only the transcendence of God[54] but also his strategy of working his purpose in the world through intermediaries rather than by direct action.[55] M. Hengel has shown that the Eastern delight in esoteric wisdom, of which apocalyptic was one special kind of manifestation, was admired in Hellenistic times, so that the rise of this literature is to be seen, not as a peculiar, isolated phenomenon within Judaism, but as part of wide cross-cultural influences in the period following Alexander the Great.[56] The basic assertion of the apocalypticists was that God, having permitted the powers opposed to him to operate to human detriment in the cosmos, was about to display his sovereignty by defeating those powers and establishing his rule. The beneficiaries of this new situation, and the only ones who truly perceived what God was about to do, were the faithful and elect members of the community to whom he had chosen to reveal his purposes in visions and cryptic messages.

The establishment of the rule of God is not conceived as taking place by God's direct action in the human sphere, but through his intermediate agents. This is implied in the simile of Dan.3.25, where the three faithful men in the furnace are accompanied by and presumably given courage by a being 'like a son of the gods'. The king himself receives his message of doom through 'a watcher, a holy one' who comes 'down from heaven' (Dan.4.13). Gabriel brings wisdom and understanding to Daniel (9.21), just as Michael comes to help (10.13), even though he must battle the hosts of evil in order to carry out his mission. In Test. Levi 18.12 the messianic priest is the one who defeats Beliar, while in Test. Judah 24.1ff. and Test. Naphtali 8.1ff. there are two anointed figures, Levi the priest and Judah the king. Similarly, in the appendix to the Scroll of the Rule (2.11–15) there are two anointed ones through whom the true worship of God and the true rule over his people are administered in the new age. The agents or the means employed are not always specified, however: in Dan. 7.27 we read:

> And the kingdom and the dominion
> and the greatness of the kingdoms under the whole heaven
> shall be given to the saints of the Most High;
> and their kingdom shall be an everlasting kingdom,
> and all dominions shall serve and obey them.

(ii) *The defeat of the hostile powers*

In considering the kingdom of God and its coming, there is no escaping the reality which it replaces: the rule of evil. We have just noted that the agents for establishing God's rule bring about Beliar's defeat. That theme is expanded upon in the Enoch literature, as in the account of the fallen angels (I Enoch 6–16) and the defeat of Satan (53–56).[57] What is remarkable in all this literature is that the apocalypticists move easily from the metaphorical representation of their historical enemies (the Seleucids; the corrupt priests) to demonic opponents, to cosmic powers. The political problems – involving both civil and religious authorities – will not be resolved until the demonic and cosmic powers are also brought under control (cf. The Song of Moses, Ex. 15, especially 4–10).[58] The very fact that the imagery used to depict the political powers is drawn from the cosmic mythology of the ancient Near East – raging waters, mysterious mountains, falling stars, earthquakes – underscores the interconnection between present realities and unseen powers.

(iii) *The redefinition of the community*

A recurrent theme in the apocalypses is that power is being abused. The royal authority has been repressive; the priestly power has become corrupt or even idolatrous (Test. Levi 16.1ff.; Ass. Moses 2.6f.; Jubilees 1.9–22, where the spirit of Beliar is assigned responsibility for the apostasy; Damascus Document 4.13–19, where the nets of Belial are described, culminating in the defilement of the sanctuary by the unworthy priests). What is called for, therefore, is the reconstitution of the covenant community, not to evade the will of God but to fulfil it properly. The roots of this notion are found in classical prophecy, both in the idea of the remnant in Isaiah (7.3ff.; 10.20–23) and the concept of the new covenant in Jeremiah (31.31–34). The remnant conception of the community is given full and explicit expression in the Damascus Document (CD 3.12b–21):

> And because of those who clung to the commandment of God
> and survived them as a remnant,
> God established his covenant with Israel for ever,
> revealing to them the hidden things
> in which all Israel had strayed:
> his holy sabbaths and his glorious feasts,
> his testimonies of righteousness, and his ways of truth,
> and the desires of his will
> which man must fulfil that he may live because of them.
> He opened (this) before them,
> and they dug a well of abundant waters (i.e., the Torah; cf. 6.4),
> and whoever despises these waters shall not live.
> But they defiled themselves by the sin of man[59]
> and by ways of defilement,
> and they said, 'This is ours!'
> And God in his marvellous mysteries
> forgave their iniquity
> and blotted out their sin;
> and he built for them a sure house in Israel (= the community)
> such as did not exist from former times till now.[60]
> They who cling to it are (destined) for everlasting life
> and theirs shall be all the glory of man.[61]

The community accordingly regards itself as a kind of colony of the end time. They have been founded as a new beginning to the age-old outworking of God's purpose for his covenant people, a purpose that was thwarted by the combined effects of human wilfulness and demonic conspiracy. Through the insights revealed to the community by its teacher or seer or prophet, it can understand the tragic events developed in the past, what its present responsibilities are, and what God has in store for its glorious future. In fidelity to this revelation, its members must live in obedient expectation.

(iv) *The certainty of the outcome*

The undergirding of the certainty of the apocalyptic community concerning the fulfilment of what it awaits is its conviction that God is fully sovereign in his creation (Dan.6.26; 7.14; I Enoch 9.3–6; 101.1–9). This theme is specified in the repeated references to the heavenly tablets on which the course of the history of the creation has been written down in advance, and therefore determined (Jubilees 5.13; 23.32; 30.22; I Enoch 81.1–3; 93.2ff.; Test. Levi 5.4; Dan. 10.21).[62] A succinct statement of this point of view and of man's place within God's creative purpose is offered in the opening part of IQS:

From the God of knowledge comes all that is and shall be,
and before beings were, he established all their design.
And when they are, they fulfil their task according to their statutes,
in accordance with his glorious design, changing nothing within it.
In his hand are the laws of all beings,
and he upholds them in all their needs.
It is he who made man
that he might rule over the earth (3.15–18).

But the predetermined purpose of God is made known on earth as
well – through the scriptures. Jubilees and Daniel build their schemes
of eschatological history on the seventy years of Jeremiah's prophecy
(Jer.25.11f.; 29.10; cf. Dan.9.2 and 24ff., where the years become
weeks-of-years). But all the apocalypses are written as expansions of
scripture: the testament of Jacob (Gen.49) becomes the basis for the
Testaments of (each of) the Twelve (sons); the brief mention of
Enoch's communion with God (Gen.5.22, 24) is expanded into the
vast Enoch literature; Moses' mysterious death (Deut.34.6) offers the
occasion for the apocalyptic material associated with Moses, of which
the Assumption of Moses is the most extensive surviving portion.[63]
From the Dead Sea Scrolls we now have abundant evidence of the
way in which the Jewish scriptures were being mined for confirmation
of the divine purpose behind the events and the persons which had
shaped the destiny of the Qumran community. This strategy is
evident both in the commentaries,[64] where allusions to the past mingle
with references to contemporary events,[65] and in the more basic
writings, such as the Damascus document, where Amos 5.26f. and
Num.24.17 are brought together to prove that the coming of the Star
from Jacob (= the founder of the community, the One who Teaches
the Law Rightly) was ordained in scripture for his role. As is the case
in CD 7.15–19, the form and reading of the biblical text is chosen
freely in order to fit the aims of the interpreter. Scripture becomes,
then, a major ground for the community's certainty about the
achievement of its eschatological expectations.

In the testamentary literature of Jewish apocalypticism, yet
another ground of assurance is offered that God will fulfil his promises
to his faithful people. In keeping with the tradition from the canonical
Jewish writings, whereby his servants are granted a vision of what is
to be in the future as they are coming to the end of their careers –
Jacob, Moses, and Elijah foretell what is to come as they approach
death – this period saw the development of the Testaments of the Twelve
Patriarchs,[66] the Testament of Abraham, and the Testament of Job.[67]
In each of these there is a recounting of the life of the central figure,
including deeds and misdeeds, culminating in a vision of the glorious

future that awaits the faithful in the new age. The vision is granted during the lifetime of the man of faith as proleptic portrayal and inner promise of the vindication that God will effect at the end.[68] The same pattern is evident in Daniel, where the eschatological visions are the basis for the prophet's confidence about the future and for the appeal addressed to him to 'be strong and of good courage' (Dan. 10.18). He possesses the understanding of God's purpose and thus can accept the injunction, 'Go your way' (12.9, 13) 'till the end'.

(v) Stand firm!

The practical aim of the apocalypticists is not to make the insiders proud because they know what others do not, but to strengthen them to persevere in the face of the mounting hostility and suffering that confronts them. The personal confessions of the author of the Hoda-yoth[69] attests this repeatedly:

> It is thou who hast created breath on the tongue . . .
> that thy glory might be made known
> and thy wonders told
> in all thy works of truth and judgments of righteousness,
> and that thy Name might be praised by the mouth of all men . . .
> And it is thou who in thy mercy and in the greatness of thy favours
> hast strengthened the spirit of man in the face of blows,
> and hast redeemed and cleansed him from much iniquity
> that he might recount thy marvels in the presence of all thy works.
>
> (IQH 1.28, 30–32)

> But to all men that fight against me
> . . . thou will give shame of face,
> and ignominy to them that murmur against me.
> For at the time of judgment thou, O my God . . .
> wilt plead my cause.
> For thou hast chastised me in the mystery of thy wisdom
> and hast hidden the truth unto the time of judgment,
> but then thou wilt reveal it.
>
> (IQH 9.22–24)

6. Conclusions

How does the Gospel of Mark fit into these literary patterns with their underlying presuppositions? Mark opens with the declaration that Jesus is a chosen agent of God to bring to fruition his purpose in establishing his sovereignty in the earth. The new situation that Jesus inaugurates (1.1) is announced as the fulfilment of the time of deliverance, the drawing near of God's rule (1.15). John, the herald of his coming, whose role is itself foretold in scripture, points to Jesus as the Mightier One, whose authority will be evident through the divine spirit that he brings. The struggles that will be characteristic, and the satanic opposition, are already announced in 1.12–23.

Thus in the fifteen opening verses Mark has announced the triumph of God's rule, identified the agent through whom it will be established, and uttered a warning about the conflict and personal suffering that the faithful must pass through as the Rule of God moves toward fulfilment. In the next pericope Mark portrays Jesus as assembling the nucleus of the new covenant community and thereby points to the active role which they must assume ('fishers of men') in creating that new people of God.

Clues to the success of the enterprise are offered in the first miracle story, where the demon itself predicts the doom of his enterprise ('Have you come to destroy us?'); and the effectiveness of the exorcism provides a clear answer to the discerning reader when 'the unclean spirits obey him'. The demands of discipleship are likewise announced from the outset in the willingness of the first disciples to leave behind the security and obligations of home, family, and means of livelihood (1.20b).

The initial public success of Jesus' ministry is balanced by his need to withdraw for prayer; that is, for constant commitment to the divine will and renewal. Not surprisingly, Mark is pervaded by references to Jesus' retirement to pray. At least 8 times Mark represents Jesus as urging his followers to 'beware'[70] – to be watchful so that they may persevere in the enterprise to which they have committed themselves in the name of the gospel of the kingdom of God.

Once announced, these themes will run like a great fugue throughout the gospel. The motif of kingdom, for example, is announced in 1.15, is declared in 4.11 to be a mystery reserved for the elect, is promised as being disclosed within the lifetime of Jesus' contemporaries (9.1), is said to be accessible only to those willing to undergo self-denial (10.14ff.; 10.23ff.), is described as being anticipated in the eucharistic meal (14.15), and is mentioned as the object of expectation by Joseph of Arimathea (15.43). And in a final irony, Jesus is put to death on the trumped-up charge of having aspired to be King of the Jews (15.2, 18, 26).

The other themes will be traced in the following chapters more completely than this minimal sketch suggests. But regarded this way, it becomes clear why no simple outline can do justice to the thematic complexity of Mark. The one architectural feature that stands out Mark has placed at the centre of his gospel (Mark 9.2ff.), the eschatological vision of Jesus' exaltation at God's right hand. He has prefaced this with the disciples' enthusiastic and ill-informed identification of Jesus as Messiah (8.29) which is immediately balanced by Jesus' assertion that his role in relation to the coming of God's kingdom can be fulfilled only through suffering and death (8.31). This is the literary fulcrum on which the gospel balances, and it is thoroughly in keeping with the literary strategy of apocalyptic. But to mistake the fulcrum, or the suffering and death associated with it, for the whole structure of Mark is to miss the richness of literary and conceptual skill by which Mark has constructed his gospel.

Written in a biographical style, like other apocalyptical writings, the Gospel of Mark addressed the critical needs of his community in his own time by telling us about the acts and words of a man who stood in a special relationship to God as his agent and spokesman, whose mission was to form about him the obedient covenant people, whose opposition included historical-political powers, demonic and cosmic powers, whose last reported utterances included prophecies of judgment on the wicked and disobedient as well as of deliverance for the persevering faithful, and whose departure from life was shrouded in mystery of a kind that faith alone could penetrate. What sort of person in what sort of primitive Christian group would have been motivated to produce this sort of writing? That is the subject of investigation in our next chapter.

IV

THE SOCIAL AND CULTURAL SETTING
OF THE MARKAN COMMUNITY

What was the *Sitz im Leben* from which and for which Mark's gospel was written? To answer that question responsibly it is not sufficient to attach a general label to Mark – such as Hellenistic-Jewish-Christian, or Palestinian-Jewish-Christian. By analysis of the text itself, but with the aid of paradigms for the study of eschatological communities as well as historical analogies with apocalyptic communities close in space and time to primitive Christianity in the first century, it should be possible to trace the contours of the Markan community. K. Koch may have demanded more than the data can deliver when he called for biblical scholarship to have 'an eye for the total historical context' and insisted that critical work can be done in interpretation 'only where the texts are illuminated by the complete political, economic, religious and linguistic sweep of the biblical world'.[1] But these factors must be kept in view at all times if the social setting of Mark or any other ancient writing is to be brought into focus, thereby enabling the interpreter to perceive the dynamics and the linguistic connotations of the writing itself.

I. THE SOCIAL DYNAMICS OF PROPHETIC MOVEMENTS

The literary analyses of the three previous chapters have pointed repeatedly to the features of Mark that are shared with the literature of Jewish apocalypticism. Most studies of apocalyptic writings have concentrated on the literary forms[2] or on the theological concepts.[3] What must be taken into account in any comprehensive analysis of apocalyptic is the social and cultural factors which gave rise to this kind of literature and this outlook on the world, as well as the kind of community in and for which such documents were produced. Max Weber's classic study is still invaluable for tracing the social dynamics by which 'break-away' movements begin, and apocalyptic groups surely fall into this category.[4]

In a situation where social and political structures have reduced a segment of the society to a status of impotence in terms of power, of moral crisis in terms of unchallenged evil or cynical exploitation of the national leadership, and of questioning of the meaning of life or of one's place in the divine purpose at work in the world, there is a yearning for a framework of understanding in which these hostile forces can be comprehended and in which there is hope of transformation and meaning.[5] The motivating force and the catalyst for such a movement are embodied in a prophet figure.[6] Especially relevant for our purposes is the 'ethical prophet' who regards himself as an instrument of the transcendent God, and whose precepts are the expression of God's will for the true religious community. His power is exerted by means of his personal gifts,[7] his claim to have been granted a personal revelation,[8] and his emotion-packed preaching.[9] The aim to understand the world and to share in the process by which it is being brought into conformity with the divine will is fostered by what Talcott Parsons has called the intellectualism of a relatively non-privileged group,[10] which stands outside the main prestige structure of the society. The disciples of the ethical prophet are an alienated people, but unlike mystics who resolve the ambiguities and discrepancies of the world by denying its reality or by retreating from it into an interior sphere, they claim the world for God, and by means of a 'messianic eschatology', they await the ultimate political and social transformation of the world.[11]

Social anthropologists have long noted similar phenomena among more modern societies living under culturally primitive conditions, such as on the Pacific Islands in the nineteenth or early twentieth centuries.[12] K. O. L. Burridge has traced the stages by which movements arise which expect radical transformation in the future, knowledge of which has been given to the members of the community through a divinely endowed prophet.[13] As Burridge has depicted it, the process begins within a generally permissive political regime, where competing sets of assumptions about power arise. These are in turn related to particular kinds of prestige and integrity, and thus are seen as providing the values and categories in which redemption of the community is sought. This is an especially potent factor when one of two groups sees itself as underprivileged and thus lacking access to redemption.

In the tensions that arise – tensions towards the other group and self-rejection within the group – the existence of a new community is proclaimed, in which new powers and new forms of existence are to be realized. As these hopes begin to take shape in tentative and unfocused ways, a prophet-leader arises who offers direction and certainty. Within the broad outlines of the culture, new assumptions emerge. Through the immediate and partial solutions to problems that the prophet can provide, confidence builds that he can solve the ultimate problems as well; indeed, the problems can be entirely transcended.[14] The revelation which he offers is conveyed in traditional terms and expressed with profound conviction. The new man gains and maintains his status as a person of integrity and prestige; his followers identify with him and yet see in him a man of wider experience and deeper insight. The details of the millennarian aspirations that such prophets offer envisage a new set of rules, new forms of obligation, and 'a new earth in which heaven is more brightly mirrored'.[15]

2. JEWISH SECTARIAN MODELS: THE SOCIAL AND CONCEPTUAL DEVELOPMENT OF HASIDISM

Are the circumstances of the origin of Mark illuminated by reference to these patterns of social dynamics within alienated religious communities? Recent studies of Judaism in the Hellenistic period[16] have drawn attention to a range of ways in which Jews reacted to the conscious, zealous efforts of Alexander's successors to impose Hellenistic culture and cosmopolitanism on the lands under their control, including the territory of the Jews. Although the evidence is regrettably sparse, Martin Hengel has made a strong case for the seriousness of the crisis that arose in Jewish Palestine during the period of Ptolemaic domination. This crisis was a result of the policies of economic exploitation of the Hellenistic rulers and of the enormous appeal of the new life-style that the pagan rulers both exemplified and encouraged among the populace. Positive 'interest in Hellenistic civilization, however, *remained predominantly limited to the well-to-do aristocracy of Jerusalem*'. But the lack of social concern on the part of the political powers and their exclusive concentration on economic exploitation served only 'to exacerbate the situation of the lower strata of the population. It prepared the ground for apocalyptic speculation and the later revolts, which had increasingly strong social elements, right down to the time of the Bar Kochba rebellion.'[17] Hengel goes on to point out that the socio-economic conditions presupposed in the gospel tradition – great landowners, tax farmers, administrators, moneylenders, day-labourers, speculation in grain, slavery for debts – 'can be understood only on the basis of economic conditions brought about by Hellenism in Palestine'.[18]

We shall return later in the chapter to the matter of socio-economic conditions in Palestine in the gospel tradition, but our immediate concern is with the question as to how the social repercussions of Hellenization could have given rise to apocalypticism. The options that were open to Jews in this period seemed to be limited to succumbing to the pressure for adopting Greek ways (as did many of the aristocrats) or accepting the theocratic state which, though it utterly lacked political power, was presided over by the priestly circles in Jerusalem.[19] The Chronicler presented this state of affairs as the way Israel ought to be, and left out of his account the historical development as well as the eschatological thrust of the prophetic tradition.[20] It was precisely this dimension of prophecy that the later additions to the prophetic writings had emphasized, as in the apocalyptic supplements in Isa. 24–27 or Zech. 9–14. The image of the revived people from Ezek. 37 was itself revived, and stress was placed on Israel as the people of God rather than as the theocratic state. If the leaders of the nation took no initiative in moving the people towards this goal, it remained for individuals to associate in voluntary groups to resist the Hellenizing pressures and to pray and plan for the end of the age, whose coming was now expected. Ironically, as Plöger has shown, the resistance to outside influences did not extend to the rejection of either Iranian dualism or of the periodizing of history that was going on in both Iranian and Greek circles – items which indeed were given central positions in apocalypticism. The beginnings of this attitude and its corresponding view of history are evident in the Isaiah Apocalypse, which may be as late as the fourth or third century BC.[21] Here the recurrent phrase 'in that day' (25.8; 27.1) refers to the time when God will execute judgment (26.21) on the creation, wreaking destruction in the earth (24.1, 18) in a manner that recalls Gen. 4 and the days of Noah. The result will be the overturning of the entire social and religious order (24.2) in judgment for violation of the covenant and adoption of a profligate, sensual mode of life (24.5). The faithful, righteous ones who will be vindicated in that day (26.2, 7) are identified as the poor and needy in 25.4 and 26.6. The overturning of the social order and the religious power structure will be accompanied by the defeat of both political and cosmic enemies (24.21), with the image of the dragon from the cosmic waters utilized as the symbol of diabolical evil (27.1).[22] The outcome for the righteous will be the day of resurrection (25.8; 26.19) and the establishment of the Rule of God (24.23). Meanwhile, the faithful community withdraws as a conventicle (26.20) until the day of judgment is past.

Similarly, in the Zechariah Apocalypse (Zech. 9–14), where the Greeks (= Hellenistic powers) are specifically mentioned (9.13), the themes are those of judgment on the faithless leaders ('shepherds') of Israel (11.4, 15, 17; especially 13.7–9), the purging punishment that the nation will undergo (12–13), and the appearance in the last days (14.4, 5, 9, 16–18) of God himself, together with the angels (14.1–5). What is evident from these late prophetic materials is that a thorough-going disaffection and hostility has set in between the acknowledged religious leaders of the Jews and certain groups who feel themselves to be alienated from what should have been their own sacred institutions and from the community that still claimed to be the people of God. The theme of the faithless shepherds who are to be punished in the end time is much more elaborately developed in the Dream Visions of I Enoch (83–90),[23] just as the recurrence of the judgment in the last days on the pattern of the flood in the time of Noah is predicted (83f.). Unlike the Zechariah and Isaiah Apocalypses, however, I Enoch 85–89 has an elaborate schematic portrayal of the course of history from the first deluge to the final judgment, a feature that was incorporated and refined by Daniel.

A Qumran text edited by J. A. Sanders (11QPs[a])[24] not only mentions that the community is to assemble – that is, voluntarily – to proclaim God's (eschatological) salvation, but indicates that this revealed knowledge is not for the learned elite but for the simple, pious ones.[25] Equally important for the understanding of the members of the community about their God-given role is the prayer later in the text that God will grant them forgiveness, and bestow the spirit that will enable them to endure faithfully, so that they will not come under the domination of the Adversary nor be led astray by evil desire.[26] The community sees itself, therefore, over against the official interpreters of the will of God, and certainly in opposition to intellectuals. There is a developing dualism, in which evil spirits and cosmic powers may lead them astray. This document is probably to be assigned to the early second century, since it seems to represent an early stage in the development towards Hasidism as a distinct movement.[27]

It is in the Book of Daniel, however, that the contours of the Hasidic movement become clear and that the features of an apocalyptic community are unambiguously apparent for the first time. The values enjoined by Daniel are maintenance of purity (Dan. 1) and persistence in piety (Dan. 6), even in the face of martyrdom at the hands of the state. To those who thus persevere God grants insight into his future purpose, including foreknowledge of the defeat of their enemies and of their own vindication (Dan. 7–12).

An important aspect of the community's self-understanding or life-world was the belief that its members were living in the penultimate phase of human history: thus in I Enoch 93.10, the elect are described as 'the eternal plant of righteousness' and are given instruction concerning the whole of God's creation. The same point is made in Dan. 8.23 ('at the latter end of their rule'), in 9.27 (where Gabriel's encouraging word comes in the last half of the last week-of-years), and in 11.40, where the last of the visions concerns 'the time of the end'. The community has a period of ongoing responsibility, even though it is convinced that the end is in sight. Its chief concern is to instruct the faithful and to warn them to stand fast in the faith, in spite of the threats and actions of the hostile authorities. Daniel intercedes and makes confession for the whole of the people of Israel, but he alone is given 'wisdom and understanding' to discern what the outcome will be (8.22).

The movement which Daniel exemplifies consists of members of a religious tradition which, in the view of the alienated group, has been violated by the majority of its professed adherents as a consequence of both pressures from pagan rulers and of compromises or apostasy from within. Confirmation of 'Daniel's' diagnosis of the situation is found by the community in the calamitous state of the Jewish people as a whole: 'He has confirmed his words which he spoke against us and against our rulers who ruled us, by bringing upon us a great calamity...' (Dan. 9.12).

It is noteworthy that the law which has been disobeyed was 'set before us by his servants the prophets'. The fact that the priestly theocracy ignored the prophetic tradition was viewed by Daniel's community as a sign of its obduracy; and conversely, the Hasidim cherished the prophets, reinterpreted them (Dan. 9.2; cf. Jer. 25.11; 29.10), and regarded their own oracles as worthy additions. Indeed, Daniel itself became the basis for further development of apocalyptic traditions, as is evident not only from well-known works such as Enoch and Jubilees, but from parts of Danielic writings found in fragmentary form at Qumran.[28]

One might suppose that the non-fulfilment of the events predicted on the eschatological timetables would discredit not only the particular set of prophecies but the apocalyptic approach as a whole. This was not the case, however, as is evident in Daniel's revisions of Jeremiah (just mentioned), in the shifts of *termini* included in the

present ending(s) of Daniel (12.11, 12), and in the continued use of
Daniel, both at Qumran and in early Christianity.[29]

The sum of the community's attitude towards the demands of an
idolatrous state is offered in the words of Shadrach, Meshach, and
Abednego, when the king asks them if they will persist in their refusal
to obey the laws of the kingdom with regard to divine honours to the
king on penalty of being burned to death (cf. II Macc. 7.1–40):

> O Nebuchadnezzar, we have no need to answer you in this matter. If it be so,
> our God whom we serve is able to deliver us from the burning fiery furnace;
> and he will deliver us out of your hand, O King. But if not, be it known to you,
> O king, that we will not serve your gods or worship the golden image which
> you set up (Dan. 3.17f.).

There is no hint here of rebellion against the state, much less of taking
up arms in a war of national liberation (cf. Dan. 6.5). After the rise
of Antiochus IV with idolatrous decrees, however, the Hasidim
apparently sided with the Maccabees initially, but broke with them
when Jonathan became high priest (after 152 BC).[30] The twenty
years of groping mentioned in the Damascus Document (CD 1.9)
would take us back to the reign of Antiochus IV Epiphanes (175–
163), which is precisely the time when the Hellenization crisis would
have been at its height. Their refusal to cooperate with the Jewish
rulers, who as priest-kings controlled both the political and religious
existence of the Jewish community, and their resistance to Helleniza-
tions left them no alternative but to withdraw completely from the
society, which they deemed irredeemably corrupt, as CD 6.6 (cf. Ms.
B, 1.34) attests and as the nature of the self-contained, remote community centre at Qumran graphically demonstrates.

It is likely at the earlier stage – before the physical withdrawal of
that wing of the Hasidim which came to be the Essenes[31] – that the
Hasidim constituted a kind of conventicle within the larger Jewish
community, and that they believed themselves to have been given
special understanding about God's plans (Dan. 7.16; 8.15–17; 9.22;
10.1; 12.10). They constitute the community of the holy and wise
ones ('the saints of the Most High', 7.18, 22, 25, 27). It is possible that
'the holy ones' refers to angels,[32] but it is much more likely a designation for the community, which regarded itself as the faithful remnant,
a theme which in the prophetic tradition connoted both promise
(Isa. 7.3–9) and judgment (Isa. 10.20–23).

The image of the nation as the planting of Yahweh (Isa. 5.1–7)
appears also in Ps. 80.8ff., where the harrassed community sees itself
as a vine that has been cut down and burned, calls upon God to
restore and preserve it, and designates itself as 'the man of thy right

hand, the son of man whom thou hast made strong for thyself'(Ps. 80.17). Using the image of the vine as the restored remnant, though not the designation as 'son of man', the Damascus Document begins its description of the origin of the community with the twin declarations: 'He left a remnant to Israel and did not deliver them to destruction . . . He visited them, and caused a root of planting to spring from Israel and Aaron to possess his land and to grow fat on the good things of earth' (CD 1.5, 7, 8).[33] Those who have given up all human security in their fidelity to God will be given the roles of power in the kingdom of God (Dan.7.27). The deprivation they have voluntarily accepted will be compensated for in their day of vindication when they receive the everlasting kingdom (Dan. 7.14).

Assurance of this vindication is provided for them by the stories of the miraculous deliverance of Daniel, the faithful servant of God (Dan.1, 3, 6), as well as by his ability to interpret dreams (Dan. 2, 4, 7) and to foretell the events of the future (Dan. 5). Highly important in the earlier stories included in Daniel is the factor of miracle, or better, sign, by which the discerning person can perceive that the extraordinary powers are not inherent in Daniel, but are given to him by God. Ironically, it is the pagan rulers themselves who bear testimony to this in Daniel. Nebuchadnezzar declares in royal decree:

> It has seemed good to me to show the signs and wonders
>   that the
> Most High God has wrought towards me.
>   How great are his signs,
>   how mighty his wonders!
>   His kingdom is an everlasting kingdom,
>   and his dominion is from generation to
>   generation (4.2f.).

Similarly, in 6.26f. Darius publishes a royal declaration:

> I make a decree, that in all my royal dominion men
>   tremble and fear
> before the God of Daniel,
>   for he is the living God,
>   enduring for ever;
>   his kingdom shall never be destroyed,
>   and his dominion shall be to the end.
>   He delivers and rescues,
>   he works signs and wonders
>   in heaven and on earth,
>   he who has saved Daniel from the power of the lions.

Miracles are regarded in apocalyptic circles, therefore, as signs of divine power, of divine approbation towards the faithful community, and as signs of the kingdom of God which is about to be established. The signs take place on earth, yet they have implications for the powers of heaven as well (6.27).

Among the Qumran material related to the Danielic tradition is the Prayer of Nabonidus (4Q OrNab), where the account of sickness and recovery of the monarch is clearly an alternative version of the story of Nebuchadnezzar's temporary insanity (Dan. 4). In line 4 of this text, *gzr* is an exorcist who both effects the cure of Nabonidus and pronounces the forgiveness of his sin,[34] as the language permits and the logic demands. In the Genesis Apocryphon, the scourge that fell on Pharaoh when he took Sarai as his wife is described as his being possessed by an evil spirit, which is expelled by exorcistic means (ch. 20).[35] In the Enoch literature, there is a recurrent theme of the fallen angels or wicked spirits which seek to thwart God's purposes but are themselves overcome in the end time.[36] In the Testaments of the Twelve Patriarchs the defeat of the wicked powers leads to praise for the θαυμάσιοι of the Most High (Test. Sim. 6.6–7); both Levi and Michael make war on Beliar (Test. Levi 5.10; 6.4); the head of the Dragon is crushed (Test. Asher 7.3, which is linked with Ps. 74.13). Test. Benj. 3.3 celebrates the triumph over the spirits of Beliar, and in the Armenian Test. Levi (B text) 18.12, the sons of Levi trample upon Beliar.

The defeat of the evil powers and the judgment of the wicked is accompanied by cosmic disturbances when the hills and the earth tremble (I Enoch 1.6; 102.2). Judgment is executed by the angels (I Enoch 1.7, 9). All the nations share in the worship of God (I Enoch 10.21), and the earth itself is renewed (I Enoch 10.7). In the final eschatological battle, the elect will be vindicated (I Enoch 90.19).

Meanwhile, however, they must expect fratricidal conflict (I Enoch 100.2). In the midst of their sufferings and deprivation they are called upon to endure (I Enoch 2.7), to stay themselves upon the Lord of Spirits (Sim. Enoch 61). They can rejoice that even now they alone have access to the throne of God (I Enoch 14.13, 20–22; 25.3–5). The Angelic Liturgy from Qumran describes a correspondence and harmony between the worship carried on by the earthly community and the heavenly liturgy performed by the angels before the throne of God.[37]

Although bits of history of the Qumran community can be gleaned from some of its more systematic documents (such as the opening section of the Damascus Document), most of the direct historical connections between the community and the circumstances that surrounded its rise are offered in the commentaries on scripture. Explicit mention is made of Antiochus and Demetrius[38] as well as of the Teacher of Righteousness and his struggles with his opponents.[39] The doom of Nineveh is interpreted as the judgment to fall on Jerusalem. In short, scripture is not quoted for its information about the past but for its insight into the present community and its expectation of future vindication. The touchstone of the community's hermeneutic is its eschatological hope. All of the fragments of *pesharim* on Isa. 10–11[40] understand the stump of Jesse, the wasted vineyard, the Shoot of David, to be near to fulfilment in the community's experience in the 'last days'. In the words of the Psalms Scroll from Cave 11, they are the many, the righteous, the faithful, the good, the pure, the righteous, the perfect, the poor, the pure, the saintly (*hasidim*).[41] J. A. Sanders has pointed out that in these texts the pious congregation is contrasted with two other groups: the wicked and haughty, from whom no response in faith is to be expected, and the senseless, careless ones to whom the many works of God are being made known in the hope that they will repent, and presumably join the community.[42]

The founder of the Hasidic wing that came to be known as the Essenes was the Teacher of Righteousness (or more accurately, the One who Teaches Rightly). As we have observed, he became disillusioned with the leadership of the nation, and broke with them about the middle of the second century BC, leading the community of his followers out into the desert ('the Land of Damascus', CD 6), where they perfected the organization of their group according to the will of God as the Teacher interpreted it for them, and where they awaited the divine intervention that would overthrow the apostate leadership in Jerusalem, thereby enabling them to institute the pure worship of God in the sanctuary there.[43] The community, judged by its rules, seems to have been strictly exclusive, even to the point of turning out members who failed to conform to the regulations (1QS 5.20–23; 7.1–3; 7.22–25).

In the Appendix to the Rule of the Community instructions are offered for admission to the community which presuppose preparatory training from childhood, and enrolment at the age of twenty, from which point members make their way upwards through the various ranks of leadership and functions within the community. Obviously, there was not thought to be any logical conflict between eschatological expectancy and organizational planning. It is likely that this supplement to the Scroll of the Rule was added as late as the turn of the eras,[44] but there is no hint of the flagging of hope or confidence that the end of the age will soon come. Indeed it is possible that the final regulations concerning the solemn meal with the 'Messiah of Israel' are a prophetic instruction for the ultimate eschatological banquet. Thus eschatology and ethics are closely interwoven in the Essene documents.

3. THE DISCIPLES IN MARK AS MODEL OF THE MARKAN COMMUNITY

(i) *The prophetic – charismatic ministry*

Unlike the Gospel of John, according to which Jesus and his associates were originally together in connection with the work of the Baptist (John 1.35ff.; 3.22–29),[45] in Mark the disciples are summoned peremptorily, abandon their families and their means of livelihood, and become followers of Jesus. They are called to be fishers of men:[46] those who gather together the community of the faithful in preparation for the eschatological judgment that is to fall on the earth. To this extent, their work is in continuity with that of John the Baptist.[47] The technical terms ἀκολουθεῖν and ὀπίσω μου[48] are used throughout Mark for those who devote themselves to the work of proclaiming the imminence of the kingdom of God by work and act, to which Jesus has been called by God.

As M. Hengel has shown,[49] the role of followers of Jesus is modelled after the call of Elisha by Elijah, whose unanticipated charismatic call to be a prophet involves a break with his family and his occupation (I Kings 19.16, 19–21). It is not at all surprising that Mark begins his account with a quotation from an Elijah tradition (Mal. 3.1, which leads into Mal. 4.5f.), and that John the Baptist appears in the traditional garb of Elijah (Mark 1.6; II Kings 1.8) and eating the food of the desert.[50] Elijah appears again in Mark (9.4) in the eschatological vision granted to Jesus and the inner circle of his followers. The coming of Elijah and the suffering of the Son of Man are linked in 9.11–13, and Jesus is reported as having been taken by some to be (eschatological) Elijah (Mark 8.28), a role which is significantly bracketed in that passage with John the Baptist and the prophets. An essential element of the role of his followers in Mark is the prophetic-apocalyptic figure whose coming heralds and even precipitates the breakdown of the family and other basic social structures.[51] The end is at hand; there is no time to lose: all human obligations and ties must give way before the urgent demands of preparing God's elect people for the last days.

Jesus is represented in Mark as the teacher of his followers; indeed, the noun διδάσκαλος and cognate verb forms appear with great frequency in Mark, chiefly in the editorial, connective material.[52] Yet his teaching is by no means that of a rabbi, interpreting the Torah. Rather, even when he deals with questions of the Law, it is with the radical situation of the new community in view as they await the new age.[53] The function of Jesus as teacher resembles that of the Teacher of Righteousness at Qumran only to the extent that both are authoritative figures who redefine the people of God and who reveal to its members the secrets of the age to come. But whereas the teacher of Righteousness outdoes the Law of Moses (as interpreted by the rabbis) in stringency, Jesus arbitrarily sets aside its claims in favour of the claims of the gospel and the kingdom whose coming he proclaims.

John's choice of the desert of Judea and the Jordan as the locale for his activities may have been in conscious continuity with the Exodus imagery. J. Jeremias has suggested that baptism may have originally connoted a new 'passing through the waters' in preparation for the establishment of a new, purified covenant people in the promised land,[54] or the imagery may have signified purification now in order that one might pass safely through the molten fires of eschatological judgment, as Kraeling proposed.[55] But John's location is likely to have evoked memories of the new era that began with the passage of the Jordan, just as later prophets attracted followers to the desert promising miracles and a New Exodus for a prepared people, as Josephus reports.[56]

The veneration accorded to John is likely to be a factor of the Markan tradition's care to represent John as forerunner of Jesus, both in eschatological message (1.7) and in his death at the hands of the hostile powers (6.14–29; 9.13). Although Jesus' prophetic role is contrasted with that of John (1.8–11), Mark obviously attaches great importance to the continuity between their respective places in the eschatological plan of God. Like the Qumran community, Mark sees the beginnings of the new people of God as launched in the desert, just as they will be miraculously fed there (6.35, 'this is a desert place'; also 8.4).[57]

The continuity between the prophetic-charismatic ministry of Jesus and that of the disciples is stressed in Mark, precisely in the summarizing or transitional passages so widely recognized as editorial.[58] Just as he 'came preaching in their synagogues throughout the whole of Galilee and casting out demons' (1.39) so they are sent to preach and to perform exorcisms (3.14; 6.12f.). As is the case with the followers of the Baptist, the prophetic movement launched by their charismatic leader survives his death,[59] as was also true of the enduring impact of the Teacher of Righteousness on the Essenes of Qumran.

(ii) *The transformation of social and economic structures*

The radicality of discipleship as Mark pictures it is evident in the demand of Jesus that all ordinary human ties and obligations be set aside, not in a retreat to the desert, however, but to go out into the world-wide mission. As we have noted, the first of his disciples abandon family, family business, and their means of support (1.20). But the instructions given in 6.7–13 require them to abandon everything except the most basic equipment for their protection and efficiency in carrying out their urgent work of preaching and exorcisms. They are allowed a single tunic, sandals, a staff, and, by implication, a girdle. Prohibited are bread, knapsack (or more likely, beggar's bag), money. The total list of items included and excluded clearly reflects the equipment employed by the Cynic-Stoic itinerant charismatic preachers reported by Diogenes Laertius (6.13, 33). In the case of these wandering philosopher-preachers, the begging bag was an indispensable factor, since it was on charity alone that they subsisted. But in the case of the Markan itinerants, charity was to be sought solely in the form of basic food and shelter. They were not to leave one home if another offered more attractive accommodation (6.10), but to remain in the first place that provided shelter until their work at that place was done and they moved on to the next village. Noteworthy is the omission in this context of any reference to cities: Jesus' work is in the circle of villages (6.6b), and the disciples move from place to place (τόπος, 6.11). What the itinerants had to offer was preaching, exorcisms, and healing (3.14–15; 6.13); in return, they could accept only the characteristic Near Eastern hospitality towards strangers in the midst.[60]

To embark on this sort of career requires a break with the one group in which the individual finds his most important attachments and his true identity: the family. Although Mark has somewhat mitigated the force of the tradition in Mark 3.20f. and 31–35 by inserting the sayings about Beelzebul at this point, thus rendering ambiguous the identity of the οἱ παρ' αὐτοῦ in 3.20, the forceful point remains that family is simply redefined. The new family, in which a man finds his true mother, brothers, and sisters, is the community devoted to finding and doing the will of God (3.35). The theme of hostility encountered from earthly families is sounded in 6.4, where Jesus is recorded as declaring that not only the prophet's own home territory rejects him, but his kinsmen and the members of his own household. The compensatory side of the situation is depicted in 10.28ff., where in response to Peter's mingled boast and complaint about having left 'all' to follow Jesus, he is promised that those who abandon family and property ('fields') for the sake of the ministry will in the present age receive a hundredfold new equivalents of these, 'with persecutions', and in the age to come, eternal life. Obviously, this can scarcely be intended literally, since marriage to more than one wife is expressly prohibited in the Markan form of the tradition (10.1–12) in the wider context of our present passage. The aim of the saying is equivalent compensation in the new community: the roles filled by literal wives and children and worldly possessions are served by new realities in the new covenant people.

Although the disciples are pictured as living off the generosity of others, the follower of Jesus was required to strip himself of all possession, according to the story reported in 10.17–22 and subsequently commented upon to the disciples (10.23ff.). Obedience to the commandments was not sufficient to gain eternal life; the rich man was instructed to sell what he had and to give to the poor what he realized from the sale (10.21). Only then, with his treasury of merit laid up before God, would he be ready to become a follower of Jesus. The man's reluctance to make this sacrificial commitment provides Mark with the transition into a general comment about wealth, which is actually a series of sayings bound together by Markan editorial seams (περιβλεψάμενος, v.23; πάλιν, v.24; ἤρξατο λέγειν, v.28). Confidence in possessions and faith in the kingdom of God seem to be mutually exclusive stances towards life. Conversely, the story of the poor widow (12.41–44) concludes with the declaration that what she gave was her entire means of livelihood (ὅλον τὸν βίον αὐτῆς).

The economic status of the Markan community cannot be determined with any certainty. The occupations of only a few of the earliest followers are indicated, most notably the four fishermen (1.16–20). It is worth observing that their father has hired servants in his employ (1.20), suggesting that the families of the disciples were not at the bottom of the economic scale. Levi, the tax-collector, was undoubtedly a minor official serving under a high administrator assigned by the Romans responsibility for supervising collection of taxes throughout the Jewish territories.[61] Allusions to the role of servant (διάκονος/δοῦλος, 10.43f.; 12.2) cannot be taken to mean that Christianity in the Markan community flourished among slaves or even that it included them. Rather, these images, as well as others drawn from agricultural and pastoral life – sheep, vineyards, grain fields – are commonplace, and would be especially appropriate among persons accustomed to village life with farming carried on in outlying fields, as implied in 13.16. Indeed, throughout Mark there is a clear preference for villages and open spaces in contrast to cities (1.38, 45; 5.14; 6.6b; 6.11; 6.31; 8.4; 8.27; 11.2, 11; 13.3).[62] In the last of these references, Jesus accepts hospitality in the village of Bethany, arranges for a donkey in a nearby village, leaves the temple to return to Bethany following his initial visit into the city and its sanctuary, and retires to the Mount of Olives *over against the city* while delivering himself of the oracles announcing its destruction.

Although some of these details are preserved in the other synoptic accounts, the motif of withdrawal is peculiarly Markan. This attitude should probably be seen against the cultural aim of the Hellenistic period – under Ptolemies, Seleucids, and Romans – to urbanize Palestine and to create a cosmopolitan atmosphere by developing Greek-style cities throughout, of which Caesarea on the coast, the Decapolis, Neapolis (near Shechem), and Herodian Jericho would be mid-first century cases in point. The conversion of Jerusalem into Aelia Capitolina by Hadrian in the second century demonstrates what the anti-Hellenizers rightly feared might occur if these policies were not resisted. Ironically, the destruction of Jewish Jerusalem was carried out in retaliation – not for primarily religious anti-Hellenizing attitudes – but for political insurrectionist action.

Further evidence of the socio-cultural outlook of Mark is to be seen in the place provided in his community for women and children. In a religious tradition dominated by adult males, this is the more remarkable. Women were given places within the community, as 10.30 implies, and as the ministrations of women demonstrate (1.31; especially 15.41, where διηκόνουν and ἠκολούθουν are bracketed). And in 9.35 the role of διάκονος is depicted as highest of all, just as the Son of Man in his redemptive death 'serves', διακονῆσαι (10.45). It cannot be inferred from these passages that women occupied the leading offices in the community of Mark, but rather that the menial tasks they performed were regarded as praiseworthy and as fully compatible with God's purpose for his people.

Two formulaic statements of a kind which can be traced to the post-Easter church, rather than to the time of Jesus,[63] represent Jesus as making provision for acceptance of children into the community of faith: Mark 9.33–37; 10.13, 16. Several technical terms employed in these passages show that more is involved than that Jesus liked small children. In Markan narratives, ἅπτεσθαι connotes contact with Jesus in faith, as is evident from 1.41; 3.10; 5.27, 28, 30, 31; 6.56; 7.33; 8.22; 10.13. Of these occurrences, six are in miracle narratives and four are in summary or transitional accounts. The remaining text (10.13) should be understood against the background of the others: to touch Jesus or be touched by him is to receive divine grace. A second technical term is used, μὴ κωλύετε (10.14), which in other contexts within the New Testament occurs as a baptismal formula (Acts 8.36; 10.47), implying that the children are fit subjects for baptism in the Markan community.

Most surprising among those admitted to the community, according to Mark, are Gentiles, including Gentile women. This factor is pointed to directly in the healing of the daughter of the Syrophoenician women and the argument that the miracle evokes (7.24–30), as well as by the indirect evidence in the accounts of the feeding and healings in Gentile territory (5.1–20; 6.53–56?; 7.31–8.10). Mark has placed the story of the Gentile woman's daughter immediately after the section dealing with defilement, the outcome of which is to dismiss the whole notion of ceremonial defilement or of kosher food (7.1–23, especially 19b, which is an awkward but unequivocal insertion in the tradition). Now the Gentile woman's request for a share in the healing powers of Jesus is greeted by what for Mark must be intended as an ironical question: Should dogs be given children's food? The woman's response evinces persistent faith, and she departs in faith to find the exorcism successfully completed when she reaches home (7.30). Her lack of cultic cleanliness was no barrier to her participation in the powers of the New Age at work through Jesus. As the beneficiary of that power, she becomes the symbol and prototype of other faithful Gentiles who will share in the benefits of the kingdom of God.

This open attitude in the name of the covenant people (14.24), and the claim made by Jesus (or on his behalf by the tradition) that he would 'sit at the right hand of Power' (14.62), could not be regarded with equanimity by the Jewish leaders, either in Jesus' time or subsequently. Even the eirenic statement by Saul Lieberman about relations in this period between individual Gentiles and thoughtful Jews and about their mutual respect is countered by his acknowledgment that it was the rabbis' great task to guard 'the true faith, the high ethics and the pure family life of the Jews against any outside contamination'.[64]

Allowing for the widespread scholarly anachronism of attributing post-AD 135 attitudes to Jews and Christians in the period before the first Jewish revolt, and hence before the triumph of the Pharisees, there was nevertheless a fundamental challenge to Jewish integrity expressed in the traditions incorporated in Mark concerning the lowering of barriers of the new people of God which could only be regarded as subversive – or affirmed.

(iii) *Avoidance of political involvement*

We have already observed that the Hasidic movement which seems to have influenced the Markan community so pervasively at first sided with the Maccabean revolutionaries and then broke with them, probably because of the increasing secularization of the theocratic state. In Mark 12.13–16 Jesus is reported to have refused to take sides with those who urged resistance to and non-cooperation with the Roman power. Assuming that this tradition was incorporated into Mark at a time when Jewish nationalism was a rising tide and when, therefore, a stand on this issue would be of paramount concern to the occupying authorities, there is no hint of an inclination to join the revolutionaries. Since messianic language is political language, since the chief image for the new age in Mark is 'the kingdom of God', and since Jesus had, according to Mark 14–15, been executed as a pretender to the Jewish throne, it was difficult for the Markan community to avoid sympathies, if not connivance, with those who were working to free Palestine from Roman control. But Mark records Jesus as refusing to make a move in that direction. Rather, in his response to the bids for power in the Age to Come advanced by James and John (10.42–45, a passage introduced, it may be noted, by characteristic Markan terms, προκαλεσάμενος and λέγει αὐτοῖς),[65] Jesus tells them:

> You know that those who are supposed to rule over the Gentiles lord it over them, and their great men exercise authority over them, but it shall not be so among you...

The route to power is here seen as utterly paradoxical: the role of διάκονος or δοῦλος – acting not merely in a servile function but as a slave – which leads to death on behalf of others (10.45).

The irony is compounded, since the title linked to the fate of the servant-martyr is one that the cardinal document of early Hasidism reserves for the one (v. 13) or ones (v. 18) to whom the kingdom of God is given: (one like a) son of man (Dan. 7.13f.). Between persons who shared this strange view of the coming of the kingdom solely by divine grace and those who seized initiative in taking it by storm there could be no common ground. We shall return to this point when we come to consider the historical setting and relationships of the Markan community.

(iv) *The esoteric aspects of the community*

Like the Hasidim of two centuries earlier, the Markan community was convinced that God had granted to it special revelation so that it could understand the goal and the intervening stages in the fulfilment of his purpose for the creation. To them alone was given the mystery of the kingdom of God, while to outsiders everything remained an enigma (4.11). This division between those to whom the secret was disclosed and those from whom it was withheld was in accord with scripture (4.12), quoted in a version which differs from both the MT and the LXX and which emphasizes that the 'parables' = enigmas have been employed in order to *prevent* the outsiders from perceiving the truth that they contain. Both Matthew and Luke omit this difficult, deterministic part of the quotation. Interpreters[66] have correctly noted that Mark uses παραβολή in 4.11 as equivalent to μυστήριον; hence parable = 'riddle, enigma', rather than a figure of speech, or an extended metaphor. While that is an accurate observation, it fails to take fully into account the way in which Mark[67] exploits the parables to serve as descriptions of the Christian community in his own time, as it awaits the coming of the New Age. The esoteric nature of the interpretation of the parables is made explicitly in 4.34, a passage omitted by Luke and fundamentally changed by Matthew (13.34) into a simple comment that Jesus used parables in addressing the crowds. Only the disciples are granted explanation of the teaching of Jesus.

That viewpoint runs throughout Mark, often with the phrase κατ' ἰδίαν to stress the private nature of the disclosure. In 7.33 the deaf and dumb man is healed away from the crowd in an act observed only by the inner circle of followers, just as the disciples' inability to perform an exorcism (9.18) is explained only to them. The full import of his teaching about divorce is reserved for his disciples in a separate explanation, as we have noted (10.10), as is the explicit declaration of the difficulty rich persons will have in entering the kingdom of God (10.23). The announcement of the necessity of the suffering of the Son of Man (8.30f.) is reserved for the inner core of the disciples, as is the vision of Jesus' exaltation in the Transfiguration narrative (9.2). Most notable of the private disclosures (κατ' ἰδίαν) is the announcement of the destruction of the Temple and the end of the age, given to Peter, James, John, and Andrew on the Mount of Olives (13.3ff.).[68]

Other indications of the clandestine nature of the Markan community are provided in the similar stories of the arrangements for the donkey that Jesus rode into Jerusalem (11.1–10) and for the final meal with the disciples (14.12–16). Both are surrounded by an aura of mystery in identification of person and place. Most mysterious of all, however, is the enigmatic series of comments about the significance of the feedings (6.52; 8.14–21). They are linked not only by connection with the bread, but also by reference to hardness of heart

(8.17; 6.52). The theme has been the subject of an extensive study by Q. Quesnell, who comes to the conclusion that the image of the bread(s) in Mark 'could be expressed as mystery, as eucharist, as death-resurrection, as knowledge of Christ'.[69] Although to proceed by free association (which links together bread in 2.26; 7.27 and the parables of the growth of grain in Mark 4), to see bread as a symbol of teaching, of kerygma, of eucharist, etc., may be an accurate assessment of 'the mind of Mark', the most evident and significant implication of these passages (6.52; 8.17) is mentioned by Quesnell only in passing, and is not adequately developed: the union of Jew and Gentile in the eschatological fellowship. The symbolic numbers, for which Quesnell offers no real explanation, appear in Acts as the leadership designations for the Jewish (12) and the Gentile (7) wings of the church.[70] The bread is a fitting symbol, therefore, not only for the eucharist but also for the unity of the body of Christ (I Cor. 10.16f.; 12.12f.), a theme which is further developed with regard to the unity of Jew and Gentile in the mystical body (Col. 1.24–27). Although the distinctive Pauline language is not evident in Mark, there seems to be a parallel development between the Pauline and the Markan views of the church as the uniting of Jew and Gentile in the community of faith.

Wrede was correct in tracing the emphasis on secrecy to Mark or to the tradition that he was incorporating,[71] but he confused the secrecy question by lumping together passages that have in common secrecy or silencing or clandestine features, but which serve quite different functions in Mark. The passages cited by Wrede fall into three main groups: 1. silencing of the demons: 1.23–25; 1.34; 1.43–45; 3.11f.; 2. instructions following the healing/exorcism: 5.43; 7.36; 8.26; 3. preservation of messianic identity within the circle of disciples: 8.30; 9.9. Only the latter can accurately be classified as 'messianic secret'. The nature of Jesus' messiahship as Mark presents it is discussed in ch. V; here it will suffice to note that in the first group of passages, the focus is on conflict with the demons and the 'rebuke' administered to them is actually the technical term for the commanding word of an exorcist,[72] the aim of which is to bring the demon under control rather than to prevent disclosure of information. Similar to this group is the exorcism in 9.14–29, where the demon is addressed by the commanding word, but where there is no injunction to silence. The second group comes from pericopes concerned with the spread of the mission of Jesus, especially to the Gentiles. Mark portrays Jesus as harrassed and pressed upon by crowds from which he seeks escape (1.37; 3.9; 5.21, 37; 6.31; 6.53–56; 7.24; 8.1, 10).

In the two stories of healing on Gentile soil (5.1–20; 7.31–37) there are two different sets of instructions to the one healed, but the results are similar. The Gerasene demoniac is told – using unmistakably Christian terminology – to go and tell what things the Lord has done for him, while the deaf mute (also in the Decapolis?) is told not to spread the word of his cure, but does so with wide results which are phrased in language that points to Isa.35.5f. with its promise of cosmic redemption. On the other hand, the advice to the father of the little girl (5.43) that the story should not be made known seems to bring to a close the mission among Jews and to point to Jesus' rejection in his homeland (6.1–6) and to the wider mission of the Twelve (6.6b–13) which follow on the healing story. The restriction on the blind man of Bethsaida about going into his village after he has received his sight similarly leads into the Markan passage where the nature of Jesus' messiahship is to be revealed to the disciples alone.

Thus, the secret for Mark is not that Jesus heals and performs exorcisms: these incidents are public and well-known. The 'mystery' is that of the messiah who is suffering Son of Man (8.30), and who is to be vindicated by God (9.9) following his resurrection from the dead. The association of Jesus with messiahship is known to the authorities, as is shown by their seizure of Jesus, his condemnation, and his death as 'King of the Jews'. Judas does not betray Jesus' messianic claim, but his location, so that he could be seized by stealth (14.2, 10, 44, 48f.). As Mark represents the disciples, even to have been given the basic information about Jesus' role as Messiah-Son of Man did not mean that it could be grasped until after the next decisive stage in God's vindication of Jesus: after the Son of Man has risen from the dead (9.9). The secret is not an apologetic or a literary device invented by Mark and employed by him somewhat clumsily to explain why a non-messianic Jesus came to be acclaimed as Messiah after his death, but is a central, pervasive element in the community's understanding of itself and of Jesus as those to whom it has been revealed that the kingdom of God is given – not to those who seize power – but to those who in faithful, suffering obedience, receive it as a gift.

(v) *The inclusive aspect of the community*

It would be a mistake, however, to assume that the Markan community thought it had only to await the imminent end of the age quietly and complacently. The end was expected within the lifetime of that generation (9.1; 13.30), even though there was a refusal to set a firm date. That was one secret that God had reserved for himself (13.32)! Meanwhile, as the transitional passages of Mark attest, the community is to carry forward the work of preaching, healing, and exorcisms that Jesus had begun (see above, 87ff.). The angelic assembling of the elect 'from the four winds, from the corner of earth to the corner of heaven' (13.27) may be either hyperbole or Mark's version of the traditional apocalyptic expectation of world-wide response to the redemptive work of God in the eschaton.[73] Even granted the stylized and hyperbolic nature of this prediction, the Markan community obviously saw its own activity reflected in Jesus' travels to Gentile regions: Tyre, Sidon, Decapolis, as well as in the areas from which seekers came: Idumaea, beyond the Jordan, Tyre, and Sidon (3.8). The Gentile mission of the Markan church has precedence and assurance of success in the ministry of Jesus as Mark portrays it. The important space devoted to setting aside the ritual laws of Jewish separateness (7.1–30) both in precept and in action shows that this was an issue for Mark's community, but one on which a firm position had been taken: the community was open across social, economic, sexual, and ethnic barriers.

4. The Historical Links of the Markan Community with First-century Judaism

As has been sketched earlier, there were four main options open to Jews of Palestine in the period prior to the first revolt in AD 66–70. 1. The first was to collaborate fully with the Roman overlords and their puppets, the Herodian tetrarchs and petty kings. That stance could take the shape of conformity to the Hellenistic-Roman way of life that Herod and his successors had sought to impose on their Jewish subjects through building stadia, theatres and baths.[74] 2. Or the Jews could assume the more passive form of acquiescence to Roman rule and to Rome's economic demands. It was this attitude that was adopted by the Pharisees, who concerned themselves largely with maintenance of personal and group piety within their own community. Wider issues, such as the political liberation of the Jewish people or even an eschatological transformation of the Jewish community, seem not to have concerned them. Josephus reports only negative political acts, such as their refusal to take part in a mass loyalty oath to Caesar (*Antt.* 17, 41–43). The rabbinic traditions tell how Yochanan ben Zakkai was carried out of Jerusalem in a coffin, which hardly qualifies as an aggressive political act. Their primary objective was to preserve the purity, ethically and cultically, of the covenant people through study and interpretation of the Law. When, therefore, Mark reports Jesus as warning his disciples against 'the leaven of the Pharisees and the leaven of the Herodians',[75] it is these two inappropriate Jewish responses to the socio-cultural situation that are in view.

3. The third position, of which we hear nothing directly in the gospel tradition but which has significant kinship with primitive Christianity, is that of the Essenes.[76] The similarities between the Markan community and the Essenes are apparent in their modes of scriptural interpretation, their conception of the covenant community as distinct from the main body of Jews, their estimate of the Jerusalem temple and its cultus as corrupt, their expectation of divine intervention in the near future to vindicate them and establish them as the central agency of God's rule in the New Age. Other shared details are the practice of depending solely on hospitality for itinerant members (cf. Mark 6.10; Josephus, *Wars* 2, 124f.) and the refusal to carry any equipment other than what was required for basic protection.[77]

The striking differences, however, more than outweigh the resemblances. The Essenes withdrew from society, clustered in their desert settlements, in order to avoid risking ceremonial pollution by contact with non-members. Their interpretation of the Law and the cult were stricter than those of the Jewish authorities in Jerusalem. Although they made provisions for novices to enter the community,[78] it was required that the candidate be an Israelite, that he agree to avoid all further contact with 'perverse men', and that he commit himself both to unswerving obedience to the Law of Moses as the community interpreted it and to its process of judicial exclusion – at the risk of death by starvation[79] – if he failed to measure up to the requirements. The Markan attitudes on defilement, on inclusiveness of the community, and on forgiveness stand in the sharpest contrast to the Essene doctrines.

4. The remaining position was that of the insurrectionists, to whose endeavours Josephus devotes much of books 2 and 3 of his *Jewish Wars*. There is a report in Hippolytus' *Refutation* (9, 26) that at the height of the first revolt, some of the Essenes joined cause with the revolutionaries, taking individuals aside who made pious pronouncements, demanding that they accept circumcision immediately if they had not been administered the rite, and murdering them forthwith if they refused. This is not inconceivable, but the only belligerence that can be documented for certain among the Essenes is in the highly stylized War Scroll, where the chief reliance for the expected eschatological victory is placed on the angelic hosts, as is attested by the document's identification of the army of the Kittim (here = Romans)[80] as the troops of Beliar (11.8; 13.2; 15.1; 18.3) who are to be defeated by the sword of the Lord (cf. 19.9). The archaeological evidence at Qumran

indicates rather that the Essenes were attacked in the midst of the ordinary routine of their community life there; there is no hint of military equipment or an actual military organization at the site.

The fight to free the Jewish people from Roman domination was by no means limited to Jerusalem and its environs, although the Roman display of the temple trophies on the Arch of Titus is the justly renowned symbol of the defeat of the insurrectionists. Josephus' detailed account shows the fratricidal aspects of the conflict and the fact that Jewish minorities in the Hellenized coastal cities, in Alexandria, in the east Jordan districts and in Syria did not escape involvement in the struggle and reprisals at the hands of pro-Roman groups. The violent reactions against the Jews throughout the Eastern Mediterranean lands seem to have been triggered by a woeful slaughter of Jews in Caesarea,[81] where ironically the most thoroughly Hellenized Jews would have lived. The Jews rose up in attacks against their Gentile fellow townsmen in 'Syrian villages and cities . . .' in Philadelphia, Heshbon, Gerasa, Pella, Scythopolis, and Kedosa, which Josephus calls 'a Tyrian village'.[82] The result was a frightful disorder throughout Syria. Even after many Jews had been killed, the residents in these cities and villages were suspicious of certain persons thought to be Jewish sympathizers, and thus 'while they shrunk from killing offhand that equivocal element in their midst, they feared the neutrals as much as pronounced aliens'.[83] Even when local Jews sided with the Roman supporters against invading insurrectionists, as at Scythopolis, it was impossible to allay suspicions and the result was further Jewish slaughter.[84] There were fears of Jewish uprisings in Batanea,[85] and the Jews of Damascus were attacked by the local populace when the report reached the city of the rout of the Syrian governor, Cestius, following a disastrous effort to take Jerusalem from the revolutionaries in AD 66.[86]

The cities of Antioch, Sidon, and Apamea, which alone 'spared the residents and refused to kill or imprison a single Jew', were noteworthy exceptions to these revolutionary and counter-revolutionary actions of the Syrian cities. They did not consider the Jewish uprisings or the local minorities to be of sufficient size or significance to constitute a threat to their large, established metropolises, 'but mainly they were influenced by pity for people who showed no revolutionary intention'.[87] Obviously Jews and those suspected of Jewish sympathies – wherever they might be living in Syria or east Jordan – could not escape involvement in and threat of life from the action of the fanatical insurrectionists in Jerusalem and its environs.

The community of Mark adopted a position that was not consonant with any of the options taken by the Jews of the 60s. The open society of these Christians would have been repugnant and unacceptable to Pharisees and Essenes alike. Their rejection of the use of political power or physical force, as shown by Jesus' denunciation of the power play by the sons of Zebedee (10.35–44) and their concurrent acquiescence in the payment of tribute to Caesar (12.13–17), would have enraged the revolutionaries. Significantly, the dilemma in which Jesus' opponents sought to place him in Mark's account is articulated by spokesmen for the same curious coalition that appeared in 8.15, the Pharisees and the Herodians. What we see in the Markan community, therefore, is a group which claims to be heir to the prophetic promises concerning the new covenant (14.24) and yet is alienated from all the Jewish parties that lay claim to that heritage and that destiny. In the next chapter we shall consider the christological titles, including 'Son of David', but it should be noted here that Jesus' refusal to accept that title as an unambiguous designation for the agent who is to establish God's rule (12.35–37) would have exacerbated the estrangement between Jewish nationalists of either the radical or the passive sort and the community of Mark that preserved and fostered this tradition.

In a time when not only Jews but Jewishness were suspect, the Markan community which put forward these prophetic claims and yet refused to identify itself with any of the wholly Jewish groups of that epoch would find itself a radically alienated social group that could expect little but suspicion and hostility from Jew and Gentile alike. It was in such an era and in this sort of climate that the Gospel of Mark is most likely to have been written, to offer understanding and encouragement to this segment of primitive Christianity. Mark selected from the tradition available to him, formulating on his own the sequence of material with the emphases that set out the disciples in their perplexity and misunderstanding, in their favoured position as recipients of divine mysteries and revelations, and as the paradigms of his own community in its critical situation.

5. THE HISTORICAL AND GEOGRAPHICAL SETTING OF MARK

As the thrust of our analysis of the situation in Judaism before the first Jewish revolt has implied, Mark was written in close chronological proximity to that event, in all likelihood before it came to an end with the capture of the city and the destruction of the Temple. The lack of precision in the prophetic description of the fate of Jerusalem in Mark 13, while not conclusive evidence, points to its having been written prior to the events which it depicts. Since there is no reason on the grounds of style or content to suppose that someone other than the author of the rest of Mark has composed the apocalyptic section in its final form,[88] and since the sense of urgency pervades the whole gospel, Mark probably assumed its present form in the late 60s. The imminence of catastrophe and the sure expectation of deliverance following the doom of the city of Jerusalem confirm this impression; conversely, the mood of Mark is inappropriate for the period after the fall of the city when the expected denouement did not occur. It was probably after this disaster that the various endings began to be attached to the gospel to offset the open expectancy with which the original concluded at 16.8.

The linguistic character of Mark as a whole points to a locale where Greek is the common language, although its cultural level is quite low and traces of a Semitic influence are evident.[89] The fact that most of the transliterations into Greek of Aramaic words have been omitted by the other two synoptists[90] and that the two direct Semiticisms in the text noted above (15, 40) have been either dropped (συμπόσια συμπόσια, 6.39) or Graecized (εἰ δοθήσεται τῇ γενεᾷ ταύτῃ σημεῖον, 8.12) shows either that Mark has reproduced the originally Semitic tradition or that he had reason to lend it a Semitic colouring. The most plausible explanation for this would be that his readers in some way identified with the Semitic linguistic background. For bi-linguals (Aramaic and Greek), Greek would have become increasingly the vehicle of commerce – and of evangelism – although formulaic expressions would continue to reflect the underlying Aramaic thought-patterns. It would be a foolish anachronism to suppose that his readers would expect linguistic verisimilitude or historical precision in reproducing the Jesus tradition, especially readers who were prepared to read Mark's unsophisticated Greek. The fact that Mark does include Aramaic terms at especially sensitive points in his narrative, such as the raising of the little daughter (5.41), the prayer in the garden (14.36), and above all, the cry from the cross (15.34), supports this inference. Indeed, this free quotation from Ps.22 in Hebraized Aramaic – converted to Hebrew by Matthew and replaced by Luke with a theologically less difficult Psalm quotation (Luke 23.46 = Ps.31.6), and then translated from LXX – is a closer indicator of the linguistic setting of the Markan community. Aramaic lies behind them in the tradition, but Greek, including the LXX, is their version of the Bible.

The same point is made by a different line of evidence: the fondness for ἀμήν.[91] The remarkable feature of this term is not only its frequency, as contrasted with its omission by Matthew and Luke as noted above, but the settings in which Mark uses it. All 13 instances of the word are found within a pronouncement formula. Four of these are in the nature of eschatological pronouncements: 9.1; 10.29; 13.30; 14.25, bearing directly on the future of the community. Four others are found in what Käsemann has called 'Pronouncements of Sacred Law':[92] 3.28f.; 9.41; 10.15; 11.23, which follow the rigid pattern, 'whoever does such and such, he will be, etc.' While these formulae may ultimately go back to Jesus, in their Markan form they regularly occur in a context of community instruction and/or utilize distinctively Christian terminology (e.g., 'in my name, because you belong to Christ'; μη κωλύετε, 9.14). The remaining five occurrences are found in predictions or solemn pronouncements: no sign will be given on demand (8.12); the widow has given away the whole basis for human support of her life (12.43); the anointing of Jesus for death will be perpetually remembered in the community (14.9); one of Jesus' companions will hand him over to the authorities (14.18); Peter will deny Jesus (14.30). Whether the term ἀμήν was preserved from the tradition or introduced in some or all cases by Mark, its presence in his text shows that he is writing from within a circle for whom Aramaic expressions would serve neither scholarly interests in historical precision nor antiquarian curiosity, but would enable the reader to identify more fully with the poignant and powerful narrative than a purely Greek account could accomplish.

In what sort of setting is such a literary endeavour credible? Although the traditional locale, Rome,[93] is chronologically possible, the preservation in Mark of cultural and linguistic features of the Eastern Mediterranean rural or village culture – features which Luke, in writing for a Gentile audience, eliminates or alters – speaks against Rome. Marxsen, following the lines of reasoning developed by Lohmeyer and Lightfoot, proposes Galilee.[94] The archaeological evidence from excavations there in recent years confirms the wide use of Greek in public inscriptions, including synagogues, so that for Mark to have written a Christian document there in the 60s as Marxsen suggests is not inconceivable. And the accurate reflection of practices having to do with agriculture,[95] housing,[96] employment,[97] and land-ownership and taxation[98] that are characteristic of the whole of Syria-Palestine in this period do indeed speak for that larger area as the place of origin and against Rome.

Paradoxically, however, the way in which Mark refers to Galilee and the surrounding cities and territories tells decisively against the gospel's having been written in Galilee proper. The place names are known and their general relative positions are understood, as for example that the Decapolis lies east of the Jordan and the Sea of Galilee. But the specific details of the locations are not accurately perceived by the author, who represents Jesus as travelling back and forth in Galilee and adjacent territories in a puzzling fashion.

The references to movements across the Sea of Galilee are impossible to trace sequentially. Mention of specific locations near the sea are either unknown sites, such as Dalmanutha (8.10), or are patently inaccurate, as in the designation of the eastern shore of the lake as the country of the Gerasenes (5.1); and in both instances the wide range of variants in the textual tradition shows that early readers of Mark were aware of these problems of locale.[99] The itinerary sketched in 7.31 – from Tyre in the south to Sidon in the north to the Sea of Galilee through Decapolis, which lies east of the lake – is scarcely credible. Since it appears in an editorial introduction to a miracle pericope, and since it corresponds to another editorial passage (3.7f.) in which Mark is apparently seeking to show the sweep of Jewish and Gentile territory from which persons responded to Jesus with faith, 6.31 should be considered as filling the same role for Mark. But that implies that the writer does not know Galilean topography accurately, even though he is acquainted with place names. A Syrian provenance could account for this state of affairs.

Does an indication of Syria require us to think of Antioch? Three factors tell against that hypothesis. First is the explicit indication in Josephus[100] that those suspected of Jewish sympathies in Antioch were not subjected to persecution by the Gentiles in the years before the fall of Jerusalem. Second, there is a clear antipathy towards the city in Mark. Not only are his images and metaphors drawn from the life of field and village, but he portrays Jesus in editorial sections as avoiding the cities, and many of the narratives are specifically located in open territory: on a hill (3.13; 9.2; 13.3), by the sea (passim), in the 'desert' (1.12; 1.35; 1.45; 6.31f.; 8.4), 'on the green grass' (6.39). Villages and fields are mentioned frequently (1.38; 6.11, τόπος; 6.36; 8.27; 11.1, 2, 11, 12; 14.3). The city is the place from which Jesus withdraws (1.45; 6.33; 11.19; 13.1). Except for the denunciation of the sanctuary and the secret gathering in the κατάλυμα (14.13–15), Jesus lives outside Jerusalem in a village, announces the city's destruction from a vantage point 'over against' it (13.3), gathers his disciples in a garden outside its walls (14.32), enters it again only under arrest as an insurrectionist (14.48–53), is condemned by its civil and religious authorities, and is led from it to be executed (14.20–22) and buried (15.46).

Consonant with this anti-city stance of Mark is his portrayal of the ministry of Jesus and the disciples as an itinerancy among villages, living on the hospitality that is provided by the inhabitants (1.38; 3.14; 6.6b; 7.24; 8.27; cf. 6.6b–13). Indeed, Mark's entire picture of Jesus' ministry is one of constant movement from place to place, emphasized by his favourite terms εὐθύς and εὐθέως,[101] and relieved only by occasional retreats for prayer (1.35; 6.46; 14.32, 35, 38, 39). The itinerant ministry depicted in Mark has two rough, partial cultural analogies: to the Essenes, and to the Cynic-Stoic charismatic, preacher-philosophers. We have had occasion to note some similar features in Josephus' account of the travelling Essenes[102] and the instructions that Mark portrays Jesus as giving his disciples at the time of their commissioning (6.8–11). Even more striking is the resemblance of this picture of the disciples to that preserved in the tradition about the Cynic-Stoic charismatics.

A most illuminating and suggestive study of the connections between early Christian itinerant prophets and the Cynic-Stoic philosophers has been offered in an essay by Gerd Theissen,[103] who draws attention to the similarity of instructions laid down for the two groups of itinerants.[104] Both are to take no money; both are to exploit local hospitality; both are to pronounce judgment on those who spurn their teachings. The only reward they may accept is food, drink, and lodging.[105] All human ties have been left behind, as Mark 10.28–30 shows to have been the case for the Christian itinerants also. Only in such a group could the sayings about abandoning family, residence, and means of livelihood be transmitted without seeming incredible,[106] unless they were transformed into otherworldliness by gnosticizing,[107] or domesticated by liberal theologizing.[108] The socio-economic factors point to a rural setting, in contrast to the larger cities which with their larger populations were home to more structured and organized Christian groups.[109] It is perhaps representatives of these charismatic groups who caused the disturbances that Paul sought to quell, especially in his Corinthian letters, or who in the early second century troubled Pliny as he sought to preserve Roman dignity and religious tradition in the face of 'superstition' in Bithynia.[110]

Pliny's comment that the disturbance was not only evident in the cities, but had spread to the villages as well, is seen by Theissen as pointing to the rural setting of the charismatic phenomena. Because Theissen is primarily concerned with the Q tradition, which he traces to a Palestinian provenance, he thinks this sayings tradition was centred there.[111] But that conclusion is neither warranted nor likely for the Markan material. Hengel has assembled an impressive array of evidence that there was vigorous philosophical activity in the Hellenistic period in Syria and the cities of the Decapolis, especially Gadara, Tyre, and Sidon,[112] with leading Stoic figures originating there or trained there or both. There is no reason to doubt that the heirs of this tradition in the first century AD would have influenced both the methods and the life-style of the early Christian prophets. It is wholly fitting that Mark should have offered one of his most vivid narratives, one which shows most clearly the formal influence of Hellenistic miracle stories, and one which is written in more nearly sophisticated Greek than most of the rest of his gospel, as a tale from a city of the Decapolis, Gerasa (5.1–20).[113]

By the latter half of the second century, the tradition of the Christian charismatic-miracle-worker-prophet was thoroughly discredited by pagan and orthodox Christian alike.[114] But it is wholly unwarranted to read Lucian's caricature of Alexander Peregrinus back into the first century and treat that figure as a standard character who could have served as a model for portraying Jesus in the gospel tradition, [115] just as it would be unjustifiable to consider Montanus (who like Peregrinus is known only through later detractors) as the paradigm of the early Christian charismatic prophet.

In his portrait of Jesus, Mark speaks to and from a community which is influenced both by the Jewish-Hasidic-Essene-apocalyptic tradition, with its belief in cosmic conflict about to be resolved by divine intervention and the vindication of the faithful elect, and the Cynic-Stoic style of gaining adherents by itinerant preaching, healing, and exorcisms from village to village, existing on the hospitality that the local tradition offered.

Unlike the Cynics, however, who sought mostly to deflate pretensions and urge listeners to reject the false values of the culture in favour of the simple, free life, the Markan community from its base in rural and small-town southern Syria held out the hope of a covenant people whose fidelity would be rewarded by God in the very near future. Like the Stoic vision of universal human brotherhood, their membership would transcend all national, religious, and ethnic barriers, but unlike the Stoics and in keeping with the prophetic belief in a faithful eschatological remnant, only those who saw in Jesus the agent of God would share in the secret of his aim and method in establishing his rule over the creation. Thus the nature of Jesus' role in the divine purpose and the role of the community in fostering that purpose were inextricably interwoven. It is to these two factors – christology and community – that we now turn.

V

COMMUNITY AND CHRISTOLOGY
IN MARK

Reviewing our analysis of apocalyptic sects, we see that the constitutive element in apocalyptic is the community which regards itself as the recipient of a revelation through a God-sent prophet concerning the destiny of the world and its own eschatological vindication, which is to occur in the near future. The forms of the literature may vary, as they do in the library from Qumran, including apocalypses proper, rule books, scriptural expositions, hymns. The agents of redemption may be differently depicted, as they appear to have been at various stages in the evolution of the Qumran community.[1] The timing of the end of the age may be variously calculated, or even recalculated, as is apparently the case in the last verse of Daniel 12. The common element is that a group that feels itself alienated from the main body of its religious heritage has drawn together voluntarily to form a conventicle to whom the secret of God's purpose has been granted, and on whose behalf those divine aims will be effected.

To treat apocalyptic as though it were to be identified with literary forms[2] or conceptual features[3] is to preclude consideration of what is basic in the apocalyptic life-world. To seize on a single notion, such as expectation of an imminent end or a dualistic view of history, and treat that as the single determinative criterion for defining apocalyptic is to mistake the part for the whole, or to confuse optional for essential features.[4] The central element is the world-view espoused by the community that produced the document.

The group is convinced that the precepts and institutions established by God have become perverted through those who now wield power. For this crisis the only solution is for those who by revelation recognize the true state of affairs to band together, to face up to the human and demonic opposition that confronts them, to accept the trials and sufferings that are sure to come, and to await vindication through a God-sent agent in the imminent future. The literary forms that the community employs, the titles it assigns to the redemptive agent(s), and the details of its estimate of the opposition and of God's plan for triumphing over it are functions of the self-understanding by the community of the place within the world that it believes itself to be destined to fulfil.

In themselves these detailed features do not constitute the community. The primary factors in apocalyptic, therefore, are the elect, esoteric community and its life-world.[5] Its enemies are a blend of human, demonic, and cosmic forces.[6] It lives in hope of imminent vindication.[7] The community was called together by a prophet sent from God; it will likewise be vindicated in the end-time by his agent.[8] Although the divine deliverance is awaited in the future, the specifics of community hopes recall the paradigmatic act of redemption in the past: the Exodus.[9] In this literature God will accomplish through his chosen agent(s) the renewal, the vindication, and blessing of his people, as well as the defeat of all their enemies. The central feature is, therefore, the community as the people of God. For this group, messianic titles and other theological questions are clearly secondary to the primary issue of its own identity.

1. Mark's Portrayal of his Community

(i) *The kingdom and God's people*

How does this perspective shed light on Mark? One central aspect of Mark – one which is not surprising in the light of the continuity that Mark saw between his community and that of Israel, but one which has often been overlooked – is that in every case the images employed in Mark to represent Christian existence are corporate. The fact that the covenant community in Mark is a voluntary association from the standpoint of human response to the gospel ('Repent and believe the gospel') does not in any way lessen the communal nature of life among the followers of Jesus as Mark portrays them. This is apparent in the first image Mark offers: the kingdom of God (1.14f.).[10] Since the time of Johannes Weiss[11] 'kingdom of God' has quite rightly been understood as an eschatological reality; that interpretation is confirmed in Mark, where the followers of Jesus are told that some of them will live to see the kingdom 'having come with power' (9.1). The futurity of the kingdom is referred to explicitly elsewhere in Mark (14.25; 15.43). In keeping with the convictions of apocalyptic communities is the announcement that it has drawn near (1.15).[12]

Yet the new reality that is breaking into the present through Jesus is not a publicly evident phenomenon; rather, it is a mystery, insight into which has been granted only to the elect community (4.11).

The secret of the kingdom is not, however, the time when the consummation will take place; indeed the day of redemption is known only to God (13.32). The kingdom to which the elect have been given the clue is a present reality as well as an event awaited in the future. It is characterized by growth and by conflict; it must be entered or received (4.26–30; 3.24; 13.8; 9.47; 10.23–25; 12.34). In the parables of Mark 4 – or rather, in the Markan interpretation of those parables – the kingdom is explicitly compared with growth phenomena, especially with seeds and plants in process of maturation and productivity.[13] Further, the explanation of the Parable of the Sower (4.14–20) pictures an ongoing corporate life in which there is a sufficient passage of time for zeal to flag, for worldly values to entice and seduce the faithful, for outside opposition or heresy-mongers to spread false teachings within the group. Self-discipline is essential if anyone is to enter the kingdom (9.47).

The conflict that characterizes the kingdom is demonic in origin (3.24; 4.15) and cosmic in its dimensions (13.8). The Beelzebul controversy passage in Mark, which is composite in its present form (3.22–29), as the characteristic Markan locutions indicate,[14] shows that it is not the external actions of Jesus but their inner meaning (ἐν παραβολαῖς, v.23) which is related to the coming of the kingdom of God. The opponents can see in the authority of Jesus over the demons only the power of Satan himself, but he explains to his own[15] that what is really taking place is the destruction of Satan's rule, the shattering of his dynasty (οἰκία), the release of demoniacs from under his control, and hence the dividing or dispersing of his powers. Jesus' exorcisms have the effect of binding the 'Strong Man' and thus presage the end of his control. The passage points, therefore, to the hidden significance of the ongoing process of defeating the demonic opposition through the exorcisms which Jesus inaugurated and which his disciples are authorized by him to continue (3.15).

The interconnection between receiving the kingdom and entering it is declared in Mark 10.15. The figures are mixed, but the use of both of them shows that no one can merit admission to the eschatological community that is experiencing the powers and joys of the kingdom even while awaiting its consummation: entrance can only be received as a gift, like the mystery of the kingdom itself (4.11). Although the particular quality of children implied in 10.14 and 15 is not directly stated, the context seems to require that it is receptivity (δέξηται . . . ὡς παιδίον). But the notion is excluded that the kingdom can be received only in the future; rather, it can be entered now. Likewise, the man who sees the commandments summed up in the law of love is described as 'not far from the kingdom' (12.34), and hence very close to entering it. Yet those who seek to enter the kingdom are reminded of the heavy demands, the abandonment of worldly security, the divesting oneself of riches, which are prerequisite to entering it.

Clearly for Mark, then, life in his community is seen as more than merely preparation for a heavenly kingdom or even for a kingdom in a new age from which the present age is somehow radically disjunct. The instructions about the rigorous demands on those who are followers of Jesus (τοῖς μαθηταῖς 10.23) explicitly differentiate the two closely related stages of entering the kingdom: 1. the present age of discipline and renunciation, in which a new 'family' is given and new kinds of possession replace those given up (10.30a), and 2. eternal life which is received in the coming age (30b).

(ii) *The eschatological family*

This leads to the second major image employed by Mark for the eschatological community: the redefined family. As we have noted earlier,[16] this new definition of the family in terms of the Christian community is apparent in Mark 3.20f., 31–35 as well as in 10.28–31. Both passages are offered by Mark as instruction to the disciples, who in Mark regularly represent the community of Mark's own time and situation rather than a simple historical recollection. The Markan phrase περιβλεψάμενος . . . λέγει [τοῖς μαθηταῖς] appears in each case (3.34; 10.23) as an indication that what is being said is for the inner circle (cf. 3.34, τοὺς περὶ αὐτὸν κύκλῳ καθημένους), not for the crowds. The crux of the statement appears in the patterned form of a prophetic pronouncement:[17] 'Whoever does the will of God, he is my brother and my sister and my mother' (3.35). All genetic, familial, and sex distinctions are eradicated in this new concept of the true family.

The corollary of the new family identity is rupture with the actual family, as the narrative of the coming of Jesus' mother and brothers to take him away clearly implies (3.31f.). Mark is explicit that the scene occurs at the home of Jesus (3.20) and his family (3.21). The pattern of a break with family that was to characterize the disciples was set by Jesus himself, though the result was to join them in a new group identity rather than to cut them loose as isolated individuals. The rewards of life in the new community are set out in hyperbolic form in 10.30 – one hundred times as many houses and brothers and sisters and mothers and children and lands – to show that the deprivations suffered by those who devote themselves to the gospel, and are thus uprooted, will be more than made up for in the fellowship and fulfilment provided in the new community.

Jesus is the paradigm for the disciples, according to Mark, just as they are the model for the uprooted, persecuted (μετὰ διωγμῶν 10.30b) members of the Markan community. Yet their destiny is not limited to the joy in suffering that awaits them in the present age; rather, they are called to look beyond νῦν ἐν τῷ καιρῷ τούτῳ to eternal life in the coming age (10.30). Eschatological existence for Mark involves acceptance of present opportunities and obligations in view of the age to come, not merely indifference towards the present as a transitional epoch.

(iii) God's new flock

Closely akin to the image of the new family is that of the flock of God. Mark includes the flock/shepherd figure only twice: 6.34 and 14.27. Yet both times the image is employed at crucial points in the gospel, and in each case the inter-relation between the leader and the group is explicitly stated. In 14.27 the terms appear in a statement of Jesus to his disciples on the night of his arrest, the eve of his crucifixion. The defection of the disciples is predicted and represented as pre-determined by God through appeal to scripture. The passage quoted is from Zech. 13.7,[18] where the prophet is describing the judgment that is about to fall on the nation because of its apostasy. The shepherd-king, 'the man who stands next to me' (Zech. 13.7), will be struck down, and only a remnant of the covenant people will survive to share in the blessings of the new age (13.8). They will be tested as by fire, and in their purified state will become in truth God's people (13.8). The quotation is far more than a vivid metaphor for a leaderless people; it depicts the eschatological community enduring persecution and suffering in expectation of God's vindication of them in the time of the end. Mark makes this explicit when he joins to this quotation a prediction of the renewal of the community under Jesus' leadership following his resurrection from the dead (14.28).[19] This promise is clearly the point of the reminder spoken by the young man at the empty tomb (16.7) that Jesus would join with his disciples once more in Galilee; whether at the παρουσία or in post-resurrection appearances is not clear.

It is tempting to assume that the Markan tradition had more of these eschatological oracles in Zech. 9–11 in mind than the single

Zachariah

passage quoted at 14.17, especially since the pervasive theme in the oracles is the smitten shepherd, whose rejection by the covenant people brings down God's judgment, but who becomes the central focus of God's compassion and the nation's penitence (12.10) and thus leads to the restoration of the people of God (10.6–12) and eventually to all nations' joining in the worship of the God of Israel (14.16ff.).

In somewhat altered form, all those features are present in Mark, but is there any indication that this section of Zechariah was consciously operative in the mind of the community? There are indeed two unmistakable allusions to the Zechariah oracles at pivotal points in Mark. One is at 11.1–10, where Jesus is depicted as riding into Jerusalem on an ass – an obvious allusion to Zech. 9.9, which is made explicit in Matthew 21.5.[20] Mark mentions directly only the shepherd aspect of Zechariah's shepherd-king, yet it is ironic that the image is used only a short time before Jesus was condemned as pretender to the kingship of the Jews (15.18, 26, 32). Thus the community is reminded of its defection and of its promised restoration and vindication as the eschatological flock.

(iv) The new Exodus

The other allusion to Zechariah in Mark occurs at 6.34, which is of course the other appearance of the shepherd/flock image in this gospel. The picture from Zechariah is that of an aimless, needy people who have been led astray by false leaders. In Mark 6, the allusion to Zech. 10.4 appears in an extended description of the circumstances surrounding the miraculous feeding of the multitude and of Jesus' attitude toward the throng (6.30–35).[21] Jesus' compassion on the crowds which have thronged to hear him and to benefit from his powers is expressed in words that recall Moses' concern for the leadership of Israel as his death drew near (Num. 27.16–23) or that of Micaiah as he saw what was happening to the people under an evil, idolatrous king, Ahab (I Kings 22.17).[22] The more specific biblical parallel for the story which follows, however, is the miraculous food that God provided through Moses for his hungry people in the desert. Mark underlines the connection by his detail, twice repeated (6.32, 35), that this was an ἔρημος τόπος.

The Gospel of John recounts the miraculous feeding, and then appends to it an explicit interpretative parallel in which Jesus as bread from heaven is contrasted with the manna in the desert (John 6.46–51). Mark, in keeping with his esoteric outlook, not only does not go that far but gives only tantalizing hints to his reader of the real meaning of the miracle of feeding (8.19f.). The overall significance of the feeding story cannot be mistaken: as once God called his people out of Egypt and sustained them miraculously until they could enter the land of promise, so God is calling together a new people, who likewise will be preserved in their time of difficulty until they enter the New Age. The orderly arrangement of the people as they are fed is either a reflection of the actual organization of the Markan community or a stylized portrayal of its eschatological organization, similar to the groupings of the 'hosts' in the Qumran War Scroll.

The fact that both Mark's version of the feeding and the one in John 6 are followed by accounts of Jesus walking on the water (Mark 6.45–51a; John 6.16–21) suggests that both were preserved in the tradition together, and that they were linked in significance as well. This impression is confirmed by Mark's introducing a comment at the end of his account of the miracle of the waters about the disciples' lack of understanding of the miracle of the loaves (6.51b–52). The twin motifs of God's command over the waters and his feeding his own in the desert appear frequently in the Psalms in celebration of God's past acts on behalf of Israel (Ps. 78. 13–25; 106.9; 107.23–31) but also in the later prophetic tradition, where the events of the Exodus serve as the model for the awaited eschatological redemption of the chastened, renewed nation (Isa. 40.12; 41.18; 51.10). Jesus is perceived as the bearer of sovereign authority granted to him on behalf of the new covenant people, therefore, when in response to the fear and perplexity that overtook the disciples as Jesus approached them walking on the water, he reportedly declared: ἐγώ εἰμι (6.50).

The theme of eschatological deliverance is implied in the technical eucharistic language which is employed in the description of the giving of the loaves to the assembled thousands: εὐλόγησεν, κατέκλασεν, ἐδίδου, ἔφαγον (6.41). These terms, or their synonyms, are used in the story of the Last Supper in Mark (14.22–25), but in the latter passage an important additional factor is present: the community is fed not merely in order to be sustained in the present, or in order to recall the saving events of the past,[23] but in anticipation of the eschatological reunion of Jesus with his people 'in the kingdom of God'. Just as messianic claimants in the years prior to the Jewish revolt of the mid-first century aspired to reproduce the miracles in the desert that accompanied the Exodus,[24] so the Christians saw in the experiences of the community convened in the name of Jesus an eschatological re-enactment of the Exodus, along the lines announced by the later prophets.[25] God will gather, feed, and protect his people, like a shepherd leading his flock (Isa. 40.11).

(v) *New vineyard, new building*

A fifth image used by Mark in picturing the community of faith is actually a mixed metaphor: vineyard and building (12.1–11). Fortunately for the interpreter, Mark has preserved the tradition in such a way as to point up both metaphorical features. The passage opens with a modified version of the familiar allegory of the covenant people as vineyard from Isa. 5.1–7. A feature important for Mark's allegory that is not found in Isaiah's is that the vineyard is the possession of an absentee owner, who has let it out to tenants to care for (12.1b). The failure then is not that of the people as a whole (= the vineyard) but of those charged with leadership or stewardship over the vineyard. They have not only been wholly unproductive (12.2), but have rejected and done harm to the emissaries (= prophets?) sent by the owner from time to time (12.3f.). The final guilty act has been their denunciation of the 'beloved son' of the owner, his execution and expulsion from the vineyard (12.6–8). Their motive in this arrogant, defiant repudiation of the owner's rights and aims was to claim the inheritance for themselves. Far from obtaining their avaricious goal, they are turned out of their responsibility and replaced by a new set of stewards. Mark's point is clear: the leadership of the official covenant community has disqualified itself and its place has been taken by the leaders of the new covenant community. Shifting the image in 12.10f., Mark then goes on to show that God is erecting a new structure, the cornerstone of which is his Son. Ps. 118.22f. expresses that conviction without the need for modification of the LXX text. The community of Mark is portrayed, therefore, in the process of construction, with Jesus as the foundation.

Later New Testament writers would elaborate that image (Acts 4.11; I Peter 2.4, 7; Eph. 2.19–22), but Mark offers it in an undeveloped form which affirms the foundational significance of Jesus as cornerstone and the newness of the enterprise, in contrast to the old covenant community that has been displaced. That the structure will be built towards eschatological completion is implied but not expressed. The figure thus expresses confidence in the corporateness, the structure, the purposiveness, the divine intention, the process of building already under way in the Markan community. The context of this image and of the psalm from which it derives is that of the worshipping covenant community (Ps. 118.26f.).[26]

(vi) *The new covenant people*

The encompassing image under which Mark presents his community is an obvious one: the covenant people. It is mentioned directly only in the Last Supper scene (14.24), and even there the reference is to the blood of Jesus, presumably as the sacrifice which ratifies the covenant. The genitival sequence in this verse is awkward – 'this is the blood of me of the covenant'[27] – but the intention is to present Jesus' death as the ground of the covenant relationship of his people (ὑπὲρ πολλῶν). And in the verse that follows immediately (14.25), the ultimate outcome of the establishment of this (new) covenant is the consummation of God's rule.

The classic statement in the prophetic tradition concerning the new covenant is, of course, Jer. 31.31ff. Two features of that expectation as set forth in Jer. 31 are worth noting. The first is the emphasis on forgiveness (31.34); the second is the worldwide scope of the covenant community as it is gathered by God in the eschatological epoch (31.7f.). Both these features are important elements of the Markan community as well. As we have observed, Mark has inserted into the middle of a story of the healing of a paralytic (Mark 2.3–5a; 10b–11) a series of statements about the authority to forgive sins (5b–10a). In the midst of the account of the conflict with Jesus' family (3.20f., 31–35) there is a string of sayings about authority to perform exorcisms, which shifts (3.28f.) into a pair of declarations about the authority to forgive sins. This was the issue posed by John's baptism and call to repentance (1.4). The inability to perceive who Jesus is or to penetrate the mystery of the kingdom has the consequence that those who do not see or hear are not forgiven (4.12). The contrast between the forgiveness which is given to the community and which is to characterize their mutual relationships, on the one hand, and the lack of forgiveness for the unrepentant religious community on the other is set forth in two texts where the polemical factor is patent.

The first of these is in the controversy over the traditions of the elders (Mark 7). A scriptural text is quoted (from the LXX of Isa. 29.13) to show that, although Israel's official interpreters of the Law of God claim to be obeying its commands, in fact their 'heart is far' from God. Here there is an implicit contrast with the new covenant as portrayed in Jer. 31.33, where what is essential in the covenant relationship is not the written law but the law written 'upon their hearts'.

Similarly, for Mark the incident of the withered fig tree (Mark 11.12–14) is not a miracle story but an allegory of the curse on faithless Israel. The lesson to be drawn from it is less of a polemic against the old covenant people than a warning to the new covenant people (11.20–25), which culminates in an appeal to exercise forgiveness towards one's fellows in order to have a claim on God's forgiveness. Clearly forgiveness is a central concern for the Markan community.

As for the encompassing nature of the covenant community, Jeremiah depicts the new covenant people as being assembled by God 'from the farthest parts of the earth' – a phrase which is echoed in Mark 13.27, where we read that the angels will 'gather his elect from the four winds, from the ends of the earth to the ends of the heaven'. In II Isaiah, however, the picture of the eschatological community goes beyond the notion of the remnant of Israel being assembled from all over the earth to the assertion that other non-Israelite nations will respond to God's word and will share in Israel's end-time blessings (Isa. 55.3–5). Even more explicit is Isa. 55. 6f.:

> And the foreigners who join themselves to the Lord,
>   to minister to him, to love the name of the Lord,
>   and to be his servants,
>   everyone who keeps the sabbath and does not profane it,
>   and holds fast my covenant –
>   these I will bring to my holy mountain,
>   and make them joyful in my house of prayer . . .
>   for my house shall be called a house of prayer for
>   all peoples.
> Thus says the Lord God, who gathers the outcasts
>   of Israel,
> I will gather yet others to him besides those
>   already gathered.

The fact that a central portion of this passage is directly quoted in Mark 11.17, in the setting of Jesus' authoritative action in cleansing the Temple of the commercial aspects of the cultic system (11.15f.), shows that for Mark[28] the inclusiveness of the community as exemplified by free access to the sanctuary of God is a pivotal concern. But throughout Mark, the point is made in both subtle and overt ways that there are no social or ethnic prerequisites for admission to the covenant community: it is indeed the 'outcasts of Israel' who are welcomed into membership. The 'dogs' are given food within the community of faith.[29] As we have noted, the enigmatic words about the leaven and the numbers of loaves and fragments (8.17–21) are intended to point to the new reality within the covenant community, presaged by the two feeding stories as Mark presents them: those of Jewish background and those who lack it are alike welcome in the household of faith. By criteria for admission that are even more open to outsiders than those of Deutero-Isaiah, with its minimum requirement that Gentiles observe the sabbath (Isa. 55.6)[30] – failure to observe the sabbath is presented by Mark as the occasion for forming a coalition to destroy Jesus (3.6) – Jesus is portrayed in Mark 1.15 as convening the new community by his word and action that lead his hearers to repent and to trust his announcement that the kingdom of God has drawn near.

2. MARK'S PORTRAYAL OF JESUS AS AGENT FOR ESTABLISHING THE NEW COVENANT

A full understanding of Mark's conception of the meaning of Jesus for the faith of his community cannot be content with an assessment of the christological *titles*. Due consideration must also be given to the *revelatory and redemptive roles* that are assigned to Jesus in the Markan tradition.

P. Volz wrote in his classic study of Jewish eschatology that so manifold was the messianic idea in Judaism during the period from Daniel to Akiba that one has not said much when one states that Jesus was the messiah. What kind of messiah? A prophet, a teacher of the Law, a bearer of angelic power, a priest-king (as in Test. Levi) or a political-national king?[31] The Qumran discoveries have served to complicate rather than to clarify the picture of redemptive-eschatological roles in the period during which Christianity was taking shape. Accordingly, when Peter acclaims Jesus as messiah (8.29), he forthwith displays that he not only does not grasp the import of Jesus' understanding of his mission as involving suffering, but to the extent that he does understand what Jesus is saying, he rejects the notion (8.32).

Similarly, the sons of Zebedee perceive that Jesus is to play a central role in the eschatological plan of God (10.36), but they wrongly regard association with him as providing them places of favour and special privilege in the new age, a confidence which Jesus tells them is not only unwarranted but wholly out of place (10.38–45). In the latter incident, no christological titles are used, yet the messianic role (using the term broadly) is being redefined. That redefinition involves directly the responsibilities of the members of the community: 'It shall not be so with you, but ...' (10.43).

These roles in which Mark portrays Jesus have their roots in the Jewish tradition, but they do not merely reproduce what one finds in the antecedents of Mark's understanding of these redemptive functions. A fair assessment of the titles and roles must move in dialectical fashion between the background of the terms and concepts and the peculiar way in which they are employed in the text of Mark. Important for this method of clarifying the roles of Jesus in Mark is the manner in which Mark pictures Jesus as rejecting or refusing to be identified with some of the ways in which those roles were viewed from within the Jewish tradition. Thus Jesus scorns his captors who have seized him as though he were a revolutionary, λῃστής (14.48).[32] He refuses to speak out in his own defence when accused of aspiring to be king of the Jews (15.4f.). The irony of the accusation is heightened in Mark's account by the repeated charge (15.12), the soldiers' mockery (15.18), the wholly inappropriate *titulus* on the cross (15.26), and the hypocritical appeals of the religious leaders (15.32). Jesus' only response was the ambiguous Σὺ λέγεις (15.2), which for Mark may mean, 'That is your designation for me, not mine.' Although we shall shortly consider the title Son of David, it is important to note at this point that Jesus never uses it of himself in Mark, nor does he accept it when used of him by others. And when one might expect the term to be used of him, as in his entry into Jerusalem (11.1–11), it does not in fact occur. Even the hallowed notion that it is through the offspring of David that God's eschatological rule will be established is dramatically redefined in Mark. What are the roles that Mark assigns to Jesus?

(i) *The prophet*

Mark's favourite designation for Jesus is teacher, as we have noted.[33] Yet Jesus does not appear as a rabbinic interpreter of the scriptures, but as a charismatic, divinely authorized spokesman for God. That is implied in most of the controversy stories of Mark, but it is expressly dealt with in 6.1–6. There the crucial verses are 6.4, where Jesus depicts himself as a prophet, and 6.2, where the substance of his role is epitomized: his wisdom and his δυνάμεις. Mark does not tell us the source of either, but by his much-favoured interrogative device (Πόθεν τούτῳ ταῦτα . . .; 6.2a) he puts the responsibility on the reader to provide the answer. Jesus makes a similar response to the request to disclose the source of his authority in 11.27–33. The hostile inquiry is in relation to his actions (ταῦτα ποιεῖς), not merely his teachings.

But the picture presented by both passages is a consistent one: Jesus is a charismatic prophet whose words and works are self-authenticating. He will not appeal to authority, nor will he perform a miracle on demand as a means of authenticating his work (8.11–13). Only from the perspective of faith in him as the messenger and agent of God can it be determined what the source of his power is. Conversely, where faith is lacking (ἀπιστίαν, 6.6), he is unable to perform his powerful works (6.5). The specific details of his mighty works recall the prophetic tradition of Israel, especially the figures of Moses and Elijah (cf. the desert feedings, 6.31; 8.28; 9.4, 11).[34]

In giving Jesus this role as prophet-teacher, however, Mark presents him as the one who interprets the will of God to the covenant people. The new covenant demands a new appropriation of the Law (Jer. 31.33) by God's new people to whom he grants a new under-standing ('new heart'). Accordingly Mark devotes extensive space in his gospel to the discussion of the Law, as well as to the reporting of wisdom and eschatological sayings of Jesus as the bearer of divine wisdom.

As we shall consider in the next chapter, the issues of sabbath, ritual purity, divorce, obligation to secular authority and to priests, attitudes towards possessions, and moral responsibility to one's neighbour are all discussed in Mark. These are not elements extra-neous to Mark's major interest – as though that were the passion[35] or christology[36] – but are an essential feature of an end-time prophet. The founder of the Qumran community, with its intense eschato-logical expectation, was called 'The One who Teaches (the Law) Rightly', as T. H. Gaster has pointed out.[37] The Teacher was a priest, but his major function in relation to the Qumran community was as the one to whom God granted understanding 'that he might interpret all the words of his servants the prophets, through whom he foretold all that would happen to his people. . . .'[38]

In the Qumran Hymns, the speaker (presumably the Teacher) declares that God has opened a fountain by the mouth of his servant, that the divine mysteries are on his tongue, in order 'that out of his understanding he might preach to a creature, and interpret these things to dust like myself'.[39] In CD 6, an exposition of Num. 21.18 is offered, according to which the 'well' is the Law, and the staff by which it was dug is the Teacher. The regulations of the Qumran community, strict as they are, are represented in CD as the inter-pretations rendered by the Teacher of Righteousness, just as his exposition of the prophets in the *pesher* commentaries explains the historical origins and trials of the community, as well as pointing to its eschatological vindication.[40] A consistent figure in the otherwise diverse presentation of the 'messianic' persons whose advent is expected at the end of the age is 'the Prophet', whose coming is seen as the fulfilment of the promise in Deut. 18.15–18, as is unambiguously declared in the Psalms of Joshua.[41] While the content of the teaching of Jesus as Mark presents it is radically different from that of the Qumran prophet, the intent is the same: to interpret past and present trials in preparation for the future vindication of the com-munity of the elect to whom these mysteries have been vouchsafed (Mark 4.11).

The prophet as seer functions throughout Mark, even though the title is not assigned to Jesus in this role. This is especially apparent in Mark 13, where we have the single extensive discourse in Mark. But it is also evident in the series of predictions of his death (8.31; 9.31; 10.33ff.) as well as in the narratives of the arrest and trial of Jesus: his death is foreseen in the act of anointing (14.3–9); his betrayal is foretold (14.18); the scattering of his followers is announced (14.27); he speaks of his impending death (14.36); he warns of his betrayal (14.14). And in the last hours before his death he announces his vindication (14.25, 62). The last promise reported in Mark (16.8) is a reminder of a prophetic word of Jesus about the reassembling of his followers after the resurrection. These prophetic functions of Jesus in Mark, as well as his associations with the prophetic figures of John the Baptist, Moses and Elijah, place him fully within the tradition of eschatological prophet (1.2f.; 9.2–9, 11–13).

There is no way of determining with finality whether Jesus saw himself in the role of eschatological prophet, and our concern in this study is with Mark rather than with the historical Jesus. But it is highly likely that Jesus did so regard himself and that it was the power of that image – perhaps reinforced by post-resurrection appearances and described as the power of the (Holy) Spirit (Mark 1.12; 3.29; 13.11, see below, 139ff.) which sustained the disciples and their followers in what they regarded as the interim until they would be reunited with the resurrected, publicly vindicated Jesus (13.26; 14.62).

(ii) *The mightier one*

Although it cannot be considered a title, John's description of Jesus as one more powerful than he helps to set the stage for the mighty acts of Jesus, both those in the conflict with the demons and those related to his mastery over the cosmic powers, as represented by his control over winds (4.35–41), and waves (6.45–52). Although Mark does not report John as disclosing the nature of Jesus' superior strength (1.7), this is perhaps to be understood in connection with the Holy Spirit in another passage which is of his own editorial creation in its present form (3.23–29). There, however, it is Satan who is the 'strong one', with Jesus implied as being his victorious opponent, his superiority to Satan becoming evident in the exorcisms which he performs. For Mark, there is a closely related point (to be discussed below): [42] namely, that exorcisms performed in Jesus' name, by the power of the Spirit, are to be regarded as phases in the dividing up of Satan's hold over the creation, as the plundering of his tools, as the binding of the 'strong one' (3.26f.), rather than as evidence that those who drive the demons out are in league with Satan, the ruler of the demons (3.22). This capability of Jesus is represented by Mark as known to the demons and acknowledged by them (1.24; 3.11; 5.7; 12).[43] There is no messianic secret in these stories, and the commanding words are not intended to preserve the secret that Jesus is messiah,[44] but to bring the demons under control and expel them.[45] It is this capacity of Jesus which lies behind the portrait of him as 'the stronger one'.

(iii) *The holy one of God*

The first of the demonic words addressed to Jesus in Mark (1.24) identifies him as 'the holy one of God' (ὁ ἅγιος τοῦ θεοῦ). Bauernfeind has rightly noted the parallels between this passage and the hostile reaction to Elijah on the part of Ahab in I Kings 17[46] in the LXX. The defender calls his attacker by name in each case (Elijah – Jesus the Nazarene), characterizes him as standing in a special relationship to God (ἄνθρωπος θεοῦ – ἅγιος τοῦ θεοῦ), and articulates the threat under which he sees himself as a consequence of his opponent having appeared on the scene ('Have you come to cause the death of my son? Have you come to destroy us?'). In the Markan story, the factor of identification is emphasized by the phrase οἶδά σε τίς εἶ. The demon thus perceives in Jesus not only his own conqueror but also the victor over the demonic rule with which he is linked.

Various attempts have been made to account for the title 'holy one of God'. Bauernfeind tries to capitalize on the term in the I Kings 17 parallel, ἄνθρωπος τοῦ θεοῦ, and on the assumption that that was the original form behind Mark, develops a theory linking this story with the speculative notion of θεῖος ἀνήρ as a fixed first-century Hellenistic term for a miracle worker.[47] But the interpreter is obliged to treat the text as it stands, there being no manuscript evidence for variants here. The phrase does occur in the LXX: it is used for Aaron (Ps. 105.16); for Samson (LXX[B]: Judg. 13.7; 16.17);[48] and for Elisha (II Kings 4.9). Of these occurrences of the approximate phrase, the Samson and Elisha[49] instances seem to be the more relevant ones, since in both cases ἅγιος has to do with extraordinary powers granted by God. In Sim. Enoch the phrase appears in the plural (38.4; 50.1f.), and in each case the point of the passage is that the faithful will be vindicated by a manifestation of divine power prior to the end time.

Here again, as in the case of the prophet, the important factor for Mark is not the title itself but the function to which it points: the defeat of the demonic powers, which began with the ministry of Jesus, and is continued in the ministry of the disciples (1.39; 3.14;

6.7). It is possible that Mark sees the Holy Spirit as the powerful link between what Jesus did in the defeat of the demonic powers and what the disciples carry forward in his name (3.29), but we shall consider this possibility below.

(iv) *The cosmic agent*

Obviously this term does not appear in Mark, but a question very similar to the one raised by Jesus' opponents concerning his wisdom and powers as prophet (6.2b) is raised by the disciples in 4.41 as a consequence of his having stilled the storm on the lake: 'Who is this, then, that even the wind and the sea obey him?' A similar response of astonishment and awe fills the disciples when Jesus comes to them on the water (6.45–52), even though he assures them that it is indeed he: θαρσεῖτε, ἐγώ εἰμι. μὴ φοβεῖσθε. Using the device of a rhetorical question, or one that only the discerning reader is prepared to answer accurately, Mark poses the issue as to who could triumph over storm and waves. As we have already observed in other contexts, these stories recall two motifs often intermingled in the Old Testament tradition: the mythological battle with the waters of chaos and the deliverance of Israel from bondage by passage through the Red Sea and the Jordan.

That the stories have taken on connotations of cosmic conflict is evident in the use of ἐπιτιμᾶν in 4.39, the technical term for the defeat of the demonic powers. Thus Mark presents Jesus as competent to overcome the threefold coalition of hostility that stands in the way of the coming of God's kingdom: the human institutions and powers, the demons, and the cosmic powers. Redemption is not seen by Mark as extrication from a hostile context in which man lives, but as renewal and ordering of that context, exemplified by these cosmic powers he described working through Jesus.

(v) *Son of God*

The textual support for the occurrence of υἱὸς θεοῦ in the lemma of Mark (1.1) is strong, in spite of patristic witnesses that omit it.[50] Unlike Hellenistic usage, where the phrase has mythological or metaphysical connotations, or both together, the term must be understood in its Markan context, with the significance attached to it implied by its functions within the narrative. In addition, the association of the title with the scriptural quotations and allusions linked with it in Mark must be taken into account as a primary source for determining the meaning for Mark of 'Son of God'.

The first clue we have in this connection is the juxtaposition of the title with the double quotation (from Isa. 40.3 and Mal. 3.1), thereby stressing that the good news concerning or proclaimed by the Son of God is eschatological in nature, pointing to God's coming to redeem his people. As modified in Mark by the shift of pronouns, it is the coming of Jesus (= Lord) that John the Baptist as messenger prepares for through his message and rite of repentance (1.4). The prophetic-eschatological scheme is developed further by the words of the voice of God which acclaims Jesus at his baptism (1.11) and later in the Transfiguration scene (9.7). Since the vision of the spirit descending and the audition of the heavenly voice are represented in Mark as purely private disclosures to Jesus (εἶδεν . . . ἐν σοι), he is called Son of God by direct address (Σὺ εἶ), which differs only in word order[51] from the LXX of Ps. 2.7.

The second part of this verse from Ps. 2, 'Today I have begotten you', which is omitted from Mark,[52] is referred to in the important eschatological supplement to the Scroll of the Rule (1 QSa 2.11f.), where the coming of the anointed king and priest is predicted for the end time.[53] Obviously, then, Ps. 2 was being interpreted by sectarian Jews of the first century as messianic and eschatological. And most important, one of the ways of designating the redemptive figure of the end-time was 'Son of God'.

The epithet ἀγαπητός recalls the language of Gen. 22.2, where Abraham is instructed to sacrifice his only son, as well as that of the Servant poems of Deutero-Isaiah, where the servant (παῖς) is the elect of God and his special delight (42.1), whose conception and birth were an outworking of God's purpose (44.1f.). In both these passages there is a further declaration that God has poured out his Spirit on the servant so that the servant's witness may go forth with power to the nations of the earth (42.1b–7; 44.3–8). The details of language differ as between Deutero-Isaiah and Mark 1, but the basic outlook is very similar, as Luke made explicit in having Jesus quote Isa. 61 in a sermon at Nazareth and then declare the passage to be fulfilled in himself (Luke 4.18f. = Isa. 61.1f.; 58.6).

Often overlooked in recognizing the kinship of the words of the heavenly voice with the Servant motif of Deutero-Isaiah is the fact that it is difficult to determine whether the Servant is an individual or the faithful among Israel. A third possibility is that the Servant is the representative figure around whom the obedient from among Israel rally, and who emulate him in his zeal and redemptive functions. There is surely precedent for this dual conception of the nation as corporately God's 'son', as can be seen in the instructions given to Moses (Ex. 4.22) to tell Pharaoh to allow 'my first-born son' to leave

Egypt. In Hosea 11.1ff. Israel in her disobedience is addressed as 'son', and depicted in thoroughly anthropomorphic terms as being taken up in God's arms and taught to walk. The metaphorical representation of the covenant people as son is firmly rooted in the biblical tradition, so that there is nothing surprising or extraneous to have a servant-child figure in Deutero-Isaiah stand as both a prophetic individual leader and as representing the people whom he leads toward eschatological redemption.[54]

Since the divine voice in Mark 9.7 is addressed primarily to the three disciples who are present, it refers to Jesus as son in the third person, but with an unmistakable echo of the earlier acclaim in 1.11. A different phrase is attached, however: 'Listen to him.' We have earlier observed[55] that this is an allusion to Deut. 18.15, where the prophet – understood at Qumran as an eschatological figure – will reveal the truth of God to the covenant people, who are instructed to heed his words. The Son of God, in this proleptic vision of Jesus' eschatological vindication, is God's spokesman for the end time.

Recognition of Jesus as God's agent is common knowledge among the demons, whose hold on the creation he has come to break. In the transitional section, 3.7–12, Mark reports that the demons prostrate themselves before him and cry out his identity as Son of God (3.11). A more elaborate recognition form is attested in 5.7 – 'Son of God Most High' – with the adjuration added that Jesus might not 'torment' the demons.

Clearly there are several factors operative in these stories. 1. The ability to recognize the exorcist and the direct address to him (Σὺ εἶ . . .) conforms to the pattern found in the magical papyri, as Bauernfeind's collected evidence shows.[56] 2. As we have noted, again in dependence on Bauernfeind,[57] the person threatened by the holy man declares to the charismatic the consequences he expects from his challenge ('Have you come to destroy us?' 1.24; 'Are you going to kill my son?' I Kings 17.18). And 3. while the title 'Son of God' is linked with messianic hopes, it has no obvious connections with exorcisms. The prophetic tradition does tell of the defeat and judgment of the 'host of heaven' in the day of the Lord (Zeph. 1.2–7a;[58] Isa. 24, esp. vv. 21–23). In Sim. Enoch 69.26–29 there is an account of the defeat of sinners and of 'those who have led the world astray' – presumably the demonic powers or fallen angels – although the agent by whom they are enchained and destroyed is the Son of Man. The theme of conflict with the hosts of Belial or the evil spirits pervades the Testaments of the Twelve Patriarchs.[59]

The clue to the significance of the title Son of God in the exorcism narratives is offered in Mark 2.23–27, which is part of a Markan complex of narrative and sayings material. There the images are mixed: a kingdom is divided, a dynasty is ruined by internal conflict, the Adversary (Satan) is seen to be opposing himself, the evil strong man is bound and his possessions plundered. As the demons' words disclose, Jesus is the agent of God empowered to bring about their defeat and to wrest control of the world from the hand of Satan and subject it to the rule of God. This is not traditional messianic language, according to strict Jewish traditions, but it is Mark's way of understanding the one ordained to be God's vice-gerent, and therefore qualified to be addressed by God as 'Son of God' – (1.11; 9.1), by his defeated enemies (1.24; 3.11; 5.7), and by a perceiving pagan (15.39).

The redefinition of messianic categories emerges at many points in Mark. When Peter acclaims Jesus as *Christos* (8.29) and then learns that Jesus sees his role as necessarily involving suffering and death (δεῖ . . . παθεῖν . . . καὶ ἀποκτανθῆναι 8.31), he remonstrates with Jesus, only to be addressed by the same commanding word with which Jesus in the tradition brings the demons under control (ἐπετίμησεν 8.33).

The second announcement of Jesus' impending suffering and death leads to a squabble among the disciples about who is greatest (9.33–37), just as the third announcement of the passion (10.33–34) leads to James and John vying for positions of privilege (10.35–45). The redemptive role of Jesus as Mark pictures it is not fulfilled by the seizure of power but by submission to the divine will, which involves suffering and martyrdom (10.38, 45).

(vi) *The Son of David*

In keeping with this programme of redefining the eschatological community, Mark breaks with the traditional forms of messianic expectation, and in so doing avoids direct, positive use of the title Son of David. The one extant text in which the Son of David is presented as a powerful eschatological king, who crushes his enemies and rules 'with a rod of iron', is Ps. Sol. 17.21–25:

> Behold, O Lord, and raise unto them their king, the
> Son of David,
> At the time in which thou seest, O God, that he may
> reign over Israel, thy servant.
> And gird him with strength, that he may shatter
> unrighteous rulers,
> And that he may purge Jerusalem from nations that
> trample her down to destruction.

Wisely, righteously he shall thrust out sinners
  from the inheritance,
He shall destroy the pride of the sinner as a
  potter's vessel.
With a rod of iron he shall break in pieces all
  their substance,
He shall destroy the godless nations with the word
  of his mouth;
At his rebuke nations shall flee before him,
And he shall reprove sinners for the thoughts of
  their heart.

Scholars have quite properly noted that this is one of the few Jewish texts in which the title *Son* of David is used.[60] More common are terms like Shoot of David[61] or Branch of David.[62] But it is not the titles of David alone which evidence the vitality of his image in the first century; from both the later prophetic tradition and from Qumran we can see that David as symbol of the eschatological reign of God functioned in a wide range of ways, some of which correspond to the figure of David in Mark and others contrast sharply with it.

The name David occurs in only four contexts in Mark: 2.25, in connection with the disciples' violation of the sabbath: 10.47, 48, where Jesus is called Son of David by the blind man seeking sight; 11.10, where those who acclaim Jesus as he enters Jerusalem rejoice in the coming of David's kingdom; and 12.35–37, where Jesus is questioned about Messiah as Son of David. Of the four, the most puzzling are the call of the blind man and the enigmatic statement about David's son, although indeed the other two passages are more provocative than unambiguously clarifying. Beginning with the story of blind Bartimaeus, we may ask why there should have been a link between David and recovery of sight. The answer is that regaining sight is one important facet of the rich image of David in the late prophetic tradition.

Actually the ground for portraying David as the one who brings light to the nations and who opens the eyes of the blind is laid in the oracles of Isaiah of Jerusalem. Among the transforming actions which are expected as God brings to consummation his purpose in the creation, none is given more prominence in both Isaiahs than light for those in darkness. In addition to general images of light/dark, the motif of sight granted to blind occurs in 9.1ff., where the scion of David brings light to those in darkness; in 29.18, the oracle addressed to the City of David promises that blind eyes shall see; the assurances that God will restore the monarchy to David (32.1ff.) in Zion culminate in the promise that the eyes of the blind will be opened (35.5) as an important feature of the cosmic renewal that will accompany the fulfilment of the promise of David.

In Deutero-Isaiah the reign of the servant king is characterized by light to the blind (42.7; 42.16; 43.8; 61.1 in LXX). And in Isa. 55.3–5 all nations are seen as sharing in the epoch of blessing that accompanies the fulfilment of the Davidic promise, based on the original covenant assurances (II Sam. 7.13, 16, 25, 29). The same themes are to be found in the appendix to Amos (9.11–15), in Jeremiah's picture of David as the Branch through whom the covenant community is renewed (Jer. 33.14ff.). Ezekiel presents David as the model of the shepherd of the renewed people of God (Ezek. 34.23f.; 37.24). Ps. 89 was understood to be a prophetic statement of the ideal rule of David in the end-time.

In several of the Qumran documents – most notably, 4Q Florilegium, 4Q Patriarchal Blessings, and in the Isaiah Commentary – the following themes are interwoven:

> The kingly promise to David from II Sam. 7;
> The eternal covenant with David from Isa. 55;
> The cleansing of the sanctuary from Isa. 56;
> The Davidic king as Son of God from Ps. 2.

In Fragment D of the Isaiah Commentary (4 Qp Is^d), which is based on Isa. 11.1–5, the Shoot of David, who will appear at the end of the age, is to be upheld by the Spirit of God. In 4Q Flor 1.1, the house of David will be built at the end time, and David as symbol of the Son of Light (1.7) will be granted respite from the attacks of the hosts of Belial. The rule of David is assured, according to 4Q Flor 1.10–14 and in the Patriarchal Blessings, where the promise made to Judah in Gen. 49 is seen as fulfilled in the Davidic kingship. And as we have noted, in IQSa 2.11, God's begetting the messiah is predicted in language that echoes Ps. 2.

From this wide range of texts which are known to date from the time of Jesus or earlier, we can infer that the figure of David was a living image embodying the aspirations of the covenant people for renewal and vindication, that David was regarded as the instrument through whom the light of the knowledge of God would go out to the nations, that through him there would be a renovation of the worship of God and the defeat of the powers of evil.

It is against this background that we can perceive the appropriateness and the import of the appeal addressed to Jesus as Son of David by a blind man who petitioned that his sight might be restored (11.47). As we have noted in our analysis of Mark's positioning of the Bartimaeus story within the gospel as a whole, the recovery of sight functions for Mark as it does for Deutero-Isaiah; that is, as a sign of the encompassing covenantal and cosmic renewal through which the divine purpose will be consummated in the creation.

In contrast to the other synoptic accounts in which Jesus is addressed as 'Son of David' (Matt. 21.9) and 'King' (Luke 19.38), Mark reports only a pair of acclamations uttered by those who preceded and those who followed Jesus as he entered Jerusalem:

> Hosanna! Blessed is he who comes in the name of the
> Lord!
> Blessed is the kingdom of our father, David, that is
> coming!
> Hosanna in the highest!

As commentators have observed,[63] Mark presents here a curious mixture of a liturgical term transliterated from the Hebrew of Ps. 118.25 ('Ωσαννά), a quotation from the LXX of Ps. 118.26 ('Blessed is he who comes in the name of the Lord'), and the phrase about the coming kingdom of 'our father David' for which there is no parallel, either for the statement as a whole or for that way of referring to David. Ps. 118, as is most clearly evident from vv. 19–27, functioned as a song sung by pilgrims approaching the sanctuary of Yahweh. In first-century practice, the psalm was recited in connection with such feasts as Booths, Passover, and possibly Dedication, and was understood eschatologically[64] as pointing to the triumph of God and the vindication of his people. That point is made explicit in the parallel utterance included in Mark.

But whereas in Ps. 118.26 the one who comes in the name of the Lord is the worshipper, in Mark the acclaim is ambiguous. Is Jesus being welcomed – presumably along with other worshippers – as he enters the Holy City? Or is he being acknowledged as 'the Coming One', in terminology similar to the phrase used by John the Baptist according to the Q tradition (Matt. 11.3 = Luke 7.19)?[65] To pose the alternatives more explicitly, is Jesus merely an honoured pilgrim, or is he acclaimed as messiah? Mark intends the reader to discern the hidden meaning of the incident behind the outward phenomenon. There is no word in this passage which sets Jesus apart from the others, and nothing which points directly to his messiahship. The esoteric flavour of the narrative is heightened by the peculiar preparations to have the ass ready for his ride into the city.

The act is one of prophetic symbolism, recalling as it does not only the oracle from Zech. 9.9, which Matthew directly quotes (Matt. 21.5), but also the announcement of salvation coming to Zion in Isa. 62.11 and the oracle about the kingship of Judah in Jacob's death-bed prophecies (Gen. 49.11). The composite scriptural allusion that this incident represents is matched by the compound quotation itself, and both are in keeping with the Markan method of documenting the career and significance of Jesus in scripture, as we considered earlier.[66]

Just as in the blind Bartimaeus incident (10.47, 48), so here Jesus does not accept the designation as Son of David, although he is certainly associated with the fulfilment of the promise to David and his descendants about the eschatological kingdom. But the concept of the Davidic kingdom is being revised, or at least shifted from the fiercely nationalistic way in which it was awaited in the Psalms of Solomon to a form closer to the inclusive outlook of the later prophetic tradition as summarized above. It is wholly consonant with Mark's perspective that when, as a pilgrim, Jesus does enter the sanctuary (11.17), he claims it as a place of worship 'for all nations' (Isa. 56.7).

In the single incident in Mark where Jesus appeals to the precedent of David (2.23–28), it is in support of his disciples' violation of the sabbath law. If the analogy is pressed, more is involved than breaking the sabbath regulation by rubbing the grain to prepare it for eating: the bread set aside for the priests was made available for common people. In the narrative from II Sam. 15, the distinction between sanctified and unsanctified persons is broken down in the interests of meeting ordinary human needs. David and his men were doing God's work, and deserved support when they required it. Analogously, Jesus' disciples should be sustained to carry out the work of God for which they have been called, even though legal standards might be violated in the process. The precedent for this setting aside of the law and for the desacralization of the priesthood – or perhaps, the sacralization of all God's workmen – is David himself.

Significantly, Mark waits until near the end of his account of the career of Jesus to raise directly the issue of the relation of messiah, rightly understood, to Son of David (12.35–37a). If the Messiah is thought of in terms limited to the scribal view – presumably exclusivist and nationalist – then there is no accounting for the import of one of the favourite messianic texts in which David, as traditional author of the psalms, refers to the messiah as 'my Lord'. One would not expect a descendant of great David, the model king in the prophetic tradition, to be David's superior – so much more exalted that David would address him as 'Lord'.

The thrust of Jesus' question here is not to deny that Messiah is Son of David, but to transmute the notion of kingship by treating kingship on a cosmic plane. Ps. 110.1 (109 in LXX, which Mark here is quoting) is referred to in response to the high priest's question to Jesus in Mark 14.61 as to whether Jesus claims to be the Son of God (the pious circumlocution, 'Blessed', is appropriately used here); there Jesus is represented by Mark as paraphrasing Ps. 110: 'sitting at the right hand of power' (another paraphrase to avoid directly pronouncing the name of God).

Mark's tradition is therefore subtly bringing together three strands: Son of God, Son of David, Lord (κύριος), all of which connote for Mark the kingly role for which Jesus is destined, not in simple fulfilment of Jewish expectations, but in transformation of them. Mark has dropped hints about κύριος as a designation for Jesus in the scriptural quotation with which the gospel opens (1.3, where the LXX's use of κύριος as a translation for YHWH is exploited as a prophetic reference to Jesus as 'lord'), and in 11.3, where 'the Lord' needs the ass for which the secret arrangements are being made.[67] Less direct, but of great importance for the Markan community (as we shall see), is the designation of the Son of Man (= Jesus) as 'Lord of the sabbath' in 2.28).[68] For Mark, Jesus is the one sent by God (9.37), destined to be exalted to the right hand of God (14.62), the place reserved for God's royal agent. Under this function Mark has subsumed the traditional titles: Lord, Son of God, and Son of David.

(vii) *The Son of Man*

In IV Ezra we have a document preserved by an apolyptically-oriented community which offers hope to a covenant people in the face of the destruction of Jerusalem by the Romans. The document's method and line of argument build on and modify the prophecies of Daniel, especially the visions of Dan. 7 (12.10–13). The present villain is not the Seleucids but the Romans, symbolized by the eagle (11.1ff.). The lion, who overcomes the eagle (11.37ff.), is declared to be the Messiah, descendant of David (12.31f.), who has been 'kept until the end of days' – that is, has been planned for in the purpose of God, and thereby reserved in the heavens. In the following vision,[69] 'something like the figure of a man' arises from the sea. In spite of recent attempts to draw a distinction between this figure and that of the Son of Man in Dan. 7,[70] the similarity in the indefinite reference to each (Daniel says 'one like a son of man' = a human being, Dan. 7.13) and the fact that the human figure appears in each instance following a series of visions of beasts who represent world empires shows that both are manifestations of the same tradition. The explicit reference in this book (IV Ezra) to its contents as a correction of Daniel (12.11f.) makes the direct link undeniable, and accounts as well for some differences in detail. The functions of the lion in ch. 12 and of the man in ch. 13 are closely similar: both have been kept in heaven awaiting their discharge of their eschatological role (12.32; 13.26); both overcome the enemy by the word, rather than by force (12.32b, 'Messiah . . . will speak to them; he will denounce them . . .'; 13.27–31, 'when all nations hear his voice . . .'). Both accomplish the defeat of the enemies and the vindication of the covenant people (12.47–49; 13.36–49). The visions, therefore, represent two ways of perceiving the redemptive figure that will come at the end of the age, rather than successive stages in the accomplishment of the redemptive purpose.

What is important for our purposes is to note that the vision in ch. 12 builds on elements from Ps. Sol. 17,[71] including the Davidic lineage of the king, while in ch. 13 the image builds on the (Son of) Man, which, though often regarded as a transcendent figure,[72] is but another way of representing the nationalistic king-Messiah (13.39ff.). The final deliverance is seen as analogous to the Exodus (14.3ff., 29) and the restoration from the exile (13.46ff.): the focus of the seer remains on the restoration of the tribes (13.40). Thus in IV Ezra there is a blending of what has been regarded by some scholars as two separate traditions: the Davidic Messiah and the (Son of) Man.[73]

This combination should not be surprising, however, since both traditions have a common base in the ancient Near Eastern conception of the divine king.[74] As F. H. Borsch has shown, the notion of a Primal Man, whose conflict with the powers of chaos and darkness at first ends in defeat, from which he is delivered and exalted on a divine throne,[75] manifests itself in the mythologies of Babylon,[76] Tyre, and Canaan,[77] and influenced not only the Israelite concept of kingship, but the cultic and prophetic traditions as well.[78]

Borsch draws attention to the fact that 'son of man' in Ps. 8.4–7 does not refer to mankind as an abstraction or to a randomly selected individual, but to the Man, to the Son of Man – that is, to the descendant of Primal Man – who has been chosen to exercise authority over the creation on God's behalf (Ps. 8.4). Outside Ezekiel, he points out, 'son of man' is used in formulaic fashion in canonical and extra-canonical texts.[79] In Ps. 146.3f. and Ps. 80.14–17, 'Son of Man' stands in parallel with royal figures, princes, and the king. Solar and cosmic imagery recalling the myth of the Primal Man is found widely in the Psalms (46.4; 50.2; 97.11; 118.27; 110.7) and in the prophets (Zech. 14.8; Isa. 60.1ff.), especially in Ezekiel, where the eschatological renewal involves the creation of a new Eden, with a river of life flowing forth from the Temple mount and vivifying the Dead Sea (Ezek. 47).[80]

The expectation of an ideal king of the nation and the hope of the coming of the Primal Man were two different strands within the one tradition, and according to Borsch, it is wrong to assume that these images only become blended in later times and among Christians. By the early second century BC there was known to the author of Daniel, and presumably to many of his readers as well, 'a kind of ideogram of an idealized, semi-divine, royal figure who would rule in the great age to come'.[81] Borsch declares that the Son of Man will do what the messiah is expected to do, but he is not an earthly hero who will rule over the earth.[82]

That last distinction does not hold, however, for IV Ezra, as we have seen, nor is it appropriate for Daniel. In the crucial passage, the judgment scene takes place before the throne of God (Dan. 7.9–10), but the kingdom is wholly of this earth, with its dominion including 'all peoples, nations, and languages' which are subservient to 'one like a son of man' (7.13f.). Just as the fourth beast devoured 'the whole earth' (7.23), so the divinely appointed agent shall rule over all 'the kingdoms under the whole heaven' (7.27).

Still more important for our purposes than recognition of the earthly nature of the rule of the Son of Man in Daniel is the assumption which runs throughout Daniel that the king and the kingdom and the subjects are inseparably interrelated. A. Jeffery drew attention to this,[83] observing that in Dan. 2.37ff. the king is addressed as the embodiment not only of his realm but of his subjects as well. That representative role of the king accounts for the easy shift in Dan. 7 from 'one like a son of man' (7.13) to 'the people of the saints of the Most High' (7.27); of both it is said that to them the kingdom is to be given. In the fullest sense the (Son of) Man is the representative of the covenant people in the kingdom of God. In this we have a phenomenon that functions in a way that closely resembles the Old Testament use we have noted above: 'son' (of God) to refer to the nation, as in Hos. 11.2 and Ex. 4.22, or to the king, as in Ps. 2.7: 'servant', which can be either the nation (as in Isa. 41.8) or an individual (as seems likely in Isa. 52.13ff.), or of indeterminate identity (as in Isa. 42.1ff.).

In the case of each of these terms – Man, son, servant – it is difficult in most contexts to determine whether an individual who represents a community is in view, or whether the community is personified or symbolized by an individual figure.[84] But in a tradition where Jacob or Israel can represent the whole of a nation, and David is the enduring symbol for the ruling dynasty, there is nothing surprising about the fluidity between individual and corporate identity. There is no sharp distinction to be drawn in the prophetic-eschatological tradition between the redeemed covenant community and the agent through whom the redemption is accomplished. Once more, function is more significant than title. We turn, therefore, to the question of the functions assigned to the Son of Man in the Markan tradition. How do they resemble and in what respects do they differ from the range of functions assigned to the (Son of) Man in the Jewish tradition?

The most obvious kinship between Son of Man in Mark and in the Jewish apocalyptic tradition appears in those Son of Man words where he is seen as coming in the future. There are three such sayings in Mark, in addition to one which points to what from the standpoint of the narrative is future (9.9). In this text the disciples are instructed by Jesus not to report the vision of the exalted Jesus that they have just witnessed until after he has been raised from the dead. This verse is not a direct saying, and is akin to the second category of Son of Man words in which the suffering, death, and resurrection of Jesus are predicted (see below). Mark 9.9 furnished Wrede with what he supposed to be the key to the messianic secret: Jesus' messiahship is absolutely a secret during his earthly life and is intended to be such; no one apart from the confidants of Jesus is supposed to learn about it; with the resurrection, however, its disclosure ensues.[85]

But what is here to be concealed, according to Mark – and 9.9f. seems to be a Markan editorial seam linking the narrative of the Transfiguration scene proper with the sayings about Elijah (9.11–13) – is not that Jesus is Messiah, nor that he is going to suffer, but that he is the one ordained of God to be exalted as God's eschatological agent. Mark, and probably the tradition on which he was drawing, regarded the resurrection as the essential prerequisite of the exaltation of Jesus. Fittingly, the biblical background of the Transfiguration scene, as we have already observed, is from Dan. 10, where the revelatory agent, Daniel, on receiving a communication about the end time from the throne of God, is himself transfigured, so that his garments glow with radiant light (Dan. 10.8), while his companions flounder in awe, confusion, and incomprehension.

Analogous to Mark's understanding of Jesus' eschatological vision is that granted to Job in the Testament of Job, where during his lifetime he was granted a secret vision of the throne of God and received assurances which enabled him to endure faithfully and unswervingly the sufferings that he was destined to undergo. Only at the hour of his death does he disclose the secret of his persistent faith, following which disclosure he is taken up into the presence of God. As we have noted, this notion of an eschatological vision of ultimate vindication, which is to be kept secret throughout one's lifetime, is likely to be a facet akin to developing Merkebah mysticism.[86] The date of the Testament of Job is almost certainly late first century BC and would, therefore, have already a long tradition behind it by the time Mark incorporated it into his gospel.

Unlike Merkebah mysticism, which was more in the nature of private piety, Mark's eschatological vision in 9.2–8 includes Moses and Elijah, and therefore stands within the tradition of the eschatological prophet who restores and renews the covenant people, as Mark 9.11f. indicates clearly. The other coming Son of Man sayings, however, point to the role of judge, both as punisher of the wicked and as vindicator of the faithful. 13.24–26 is a collage of prophetic texts, including direct excerpts from Isa. 13.10; 34.4; Ezek. 32.7f.; Dan. 13–14; allusions to Joel 2.10, 31; 3.15; and possible links with IV Ezra 5.4; Ass. Mos. 10.5.[87] The main point is that in the midst of cosmic disturbances and the battle with the demonic powers, the redemptive agent, the Son of Man, will appear 'coming in the clouds', and characterized by much power and glory. His role is that of cosmic rectifier: reordering the creation, defeating the hostile powers, disclosing his power and glory to all the earth. From this position of authority he sends out the heavenly messenger-agents to gather the elect who are scattered throughout the creation (13.29).[88]

The more negative aspects of the Son-of-Man-Judge are evident in 8.38. This verse, which is a *crux interpretum* on the issue of authenticity of the Son of Man words,[89] gives evidence of having been at least reworked in the Christian community. The criterion by which the eschatological judge will evaluate those who come before him in the Last Day will be their response to Jesus *and his words*. We shall consider below the important question of the form of this saying, but now we must concentrate on what it means 'to be ashamed' in this passage.

Käsemann considers the Markan form of the saying to be secondary to that of Matt. 10.33, which reads:

So everyone who confesses me before men, I also
    will confess before my Father who is in heaven;
But whoever denies me before men, I also will deny
    before my Father who is in heaven.

But that is an untenable inference, since the crucial term, Son of Man, is missing, and since twice there appears the favourite Matthaean phrase, 'my Father who is in heaven'. Even more telling against Käsemann's theory – and in favour of the priority of the Markan form – is the fact that, unlike the technical Christian language, 'confess/deny', that appears in Matthew, Mark has preserved the characteristic eschatological language in the play on the word 'ashamed'. If one interprets this as a psychological term, the first part of the verse is dealing in the realm of feelings, and the second part is so trivial as to be nonsense.

Why should a little embarrassment about association with Jesus bring about eschatological judgment? And why should eschatological judgment amount to nothing more than reciprocal embarrassment on the part of Jesus? As I have shown elsewhere,[90] the root ἐπαισχυν – = בוש is used in the Old Testament with a range of meanings, chiefly to express disillusionment, as in the wisdom and prophetic tradition.[91] In the psalms of lamentation, however, the word appears in contexts which point to God's judgment on those who fail to stand firm in faith, or by contrast, with those who are 'not ashamed' because God vindicates them before their enemies.[92] This meaning leads, however, in the later prophetic tradition to the connotation of hope for vindication of the righteous and defeat of the enemies in the eschatological time.[93]

Against this background, Mark 8.38 may be paraphrased as, 'Whoever becomes disillusioned concerning me and my teachings, and thus fails to endure in the faith, he will be brought under judgment by the Son of Man when he appears in his exalted role with his heavenly retinue of agents.' The scene is wholly compatible with Jewish apocalyptic, and the criterion for judgment in the Last Day at the hand of the Son of Man is whether or not one has persevered in fidelity to Jesus and his prophetic teachings[94] during the time of persecution and suffering that will precede the end of the age. Solidarity between Jesus and his community is the paramount consideration when the eschatological Son of Man appears.

The last of the Markan words concerning the coming Son of Man is found on the lips of Jesus at the time of his hearing before the Jewish council and the High Priest. In response to the High Priest's question as to whether he claims to be Messiah (14.61), Jesus is reported by Mark to have given a complex answer (14.62). It consists of an affirmative statement: ἐγώ εἰμι,[95] and a blended scriptural quotation, including parts of Ps. 110 and of Dan. 7.13. The scriptural quotations are based on LXX, but are freely adapted. While it is possible that there was an earlier form of the saying in which reference was made only to Ps. 110,[96] the combining of scriptural references is a central feature of Mark's literary-theological method, and it is likely that the saying in its present form is Markan in origin, the point of which is to declare that when Jesus is publicly vindicated at the παρουσία he will take on the role of judge over all the earth, including those who in the narrative are standing in judgment over him.[97]

The point of the passage is not his heavenly location but his earthly visibility, both to those who will be vindicated and to those who will be judged by him. What is now known only to the inner circle of the followers of Jesus – that the Son of Man must suffer (8.31; 9.31; 10.33f.) in fulfilment of his ultimate eschatological role – will be publicly revealed at the Last Day. And in the days immediately preceding the suffering, even the disciples cannot grasp this, as 8.32f.; 9.32; 10.37, 42–45, and their defection on the night of his arrest make clear.

In 14.62, therefore, several strands of messianic expectation are interwoven. The kingly tradition associated with the Davidic dynasty is implicit in the allusion to Ps. 110. The divine bestowal of the rule over the kingdoms of earth by the Ancient of Days to the Son of Man and his people is behind the component of 14.62 which reflects Dan. 7.13. The acceptance of the title Son of God provides an umbrella under which the various terms for eschatological redemptive agent can be gathered and synthesized by Mark. Colpe's analysis has shown that the Son of Man tradition existed in Judaism prior to its emergence in any of the three documents in which it now appears: Daniel, Enoch and IV Ezra.[98] And it is fused in Mark with the conception of an earthly king who, exalted by God to a role as royal judge, is ultimately revealed to the world over which he exercises authority in God's name.

The sayings which refer to the suffering of the Son of Man are found in Mark in two groups: those which are formulaic in nature and those which are not. The former group includes 8.31; 9.31; 10.33f. The second group includes 9.12 and 10.45. The fact that the notion of a Son of Man or any other kind of Messiah that was required by God to suffer is represented as problematical for the disciples (8.33a)[99] suggests that this was not a widely held conception in first-century Judaism. Scholarly attempts to demonstrate that Jesus' sense of mission combined with messiahship a role as the suffering servant of Isa. 53[100] fail to carry persuasion, both because of a lack of New Testament exegetical evidence in support of it and because of the absence of precedent for this synthesis in pre-Christian Jewish interpretation of Isa. 53 or of other messianic titles.[101] Both the Lord's Supper tradition in Mark (14.24) and 10.45 manifest the same community concern to interpret the death of Jesus in terms of Isa. 53, but there is here no developed doctrine of atonement; rather, the main intent is to demonstrate that the death of Jesus was in accord with the scriptures.[102] Both 10.45 and 9.12 are presented by Mark in contexts in which the problem is the necessity for Jesus to suffer.

As we have noted earlier, this is set against the background of the request of the sons of Zebedee for special favour in Jesus' coming hour of exaltation. In 9.2–12 it occurs in a section loosely tied together that opens with the proleptic eschatological disclosure of Jesus' exaltation, moves to a report of the disciples' inability to grasp what is meant by Jesus' resurrection (9.9f.), and concludes with the series of sayings about Elijah and his relation to the consummation. Commentators have marked the awkwardness of the Son of Man saying; the passage would read more smoothly if one went directly from 11 to 13, and only slightly less smoothly if 12b is omitted. The obtrusive element – and one which is difficult to account for – is 'and how is it written of the Son of Man that he must suffer many things and be accounted as nothing' (9.12b). The term ἐξουδενηθῇ has been explained as deriving from Isa. 53[103] or as an allusion to Ps. 22.1–18, but in truth there is no convincing scriptural documentation for this concept as found in 10.45.

Borsch seeks to account for the theme of suffering in relation to the Son of Man on the ground that in the mythology of the Near East the Primal Man was humiliated and endured suffering before he was raised up to sit on the throne as God's vicegerent. That is an appealing solution, and the mythological evidence he adduces makes a good case for this notion of suffering as a necessary stage on the way to attainment of divine kingship.[104] The difficulty lies, however, in the fact that in the extant Jewish Son of Man sources we have no such direct connection between suffering and ultimate triumph.[105] The closest we come to a link between suffering and Son of Man is in Daniel, and even there the tie is only indirect and implicit.

The first part of the book (1–6) is occupied with accounts of the trials to which the pious faithful were subjected by their pagan rulers, who sought to coerce them into eating unclean food, sacrificing to idols and abstaining from prayer to the God of Israel – all these threats under pain of death. In every case, true faith was rewarded by divine deliverance. Written as the book was, in connection with the attempt at forced Hellenization under Antiochus IV, the issues of fidelity and martyrdom were not theoretical problems, but pressing in their immediacy. Suffering is seen as an inescapable aspect of enduring faith, but the redemptive agent himself – unless we limit the meaning of Son of Man to the community alone, without a representative leader – does not suffer, nor is there any hint of atoning value in the death of martyrs. Nevertheless, in his reinterpretation of the Son of

Man figure and under the influence of the interpretation of the Last Supper as a symbol that Jesus' death has sealed the (new) covenant (14.24), Mark seems to have expanded on the notion of the martyrs as vindicated through suffering,[106] and thereby viewed the death of the Son of Man as foretold in scripture and as expiatory in its effect.

The most likely candidates for pre-Markan traditions in which Jesus speaks of his coming death are Mark 2.18–20 and in the double image ('cup', 'baptism') of 10.38. In neither instance is there a direct reference to death, much less a sequential summary of the passion-resurrection events, as in the Son of Man sayings discussed below.[107] But these passages, if authentic, show that Jesus expected that his prophetic ministry would culminate in his violent death, presumably at the hands of the authorities. Whether they originated with Jesus, however, or in some segment of the Christian community prior to Mark, they could have provided the groundwork on which the interpretation of Jesus' death as Son of Man could have grown, even though the title itself was not used in them.

Of the three summary statements about Jesus' passion which Mark locates so as to delineate the successive stages of Jesus' progress towards Jerusalem – 8.31 following the confession of Caesarea Philippi; 9.31 in preparation for the final departure from Galilee; 10.33f. on the way to Jerusalem[108] – it is the second which is the least specific concerning his death: it reports that he will be handed over to 'men' and that he will be killed. 8.31 mentions elders, chief priests and scribes, while 10.33 recounts details of the torture to which Jesus is to be subjected.

It is probably not warranted, however, to assume that 9.31 is accordingly more reliable historically than the others.[109] Rather, they all appear to be products of the Markan community with its conviction that every detail of the suffering and death of Jesus, as well as of his resurrection and future vindication, was in accord with the plan of God and therefore not only foretold in scripture but announced in advance to his uncomprehending disciples. Their own retrospective understanding of that death, including their own exposition of scripture in support of that interpretation, is now placed back into the situation of Jesus, in confidence that it was after all only the outworking of the divinely foreordained plan. Whether that community developed its notion of the suffering Son of Man on the basis of older Christian tradition, or whether it interpreted the death of Jesus as Son of Man by utilizing a facet of the Primal Man tradition which pictured him as humiliated and raised up by God,[110] is not possible to determine with certainty, though the former seems more likely. In any event, it is the Markan tradition that embedded this understanding of

Jesus' death in early Christianity, and it is with that paradigm of suffering and that promise of vindication by the coming Son of Man that Mark calls upon his community to obey the gospel.

The two sayings in Mark which speak of the Son of Man as active in the present on earth are 2.10 and 2.28. The controversy as to whether they refer only to man in general[111] or represent an over-literal translation of an Aramaic term by which one refers to oneself indirectly[112] need not concern us here, since for Mark the term is clearly a title, as the contrast with ἄνθρωπος in 2.27 clearly implies. 2.10 occurs in one of the Markan interpolated sections, so that we are alerted to look here for special Markan meanings. 2.28 is an addition to the earlier form of the saying, which was originally rounded off nicely with the balanced, wisdom saying of 2.27.[113] Each of these sayings has been located by Mark in a context where an issue of paramount importance for the early church was under debate: the right to pronounce now (rather than to await the judgment day) that sins are forgiven; the right to set aside the sabbath law. While there is no basis for determining whether these questions arose during the lifetime of Jesus or whether he dealt with them in the course of his ministry, in the form in which they now appear in Mark, they have their *Sitz im Leben* in the Markan community.

In the first of these, the flow of the narrative of the healing of the paralytic is interrupted by the introduction of the issue of forgiveness (2.5b–10a). Mark reports Jesus as authorizing (ἐξουσία) the community in the name of the Son of Man to forgive sins. Implicit in this declaration is the belief that sin and sickness are simply two aspects of the evil-dominated world in which mankind lives. Redemption must deal with bodily as well as moral needs if humanity is to be restored to the wholeness for which God intended it. Jesus as Son of Man is God's agent (2.7) to inaugurate the new age in the present as well as to bring it to consummation in the future. This is what Mark understands to be implied by the declaration that 'the kingdom of God has drawn near' (1.14). But that authority is now extended through the community of the Son of Man, whose members are linked with him as are the 'people of the saints of the Most High' to 'one like a son of man' in Dan. 7.

As we observed earlier, the disciples' violation of the sabbath law against work is not justified by Jesus (in 2.23–27) merely on the ground that they were hungry. The precedent called upon is from I Sam. 21.1–6, where the bread that was offered to David and his rebel band was that normally reserved for the priests, and was intended to be eaten only by sacral persons (Lev. 24.5–9). What is at stake, therefore, is not only the right to abrogate the sabbath law in the new community, but also the obligation to provide support for its free-wheeling, non-traditional leadership. As in the saying about forgiveness of sin, the authority for these actions which set aside the normative patterns of Jewish law and cultic practice is claimed in the name of the coming judge, the Son of Man, The authority derived from him and exercised through the leadership of the Markan community, as the title implies, will be confirmed in the Last Day when Jesus is disclosed to followers and enemy alike as Son of Man.

(viii) *Jesus and the Holy Spirit*

Mention of forgiveness, however, calls to mind another series of sayings interpolated by Mark within a narrative: 3.23–29. We have already considered above the force of those sayings in the context which treats of the conflict between Jesus and the kingdom of Satan.[114] But in 3.28–30 the question of forgiveness – actually, here the impossibility of it – is the issue. Here is expressed the generous notion that all human misdeeds and wicked thoughts, sins, and blasphemies, will be forgiven in the day of judgment, *except* those who 'blaspheme against the Holy Spirit' (3.29). The only firm clue we have as to what is involved here is to be derived from the context: Jesus' opponents have accused him of being in league with Satan (Beelzebul) and thereby gaining power to perform exorcisms (3.22). To attribute to Satan ἐξουσία that comes from God through Jesus is the ultimate and unforgivable sin. The community, which saw itself as the extension of the ministry of Jesus – specifically in performing exorcisms (6.7; 9.14–29, 38f.) – is here appealing to a word of Jesus as guarantee that it is carrying out its ministry by the power which comes from God.[115] To attribute to its members satanic powers is, as it was in the case of Jesus, a slander[116] against God's spirit.

The Holy Spirit as the instrument of God[117] at work through Jesus is implied in the outpouring of the Spirit that accompanied Jesus' baptism (1.10). All that is specifically stated in Mark's account of the coming of the Spirit is that it was accompanied by a voice acclaiming Jesus as God's Son (1.11), and that it led or drove him (ἐκβάλλει) into the wilderness. Significantly, the place to which the Spirit led him is the arena of the initial conflict with Satan, precisely the theme that recurs in the Beelzebul pericope (3.22ff.). It is the Spirit who will sustain the followers of Jesus when they are summoned for trial before the authorities (13.11), just as he was. The Spirit will instruct them how to offer their testimony and defence in their trials, as Jesus was led by the Spirit and sustained by the angels in his temptations.

(ix) *The name of Jesus and the authority of his words*

Yet 9.38 demonstrates another way of expressing the power by which the followers of Jesus carried forward the ministry he had begun and to which he called them (1.17f.): demons are cast out *in his name*. Similarly, the works of mercy which his followers perform are carried out 'in his name' (Mark 9.41). And it is because of 'his name' that his followers will be hated, persecuted, and perhaps martyred in the last days (13.13). Conversely, false disciples will try to profit from his power or to pervert his aims for his people by coming 'in his name' (13.6), and for them the community must constantly be on guard. The name of Jesus is, therefore, another way of grasping the continuity of power and purpose which had its ἀρχή (1.1) in Jesus and moves forward towards the consummation through the instrumentality of the disciples.

But more pervasive throughout Mark than the Holy Spirit or the name of Jesus as the link with the authority of Jesus is his 'word' among them. In a seminal essay, first published nearly twenty years ago, E. Käsemann drew attention to the presence in Paul of certain judicial pronouncements, consisting of protasis and apodosis, of which I Cor. 16.22; 14.38; Gal. 1.9 are examples.[118] These he called 'sentences of holy law'. Käsemann noted a link (through the word 'shame') between Rom. 10.11 and Mark 8.38, although he wrongly supposed that Matt. 10.32 was an older form of the latter saying.[119] These pronouncements, of which Mark 8.38 is a prime example, all constitute legal or ethical pronouncements. We have had repeated occasion to observe that they are uniform: they regularly are introduced by ὃς ἄν . . . followed by a subjunctive in the protasis, with the judicial/eschatological pronouncement in the apodosis.[120]

There are at least fifteen of these formulaic pronouncements in Mark, which we shall examine below. But how are we to understand their origin? In every case either they occur within – usually at the end of – a complex of sayings in which Markan editorial style is evident, or are connected with another saying or narrative by a characteristic Markan editorial seam. Without prejudice to the question of their authenticity, it can be stated that in their present form they represent binding pronouncements of matters of grave importance *for the Markan community*. These we shall explore in detail in the next chapter, but it may be useful to examine representative examples both for their content and the ground of their authority.

Although all these sayings could be included under the general category of sentences of holy law, there are significantly different functional emphases among them. The first group comprises those which define the community and describe the qualifications for admission to it. Mark 3.35 forms the climax of the incident in which the tensions and misunderstandings provide the occasion for Jesus to redefine the family as those who unite in doing the will of God. It is these who are the true brothers, mothers, sisters. Similarly, the pronouncement of Jesus in response to Peter's reminder that his disciples have left everything to follow Jesus (10.28) is expressed in a more elaborate version of the declaratory pattern (10.29f.). It is important for our purposes that the *Sitz im Leben* of this pericope in its Markan form is clearly Mark's own time (ἐν τῷ καιρῷ τούτῳ) with the values of Mark's own situation (ἕνεκεν ἐμοῦ καὶ ἕνεκεν τοῦ εὐαγγελίου) and with the day of eschatological reward still ahead in the future (ἐν τῷ αἰῶνι τῷ ἐρχομένῳ).

To enter the community of Jesus' followers is variously described as following him (8.34), finding one's life (8.35), receiving Jesus (9.37), or receiving the kingdom (10.15). In every case, these qualifications are expressed in the formula of the sacred pronouncement or a variant of it. The willingness to accept martyrdom as a consequence of being identified with Jesus is requisite, as 8.34f. shows. Self-denial is taking up the cross, not leaving off some trifling peccadillo. To find health and wholeness ('save' one's life) is to be willing to give it up. Here, as above, the issues are those of the Markan community: 'for my sake and that of the gospel.' To receive a child is apparently meant literally as accepting children into the membership of the community,[121] especially as the act of acceptance is in the name of Jesus, the authority for which derives from God himself (9.37b). In the rejection of a child who is the object of God's concern, not only is God's messenger spurned but God himself is rejected.

Another negative corollary of the refusal to accept children, or perhaps the failure to follow the children in their accepting attitude towards the kingdom, is that those who do not receive it on these terms will never enter it at all (10.15). Clearly, for the Markan tradition, 'kingdom' is not only the eschatological reality about to be consummated in the future (9.1), but it is also the colony of the new age in the present time. These pronouncements provide the norms for sharing in the community life of that eschatological colony now.

We have had repeated occasion to note that the disciples are represented in Mark as fulfilling roles in extension of the ministry of Jesus. The same point is made in the formulaic pattern we are considering in 6.10f. The norm for the disciples' acceptance of hospitality

is determined by a pronouncement, not merely by an optional proposal, just as the condemnation symbolized by shaking the dust from
the feet is directly commanded in the structure of the legal formulation. The sanction for what the disciples are doing is provided through
these pronouncements, both their avoidance of the distractions that
might arise from their seeking out more comfortable accommodation
than that offered them on their arrival at any given village, and also
their public enactment of an eschatological witness against indifferent
or hard-hearted villages.

Not surprisingly, the majority of these pronouncements have to do
with relationships within the community – ethical, interpersonal, and
marital – while others concern the relationships of the community to
others. The problem of leaders jockeying for positions of favour or
prestige is dealt with (10.43, 'whoever wishes to be great among you';
10.44, 'whoever wishes to be first among you'). Others are warned
against a lack of concern for the moral and spiritual welfare of their
fellow members of the community (9.42) or for their non-member
neighbours who may have done an act of kindness to the disciples or
to the followers of Jesus (9.41). In each case there is a direct link
between the actions and attitudes of the disciples on the one hand and
the attitude towards Jesus on the other. The cup of water is offered 'in
my name'. The little ones are described as those 'who believe in me'.
The answer to the ambition of the disciples is the paradigm of Jesus'
suffering and death on behalf of others (10.45).

Even the intra-community problem of marriage and divorce is
dealt with; the authority by which it is handled is direct, strict appeal
to the Torah (10.2–9).[122] But the ultimate basis for every decision lies
in the pronouncement of Jesus, presented by Mark as offered privately
to the disciples (10.10), and therefore to be regarded as a regulation in
force within the community itself (10.11). Its stringency extended
beyond the circumstances envisioned in the Law of Moses to speak to
the rights of women within the congregations. The very fact that
women's rights are taken into account shows that this logion has been
adapted by the Markan tradition to meet the needs and lifestyle of
non-Jewish communities. Most significant, however, is the grounding
of this regulation *in the word of Jesus rather than in a position based on an
interpretation of the Torah*. This is the case even though it is preceded by
a consideration of the viewpoint of the Mosaic Law on the subject.
The position of Jesus is consonant with the Law as far as it goes, but
transcends it in the light of the community needs.

The apodosis of 9.41 shows where the ultimate sanction lies for the
fulfilment of all these pronouncements: those who fail to measure up

will 'lose their reward'. Even more emphatic than the first of these pronouncements is the one that we have already considered above: Mark 8.38. From this we learn that the coming of the eschatological judge will humiliate in judgment those who through disillusionment or worldly distraction (4.19) failed to persevere in the faith of the community (in Jesus as Son of Man) and in his precepts ('my words)'.

Presumably those who do endure are to be vindicated,[123] but there is no converse in Mark to the eschatological warnings of 8.38. The solemnity of this prediction is underscored by other pronouncements, such as that which speaks of losing one's life (8.35). Even more completely categorical in its announcement of doom on those who fail to recognize Jesus as the agent of God, is the warning about those who attribute his mighty powers to Satan. Presumably this is understood in the Markan tradition to have been raised up to the general principle that anyone who ascribes to Satan the power of the Spirit at work in the exorcisms and healings of the followers of Jesus is defaming the Holy Spirit and thereby committing a sin for which there is no pardon (3.29).[124]

The motif of eschatological judgment is not a future abstraction for the community, however, but is anchored to a present, potent reality in its midst: the name of Jesus. As we have remarked, in 8.38 it is those 'ashamed' of Jesus and his words who fall under eschatological judgment. Conversely, it is the adherence to the name of Jesus that is the continuing source of power within the community. Even those who are not official followers of Jesus share in his power by appeal to his name in performing exorcisms (9.38f.). Acts of mercy performed for the benefit of Jesus' followers *in his name* qualify for eschatological reward (9.41). The demands of discipleship require leaving behind all ordinary relationships, possessions, and security *for his sake and that of the gospel*. The power of his name will be exploited for their own ends and to their own ultimate destruction by evil men in the last days (13.6), which suggests that the counterfeit practice may well have been evident already in the time of the evangelist. On the other hand, the hatred of the Christians – to which the pagan writers of the era bear testimony[125] – arises because of the devotion of his followers to the name of Jesus (13.13).

Neither conceptually nor in literary ways is it possible, therefore, to draw an absolute distinction in Mark between Jesus and his followers, or in theological terms, between christology and ecclesiology. That the 'words of Jesus' derive ultimately from his authentic teaching is highly likely. But in their present form and extent they are shaped by and developed by the words of Christian prophets[126] and adapted to the changing needs of the various segments of the Christian community in its diverse social and cultural situations, of which the Markan group is the example with which we are immediately concerned.

The christological titles, however they may have arisen, are employed in the Markan tradition to highlight the continuity between Jesus' inaugural role in the redemptive purpose of God (ἀρχή, 1.1) and the work in his name that the community has been commissioned to carry forward. Hence the corporate metaphors for the community; hence the designations Son of Man and Servant, which alternate in the Old Testament tradition between representing an individual and a community. As initiating agent and paradigm for the community, Jesus is clearly unique: You are the Christ (8.29). But the ὃς ἄν pronouncements show that to become identified with his name demands the assumption of a wide range of responsibilities, though it offers a profound set of resources for fulfilling the new obligations. It is to these that we direct our attention in the final chapter.

VI

ESCHATOLOGY AND ETHICS IN THE MARKAN COMMUNITY

With admirable aims but with unconvincing results, several modern interpreters of the gospel tradition have tried to save Jesus from apocalypticism.[1] Yet the basic perspective of W. G. Kümmel is sound: in the Jesus tradition, he appears as one who sees the kingdom inaugurated in his words and actions, with the fulfilment of the promise yet to come.[2] As our survey of the historical models and the sociological paradigms has shown, the Markan community regarded itself as an eschatological covenant people called into being by Jesus, the eschatological prophet, and charged by him to carry forward its mission in the world. Now it must order its life in accord with the will of God if it is faithfully and effectively to discharge its God-given commission.

As in Daniel, that role may eschew direct political involvement, though it may well include fidelity to divine decrees in opposition to political requirements to the extent of martyrdom. Or it may require withdrawal from society until God's final battle with his enemies is launched, as was the case at Qumran. But the present life – in this epoch in which the community is being both challenged and tested – is the centre of historical meaning, rather than a meaning being projected solely into an other-worldly future.

The concept of the 'time between', with its new view of past and future, which Funk has attributed in a general way to the early church, is indeed the essence of the Markan apocalyptic community's understanding of itself. It is true that the early church diverged from earlier Jewish sectarian communities in important details of its view of itself, but the basic pattern is that of any apocalyptic community, Jewish or otherwise. The reason that Mark does not make a sharp distinction between 'the time of Jesus' and 'the now of the church'[3] is that he sees the latter as the divinely commissioned extension of the former.

As a sectarian group, with the characteristic sense of alienation and lack of power, the Markan community feels obligated to define itself with respect to the established authorities of its social context. Several chapters of Mark are devoted to precisely this purpose. It is not surprising that the two types of movement which we have seen to provide the best historical analogies to the Markan community – the apocalyptic conventicles and the Cynic-Stoic itinerant charismatics – were likewise sharply critical of the establishment and in large measure defined themselves over against the institutions and conventions of the time. Mark is to be seen in a similar light.

1. MARKAN ATTITUDES TOWARDS ESTABLISHED AUTHORITY

In keeping with the passivist tradition of the Hasidim, Mark portrays Jesus as refusing to take any initiative against the political authority, and even as declining to defend himself against its accusations (15.2–5). There can be no mistaking Mark's intention to assign responsibility for the death of Jesus to the Romans, based on the charge that he aspired to be king of the Jews. The entire account of the crucifixion, including the mocking treatment of Jesus by the soldiers and the *titulus* on the cross, asserts this.[4] Just as clearly as Mark holds the religious authorities accountable for handing Jesus over to the Roman officials, so he represents the civil power as solely responsible for his condemnation and execution. The 'deliverance' or 'handing over' of Jesus by the religious leaders is first announced in 3.6, is implied in the first passion prediction (3.31), but is made explicit in 9.31 ('into human hands') and in 10.33f. ('to the Gentiles'). In the circumstances, Jesus' refusal to speak in his own defence (15.2–5) arouses even Pilate's astonishment. The reader of Mark has already been alerted by the story of the beheading of John the Baptist (6.14–29) that this is what the messenger of God can expect at the hand of the civil authorities.

We have had occasion to note that for Mark the stance of Jesus towards the state is to be paradigmatic for his followers. That is stated explicitly in response to the bid for power and prestige made by the sons of Zebedee (10.37), when they are told that they will experience the cup/baptism which is martyrdom, and are called to fulfil the role of a servant (10.43–45). It is expressed in didactic fashion in the answer to the inquiry addressed to Jesus about paying tax to Caesar (12.13–17). The point is that the follower of Jesus must sort out his obligations and then fulfil them: he must render to God what is due to him, and to Caesar what is due to him. One can readily imagine that these two sets of obligations could come into conflict with each other, but in principle, at least, there is no hint here of subversion or even of civil disobedience. It is only from the rest of Mark that one could infer that when obeying God conflicts with the demands of the state, the result will be martyrdom.

That is the situation which is envisioned in Mark 13, where in the midst of political and cosmic upheavals (13.8), the disciples are told to expect arrest and trials before both religious and civil authorities (13.9). They are to rely on the Holy Spirit in these circumstances to give them the words appropriate for their witness in the presence of the earthly powers (13.11). There is no hint of opposition or resistance to the state; only a promise of divine assistance when the opportunity comes to bear testimony before the authorities.

A considerably more negative attitude is evident in Mark towards the religious authorities. From the outset of his portrait of Jesus' ministry, Mark suggests that the Jesus movement is conscious of standing over against the Jewish establishment. This is hinted at in the references to 'their' synagogues (1.23, 39) – presumably in contrast to the congregations to whom Mark is addressing his gospel. Although the identity of αὐτοῖς in 1.44 is unspecified, it apparently is intended as a reference to the religious authorities, since they will be forced to make some kind of decision about Jesus as a consequence of his demonstrated power to heal the leper. Εἰς μαρτύριον αὐτοῖς functions as a challenge laid down by Jesus.[5]

In their present form, Mark 2 and 3 consist almost entirely of controversy stories, even though at an earlier stage of the tradition some of the narratives were simply healing or discipleship stories. As we have observed,[6] the story of the healing of the paralytic has been transformed into a controversy story by the intrusion of the issue of Jesus' authority to pronounce the forgiveness of sins (2.5b–10a). By appending to the account of the call of Levi (2.13f.) a description of the consorting of Jesus with 'many tax-collectors and sinners (2.15), Mark leads into a confrontation scene with the scribes and Pharisees challenging Jesus' defiance of the laws of table purity (2.16). Of that challenge Jesus hears a report (ἀκούσας ὁ Ἰησοῦς 2.17), and accordingly utters a pronouncement about his mission of calling sinners.[7] Clearly the composite story is presented by Mark in its present form as a way of justifying the openness of the community to those who would have been considered unworthy or unclean by Jewish standards.

The story of the healing on the sabbath (3.1–5) is much more cohesive syntactically than the story of the paralytic,[8] but the present conclusion of the pericope (v.6) has been added by Mark in order to introduce the motif of the plot to destroy Jesus. The strange coalition of Herodians and Pharisees serves, as we have noted,[9] to show that both the collaborationists with Rome and those who lived in pious enclaves within Roman-dominated society are seen by Mark as having been threatened by Jesus, who did not conform and who discouraged his followers from conforming to the other options open to Jews for coming to terms with Roman domination.

The most overtly hostile response to Jesus is represented by Mark as arising from the accusation by religious leaders that Jesus – and by extension, his followers (3.15; cf. 9.38) – performs exorcisms through an alliance with Beelzebul, so that it is by the power of Satan (3.23) that demons are cast out in Jesus' name. The most solemn form of eschatological judgment is pronounced on those who attribute to Satan what is seen by the Markan community as evidence of the downfall of Satan's rule (3.24).

Obviously Mark represents his community as in a polemical situation, an understanding for which is provided for the community by appeal to a series of words of Jesus. The exorcisms are the means by which the community, authorized by Jesus through precept and example, is even now wresting control from Satan (3.27). Those within the religious establishment who call in question the validity of this claim are undermining one of the most important elements in the community's understanding of its mission. The opponents' inability to grasp the significance of the mystery of the in-breaking kingdom is regarded by the community as itself evidence of a divine withholding of insight (4.12).

The conflict with established authority and religious principle is still more intensified in Mark 7–8, however. In a passage which shows both that the base of the covenant community in Mark was in contact with a Jewish milieu – hence ritual cleanliness is an important issue – and that the kosher laws serve the Markan community as a point of departure into an understanding of purity as an exclusively moral quality, we have evidence that those addressed in Mark are not expected to have detailed knowledge of the laws about what is clean and what is unclean (7.3f.) and that they make no attempt to observe them (3.2). The Jewish detractors of Markan Christianity presumably charged that if its adherents were going to lay claim to being the covenant people of Israel's God, they could at the very least demonstrate their unique identity by observing the laws of ritual separation.

The composite section of Mark on this general theme (7.1–23)[10] does not deny that there is a real issue in the matter of purity; rather, it redefines purity as having nothing to do with ritual matters or with food (7.19b). It attacks the views of the opponents as hypocritical (7.6) and seeks to clinch its point by appeal to scripture (7.6f.), which is quoted significantly from the LXX. While the issue at stake is that of the purity of the covenant people, the outcome of the argument is a redefinition of who the true covenant people are. Although the line of reasoning in 7.9–13 may be at some points a caricature of rabbinic interpretative method,[11] the outcome is the paradox that by appeal to Moses (7.10), the Mosaic ritual requirements are set aside.

Located as it is at this point, the story of the Syro-Phoenician woman's plea for 'crumbs' (7.28) in the form of expulsion of the unclean spirit causing her daughter's illness, shows that confident faith is sufficient criterion for admitting even 'little dogs' (= Gentiles) to the fellowship and benefits of the newly-defined covenant people. In contrast to the faith evoked in Gentile territory,[12] Jesus on returning to Jews in Galilee is met with mocking doubt in the demand for yet another sign from God to prove what is the source of his authority (8.11f.). Coming as it does on the heels of the string of miraculous acts that Mark pictures Jesus as having just performed, it is an ironic challenge and one that he simply refuses to engage. As noted above (101), the Semitic form of the refusal (εἰ δοθήσεται . . .) is appropriate both to Jewish opponents and to readers in a land like Syria, where Greek was the common language, but where a substratum of Aramaic seems to have survived.

Just before the prediction of the destruction of Jerusalem (Mark 13), Mark juxtaposes a denunciation of the scribes and two brief sketches of authentic piety manifested by the common people (12.37b; 12.41–44). The Markan passage, which has been greatly elaborated in Matt. 23.1–36 with an intensification of hostility and a specifying of the divine judgment (esp. Matt. 23.32–36), is simply a warning about the hypocritical disparity between the pious ostentation of the scribes and their inward secret avarice and inhumanity. It is possible that this vivid vignette of religious charlatans is offered by Mark because in his own community there was already a tendency to prefer honour and rank to integrity and responsibility to the neighbour.

Mention of the enigmatic 'leaven of the Pharisees and the leaven of Herod' (8.15), which as we have seen[13] was probably a double-edged warning against either collaboration with the Romans or pious retreat, leads into Mark's direct presentation of the crux of the conflict with both civil and religious authorities: Jesus as Messiah. Confessed by Peter without his understanding what was involved

(8.29, 32f.), explained repeatedly by Jesus to his uncomprehending disciples (8.31; 9.12; 9.31; 10.33f.), the claim made on his behalf threatens both Roman provincial peace and Jewish religious authority. Ironically, Mark juxtaposes the eschatological hopes of Israel for restoration of the Davidic kingdom (11.9f.) and the denunciation of the abuse of the temple (11.15–17). The sanctuary, which had been intended as a place where God would dwell and be accessible not only to Israel but to all the nations (11.17), had become a place of greedy, busy commerce. And even this defilement is seen as being in fulfilment of the divine plan as set down in scripture (Isa. 56.7; Jer. 7.11)! Mark declares that these arrogant acts and utterances of Jesus confirm the religious authorities in their determination to destroy him (11.18).

The hostility on the part of the religious leadership is intensified in Mark's account by the denunciation of them in the parable of the wicked tenants (12.1–12) and by the scathing critique of the scribes in 12.38–40. In private information to the disciples, not only is the destruction of the sanctuary predicted (13.2), but the cursing of Israel as the planting of God is implicitly asserted (11.12–14).

There is for the reader no surprise, therefore, when the plot to have Jesus killed is actually put into action (14.1). Mark makes clear that there was no possibility of peaceful co-existence between Jesus and the political or religious authorities. And obviously he draws from this evidence the conclusion that there is none for the community of Jesus' followers in his own time. Rather, they have before them the prospect of unprecedented (13.19) tribulation – which is nevertheless according to scripture (Dan. 12.1) – arising from disturbances which are political (13.7–8a), cosmic (13.8b), and religious in origin (13.9). From this they will be delivered only by the appearance of the Son of Man (13.26), whose messengers will gather the elect from the ends of the earth (13.27).

What has sometimes been overlooked in this familiar picture is that only those members who endure throughout the time of testing will ultimately be delivered (13.13b). Perseverance is demanded not only in the face of tribulation and suffering, however: there are also the severe problems of deception of the elect by false claimants to messianic authority or prophetic powers (13.5f.), of treachery within households (13.12), and the temptation of succumbing to worldly anxieties or allurements (4.19).

Thus *the life of the community in the present age is of paramount significance*: only as it remains faithful and zealous in its witness will the message go forth, and only as it endures through tribulation will it enter the life of the age to come (13.30). Far from being negative or even indifferent, the history of the faithful community in the present age, with its confidence in the fulfilment of God's promises in the past – through the scriptures and through the career of Jesus – is pivotal for the eschatological future. It is in this confidence alone that the community has the courage to stand against the opposition of the established religious and political authorities.

2. Responsibilities within the Markan Community

Like the Qumran community, the Markan group is well aware that in the intervening period before the end comes (οὔπω τὸ τέλος, 13.7) there is a range of human obligations and inter-relationships to be dealt with in accord with God's will for his people. From the Damascus Document and the Rule of the Community it may be seen that the eschatologically-oriented Essenes were a voluntary association with which one became affiliated by repentance, probably symbolized by baptism. Property was not to be retained by the individuals, but was to be placed in the common fund. They looked back to the struggles and persecution of their founder as the point of origin of their community, and meditated on his hymn-confessions as well as on his eschatological interpretations of the scriptures.

The members were accustomed to uttering 'Amen, Amen' in solemn asseverations; they relied on the Holy Spirit to illumine and instruct; they rejoiced in their election by God and in the special knowledge he had given them of his mysteries; they celebrated both their unity and their destiny in a common meal which looked forward to the imminent day of their vindication and the defeat of their enemies. Meanwhile they sought to live in purity, withdrawn from sinners, preparing in the desert the way of the Lord, excluding unworthy members from their midst, carrying on a daily regimen of prayer, organizing the community into ranks and duties, convinced that until the last days came, God's dwelling place was within their community, for which he had laid the cornerstone.

The literary forms of these documents are strikingly different from Mark or from any other Christian documents, and there is in Mark nothing of the withdrawn exclusivist attitude that characterized Qumran, but there are fundamental similarities in the way in which these two sects saw themselves as the true heirs of the covenant promises and as those destined to prepare for and to enter the new age when God brought it to pass in his own time. One of the most urgent needs, therefore, was to endure in order to share in the impending

eschatological reality which was already being experienced pro-
leptically within the community.

(i) *Community roles*

Unlike the Qumran community, however, with its carefully numbered
and delineated ranks both for the present[14] and in preparation for the
final battle,[15] the Markan community offers nearly no evidence of
organization. The number twelve[16] is central for Mark (3.14; 6.7) in
connection with the community's mission in the world, just as a
council of twelve has an important place at Qumran (IQS 8.1). The
sending out of the disciples in pairs may be in continuity with alleged
Jewish custom,[17] or it may be an appeal to the Deuteronomic
principle of dual attestation (Deut. 17.6), or it may be a simple
provision for mutual protection, just as the permission to take shoes
and a staff provides for at least minimal comfort. Otherwise, Mark
depicts the disciples as simply going out two by two to carry forward
the message and ministry of Jesus. They move from place to place,
with no evidence of advance planning or organizational structure to
expedite their itinerant ministry or to consolidate the results.

There is a hint of another kind of role in the Markan community:
that of διάκονος. It is possible that Peter's mother-in-law, who on
recovery from her fever ministered to the needs of Jesus and the
disciples (1.31), was merely fulfilling the obligations of village hospitality, but the use of what was to become a technical term in early
Christian usage (διηκόνει) at least raises the possibility – perhaps reinforced by the appearance of the verb in the imperfect – that she
took care of certain of their needs on a regular basis. That is clearly
the case with the other Galilean women mentioned in 15.41, who are
reported as being not only followers of Jesus (ἠκολούθουν αὐτῷ . . .)
but as having regularly cared for his needs (διηκόνουν αὐτῷ). The role
of διάκονος is urged upon the ambitious sons of Zebedee (10.43, 45),
although it is difficult to tell whether it is meant in a more figurative
sense, as referring to performance of menial tasks in the community
life and work or whether it was a specific, lowly office often filled by
women.

There is, on the other hand, a hint of roles of special favour in the
importance attached to Peter, James, and John (8.29; 9.1; 10.35ff.),
but there is no way to determine whether their being singled out is
simply the result of their prominence in the pre-Markan tradition or
whether they indeed enjoyed places of special favour in the life or the
memory of the Markan group. Since they figure in the Markan
narrative both as recipients of special insight and as shameful

examples of pride and cowardice, they function for Mark as models of the sort of behaviour that is to be avoided rather than as paragons of virtue.

(ii) *Severing family ties*

Clearly one of the severest tests of fidelity exacted of followers of Jesus as Mark depicts them was the break with family and home. There is an element of disparity in the Markan tradition on this point, since at the outset of the narrative, Peter is at home with his extended family, including at least his mother-in-law (1.29f.). Yet Peter's mingled boast and complaint later on in the gospel (10.28ff.) is that he and his fellow-disciples have left 'all' in order to pursue their new life in the ministry to which Jesus called them.

What is included in the 'all' that has been left behind is specified in what follows: brothers, sisters, mother, father, children, and lands (10.29). There is no clear indication in Mark whether this separation was to be considered as permanent – which would be the case if the model were that of the Cynic-Stoic itinerants – or whether it was for certain periods of time during which the followers devoted themselves exclusively to the itinerant ministry.

It can be inferred from Paul's sarcastic rhetorical question in I Cor. 9.5 about his right to take a wife about with him, as did Cephas and the brothers of Jesus, that in some segments of the early church travelling preachers were accompanied by their spouses. Peter's challenge as reported in Mark 10.28, however, suggests that in the Markan community the break with family, home, personal, and economic security, and even the seeming irresponsibility towards one's own offspring, would be compensated for in the new pattern of relationships and identity that would develop in the Christian community, culminating in the full achievement of blessedness in the Age to Come (10.31).

In a village culture like that of Galilee and Southern Syria, and especially among Jews with their strong sense of family identity and genealogical continuity, this kind of separation would be a severely demanding sacrifice. And it is rendered the more severe in Mark by the added phrase, 'with persecutions'. Gratifying and fulfilling as the personal associations within the new community might be in the present age, it was only in the eschatological perspective that any compensations were to be seen.

(iii) *No reliance on possessions*

The sayings about abandoning the security of home and family in the service of Jesus and the gospel (10.29b), though presented as having been addressed privately to the disciples (10.23), are linked by Mark appropriately with the story of Jesus' conversation with the rich man seeking eternal life (10.17–22). This pericope is completely unified and constitutes what Bultmann has called a genuine apophthegm.[18]

In the context of Jewish piety, the inquiry and the aim that lies behind it – to obtain a share in the life of the age to come – is wholly understandable and legitimate. It was considered prudent to adopt in the present a pattern of life and a set of values that would offer assurance that in the eschatological judgment one could be confident of being rewarded by entering the new age. The rich man's verbalized reliance is on his faithfulness to the commandments of the Law (10.19), but his unacknowledged confidence lies in the wealth that he has amassed (10.22). It possesses him, so that he cannot break with it in order to follow Jesus. When the choice comes down to obtaining eternal life in the future or clinging to his possessions now, he turns aside from his quest for a share in the age to come.

The pericope does not present an absolute denunciation of wealth; it makes, rather, a relative judgment that commitment to following Jesus must have a radical priority over devotion to one's possessions. The only worthy possession is the eschatological reward that is even now reserved (θησαυρὸν ἐν οὐρανῷ) for those who leave behind earthly security in the service of the gospel.

To this pericope Mark has appended a string of sayings of Jesus about wealth as an obstacle to entering the kingdom of God (10.23, 25) or to being saved (10.26f.). It is possible that in an earlier form these sayings had in view exclusively the age to come and how to enter it, but in the light of the two stages of reward in the passage with which Mark brings the section to a conclusion (10.30), it is impossible to determine categorically what is meant by 'entering the kingdom', whether present or future. The likelihood is that for Mark the commitment to the gospel and participation in the ministry establishes a link with the covenant people who are even now assured of a share in the age to come. The future of the kingdom confirms the commitment in the present. The gravity of the problem that earthly possessions constitute is asserted in the form of a rhetorical question (10.24) and in the vivid metaphor of the ungainly camel managing to crawl through a needle's eye (10.25).[19]

Mark's own understanding of both the question and the metaphor are indicated in the flat statement of 10.27, where Jesus declares that salvation is God's action, not human achievement. That confidence in possessions as evidence of personal achievement was indeed a problem in the Markan community is evident not only from the

passage under discussion, but from the interpretation of the parable of
the sower (4.19), where the thorns that sprang up and choked the
seeds (4.7) are explained as 'concerns for this age, *the seduction of
wealth*, and *lusting after other things*'.

There is no suggestion that the material world is inherently evil, as
was the case in some segments of later Gnosticism and other sectarian
adherents of ontological dualism. The rich man is not told to destroy
his possessions but to divest himself of them and their claim on him
by selling them and giving what he realizes from the sale to the poor
(10.21). Apart from the hospitality that the itinerants are offered in
receptive villages (6.10), the only tangible reward the disciples are to
expect is an eschatological one (9.41).

(iv) *Divorce and women's rights*

Rather than adopting either the more liberal interpretation of the
Mosaic prescription about divorce of the Hillelites or the stricter one
of the Shammaites,[20] the Markan version of Jesus' pronouncements
on this subject is critical of the legal provision for divorce as a
concession to human obstinacy (10.5) and adapts the provision to care
for the rights of women in a way that Jewish practice (at least in
Palestine)[21] did not allow for. It is noteworthy that the direct modification of the Mosaic Law, which consists in parallelling the man's
rights with those of the woman, is in a section of the passage that has
been attached by unmistakably Markan editorial connectives
(10.10f.).[22] That conclusion is confirmed by the appearance at the
end of the section of the formulaic pronouncement ὃς ἄν (10.1f.).

The import of the whole passage is to declare that marriage is an
essential part of God's plan in the creation of the world and that it
was intended to be indissoluble (10.6–9). The private addendum to
this public declaration allows for divorce, but not for remarriage.
And it offers both this possibility and this restriction to women as
well as to men within the Markan community. The woman is sinned
against if her former husband remarries, and she sins against her
former mate if she marries again. Thus, unlike Judaism in the period,
there is in this Markan passage on the divorce issue a conception of
something close to full equality and mutual responsibility between
members of both sexes.

(v) *Resurrection of the dead*

Curiously, the issue of multiple marriage figures prominently in the
challenge issued to Jesus by the Sadducees concerning the resurrection (12.18–27). In what is apparently a stock story, the procedure

required by the levirate law is employed in the attempt to reduce to absurdity the concept of the resurrection. The woman who has been taken as wife by a succession of seven brothers will have difficulty choosing one among them as her husband in the age to come, the sarcastic anecdote concludes (12.23).

Jesus' response is in two parts. The first denies that persons are married or become married in the time of resurrection. The analogy with the angels of God is puzzling, but it may have referred to a commonly-held notion of asexual angelic existence.[23] While the Markan community does not regard marriage as inherently evil, it does consider it as a lesser value which must be sacrificed in a life of full commitment to the work of the gospel in the present age, and which will be out of the question in the new age.

The argument in support of the resurrection is perplexing on at least two counts. First, it offers no hint of a link with the resurrection of Jesus – a point which is central to Paul's teaching on the subject, for example (I Cor. 15.20–49). Second is the strange line of argument itself. The dismissal of the Sadducees' *reductio ad absurdum* causes no problems, since it simply asserts that life in the age to come has a significantly different quality from what obtains in the life of the present age, so that the antagonists' objection to the resurrection falls to the ground when its true nature is apprehended. The difficulty lies in the fact that there are a number of apparent logical gaps in the second part of the argument which seeks to prove the resurrection by appeal to Ex. 3.6.

As Haenchen has shown, the thrust of the psalms and prophets[24] is to declare that man can serve and honour God only during life. When man is in the grave, that relationship of honour and dependence comes to an end.[25] What seems to be implied is that Yahweh did not say, 'I *was* the God of Abraham, of Isaac, and of Jacob, and I *now am* your God,' but that on the same plane of being God says to Moses at a point in time chronologically remote from the days of any of these patriarchal figures, 'I *am* the God.' . . . This point could not be made at all on the basis of the Hebrew text, which contains no form of the verb 'to be', but it makes a kind of sense in the LXX, where the passage opens with the solemn declaratory self-identification, ἐγώ εἰμι. But curiously, εἰμι is not found in the text of Mark either, so that one can only conclude that it is understood implicitly, and that what is being asserted is the identity of relationship between God on the one hand and the succession of patriarchal figures on the other. That this relationship is described, by implication at least, in the present tense, is presumably understood by Mark as affirming that God's association with his people is an ongoing reality, rather than merely a memory from an irrecoverable past.

In a way that stands on its head the despair and finality of the psalms concerning death, the Markan tradition here argues that, since God is not the God of the dead (12.27a), these persons are alive and he is their God. An explicit doctrine of the resurrection is not taught, but both the mistaken notion that life in the age to come must be defined in terms of present limits and patterns, and the excluding of a continued relationship to God beyond death in an age to come are combatted.

The specific details of the argument and the method employed show that the Markan community had to debate by scribal rules issues arising out of scriptural interpretation in order to justify its belief that it was in fact the true heir of the covenant promises. It is somewhat surprising that the LXX, which proved so useful in other arguments with Jewish interpreters, was not employed here, as it might have been to good effect.

(vi) *Forgiving one another*

As was the case at Qumran, much of Mark is taken up with laying down guidelines for intra-community relationships.[26] The prominence given from the outset to the question of forgiveness is indicative of its importance for the community. It may be assumed from the literary way in which Mark linked forgiveness of sin with healing of disease in 2.1–12 that his community saw them to have a causal relationship. It was not sufficient to overcome the disease; the sin which manifested itself in the disease had to be dealt with as well, and to this end the community's pronouncement of forgiveness in the name of Jesus seems to have been a basic practice for which sanction was sought in the precept and precedent of Jesus. It is likely that the words of Jesus ἀφίενται σου αἱ ἁμαρτίαι (2.5) resemble or even represent a liturgical formula employed in the Markan community.

In the Beelzebul controversy passage (3.20–30), the withholding of forgiveness from those who attribute to Satan the power of Jesus – and by extension, of his followers – echoes a theme in I Enoch 12–14, according to which, in spite of intervention in their behalf, the wicked angels are banished for ever from the presence of God. An important feature of the Markan community which distinguished it from the outlook of Jewish sectarian groups that were also apocalyptic in their outlook was that, just as entering the kingdom was a proleptic possibility for the community in the time before the eschaton, so the forgiveness of sins or the withholding of forgiveness could be pronounced in the church in the present without waiting for the eschatological judgment. The coming Son of Man, therefore, would confirm judgments that were made within the community in the present age.

In connection with the teaching of Jesus about prayer (discussed below, 160ff.), forgiveness is said to be a prerequisite to efficacy in prayer. Unless the petitioner who addresses God has forgiven his neighbour beforehand, he is in no position to seek God's forgiveness. The basis for antagonism with the neighbour is stated in broad terms – 'if you have anything against anyone' (11.25) – rather than being limited to some specific form of grievance or having been wronged. Not only overt misdeeds or violations of one's rights but even resentments or distrustful attitudes would come under the blanket description, 'anything against anyone'. In the Markan community there is no place for such divisiveness, and the only cure for it is to manifest forgiveness. Thereby divine forgiveness may be granted and received, as well.

(vi) Love for neighbour

The chief virtue which the Markan community is exhorted to manifest is love of neighbour. Like the rabbis who spoke of ways in which the essence of the Law could be summarized,[27] Jesus is pressed to state his own priority among the commandments. In response he combines the *shema*, the closest approximation to a creed in Judaism, with[28] an injunction from the Holiness Code of Lev. 19. Like other appeals in that code, the love command of 19.18 has as its sole sanction the nature of God Himself: 'I am Yahweh.' It is accordingly wholly compatible to bring these two strands of the legal tradition together and thereby offer a non-legal ground for obeying the commandment.

As Mark presents the tradition here,[29] the 'first' commandment is not a matter of one having priority over the others, but of this combination of elements from the legal tradition of Judaism placing ethical responsibility on a plane where precepts no longer have absolute significance. By shifting moral obligation from the realm of the prescriptive to that of the affective, legal norms have lost their primary function as defining the obedient person.[30] The closest remaining approximation to guidelines is the pair of questions, 'What does the nature and purpose of God require of me in this situation?' and 'What does love for my neighbour demand of me in this moment?' The scribe's comments and elaborations of the implication of these twin love commands add little to what is implied in the sayings themselves, except to lift up from I Sam. 15.22 the judgment about the relative unimportance of the sacrificial system as compared with obedience – in this instance, to the command to love God and neighbour (12.33). The scribe's reply draws from Jesus the assurance that he is near the kingdom, which in the Markan context of meaning seems to assert that his perception of ethical responsibility closely approximates to that of the true covenant community awaiting God's kingdom.

(viii) *Threats to the integrity of the community*

Side by side with the appeals to love and to forgive in Mark are solemn warnings about the hazards that the community faces, some from without and some from within. The account of Jesus' temptation (1.12f.) and the repeated protests of the demons against Jesus as their conqueror serve to remind the members of the community of their Satanic opposition. But they are also warned against traitors at work within the congregations themselves. The birds who devour the seed (4.4b) are described in the allegorical interpretation of the parable of the sower as Satan, who comes and takes away the message that has been sown among the members. Judas the traitor and Peter the coward, as well as all the fugitive disciples on the night of Jesus' arrest, stand as paradigms of what happens to the most stalwart followers, protesting their fidelity but collapsing when the pressure is on. More specific about the internal problems of the community are the warnings in Mark 13 about the false claimants who declare themselves to be the messiah (or Jesus, or both) (v.6) or to know where he will appear (v.21) or to be messianic prophets performing eschatological signs in his name (v.22). To the end of the age, the members of the community must be on guard against messianic fakery.

But they must also be on the alert concerning lethargy, preoccupation, or disillusionment within the community. The seed on rocky ground (4.5) is interpreted in Mark 4.17 as the adherents of Jesus whose faith withers under pressure, who cannot endure when persecution overtakes the community because of its faith in the word of Jesus. Others, symbolized by the seed sown among thorns (4.7), are those beguiled by wealth and worldly involvements, the power of which chokes out the life of the kingdom.[31] The only adequate response to these severe challenges, as to treachery within one's own household, is perseverance until the end of the age (13.13b).

(ix) *Discipline within the community*

Various kinds of personal discipline are also enjoined on the members of the community, of which the most severe details are offered in

Mark 9.42-48. The first of the string of sayings is in the form of an eschatological pronouncement (9.42) and the others are in protasis/apodosis form. It is impossible to determine with certainty whether the 'little ones' who are caused to stumble are literally younger persons, more recent converts, or simply weaker members, but the penalty proposed is far more severe than those for offences against fellow-members of the Qumran community. Furthermore, it is not only sins against one's fellows that are to be visited with judgment, but sins against one's self: the member is told in vivid hyperbole not to allow hand or foot or eye to lead him from the path of faithful obedience. The alternatives are radical self-discipline or the torments of Gehenna (9.48). Those who do learn self-control may enter the kingdom, or 'life' (9.43, 45).

Mention in 2.20 that the followers of Jesus will fast in the day 'when the bridegroom will be taken from them' is rightly understood by most commentators as pointing to the fact that fasting had become a fixed practice in the Markan community. The context suggests that it is a reminder of the absence of the Lord and his awaited return, when joy will again reign in his presence (2.19). There is wide textual support for καὶ νηστεία following προσευχή in 9.29,[32] which suggests that fasting was indeed a type of discipline practised in the Markan group, and was considered essential as a prerequisite for effectiveness in the ministry. If the reading is original, then failure to fast was a part of the reason for the disciples' inability to perform successfully the exorcism on the boy (9.18). The fact that Mark has bracketed what may have been a straightforward exorcism narrative told about Jesus alone, surrounding it with an account of and an explanation for the disciples' inability to perform, suggests a heightened importance of this factor for Mark's community.

(x) *Watchfulness and prayer*

The most frequently repeated advice to Mark's readers is that they are to watch and pray. Mark uses three terms: προσεύχειν, γρηγορεῖν, βλέπειν. The latter is used in some important passages in the sense of 'perceive'. Actually in 4.11 and 8.18 it describes the inability of the non-elect to discern the truth about Jesus even when they observe it. Ironically, it is the blind man in 8.23f. who is able to see who Jesus is. But βλέπειν – apart from where it is simply 'to see' – more frequently occurs with the connotation, 'look out!' as in 'look out for the leaven' (8.15) and 'look out for the scribes' (12.38). In 4.24 there is the strange counsel to look out for what one hears. Occuring as it does in the midst of a cluster of sayings, bound together by Markan editorial links[33] and culminating in an eschatological pronouncement (4.25), the imagery of the whole complex is that of light. The light of the gospel is to be displayed, not concealed. The discerning will take care as to what he hears and heeds, while the one who lacks divinely granted perception will discern nothing.

It is in the apocalypse of Mark 13 that the warning about being on the lookout occurs most frequently (13.5, 9, 23, 33), and there it is linked with being on guard (γρηγορεῖν) as well (13.34, 35, 37). The motif of watchfulness is repeated in the Gethsemane scene (14.34, 37, 38). But the basic point is consistent throughout: only the one who is privy to the divine purpose of the suffering, crucified Jesus, who is to be raised from the dead and publicly vindicated by God in the last day, can perceive either what truly occurred in his passion or the significance of the days of tribulation through which his followers must pass in the final phase of the present age, prior to his parousia as triumphant Son of Man (14.62; 13.24–27).

In the Markan tradition, prayer functions in two essential ways: as a mode of commitment and as a channel of power. In 1.35 and 6.46, Jesus is pictured in the context of Markan editorial material as withdrawing from the crowds for strengthening and renewal as he faces the next stage in his ministry. Prayer figures prominently in the Gethsemane scene as the means by which Jesus both commits himself to the will of God and seeks strength to obey that will (14.35, 38, 39).

The emptiness of prayer where the factor of commitment is lacking is described satirically in 12.40 as a sham (πρόφασις). An even more sweeping critique of Jewish religious practice is offered in the story of the cleansing of the temple, when Jesus declares that the sanctuary was intended as a *house of prayer* for all nations (11.17). He speaks within the Court of the Gentiles, as the commercial activity implies (11.15f.), in an area beyond which 'foreigners' were not permitted.[34] The huckster atmosphere and the money-changing enterprises rendered the place wholly unconducive to approaching God there.

In both the apocalyptic section and the Gethsemane sequence, the disciples are enjoined to pray in order that they may endure their own hours of tribulation (13.18; 14.32). But the positive function of prayer as a medium of power for carrying forward the ministry of Jesus is pointed up concretely in the story, referred to above, of the disciples' inability to perform an exorcism (9.14–29). The explanation for their failure, appended to the earlier form of the narrative in characteristic Markan fashion (9.28) as a private disclosure to the disciples, is that exorcisms of this sort can be performed only 'by prayer' (9.29). That prayer is indispensable to a wider range of needs than merely exorcisms is evident in the response of Jesus to the disciples when they drew his attention to the fig tree that had withered under his curse (11.12–14, 20f.). There is no verbal or seemingly logical connection between the situation and his response; the curse itself is offered by Mark as a symbolic act, pointing to God's having visited judgment on the unrepentant and unperceptive members of his covenant people, who are about to reject and call for the death of God's eschatological messenger to them.

The instruction, however, is to be bold in faith, having full confidence that what is requested of God in prayer will indeed take place, here expressed in hyperbolic form as throwing a mountain into the sea (11.23).[35] There is a close link between faith and prayer: what is affirmed in faith is to be requested in prayer (11.24). Prayer in Mark is not acquiescent acceptance of the situation as given by God and therefore inevitable, but petition in faith that what is lacking – such as strength to endure – may be provided by God, or what is wrong about the present – even a mountainous obstacle – may be removed. Prayer is not resignation but urgent request, with prompt service expected.

3. The Self-Image of the Community and its Stance towards the World

Bryan R. Wilson, in his study of millennarian movements,[36] has suggested that the most useful criterion of classification of a sect 'is in terms of a movement's *response to the world*',[37] which 'may be manifest in many relatively unfocused, unpurposive activities, and not only in activities, but also in life-style, association and ideology'.[38] Whereas orthodoxy accepts the world and its values, 'concern with transcendence over evil and the search for salvation and consequent rejection of prevailing cultural values, goals, and norms, and whatever facilities are culturally provided for man's salvation, defines religious deviants'.[39] These are precisely the factors that are operative in the Markan community's definition of itself over against the religious, political, and cultural institutions of its time.

Unlike the Pharisees, whose passive acceptance of the social and political order gave them the privilege of devoting their energies to the contemplative life of refining and updating their religious tradition as an end in itself, and unlike the Essenes, whose zeal for God and despair of human institutions led them to withdraw until such time as God would set things right for them by catastrophic intervention, *the Markan community is discernible from the pages of Mark as at once esoteric and evangelistic, as both inclusive and voluntaristic,* as affirming both divine determination and hard decisions to be made by its members.

(i) *Evangelistic outreach and voluntary participation*

The evangelistic outreach of Mark is evident from the opening words of the gospel (1.10), which speak of the inauguration or launching of the gospel enterprise, an undertaking grounded in scripture and prepared for by the work and message of John the Baptist. With John's arrest (1.14), the gospel activity begins on its own with Jesus' announcement of what God has begun to do (κηρύσσων τὸ εὐαγγέλιον τοῦ θεοῦ), including the declaration of the nearness of the kingdom and the consequent call to repentance (1.15). The events which have begun to occur, leading on to the fulfilment of God's purpose, are not dependent on human decision, but to share in them in a beneficial way requires repentance (1.15b).

Likewise, to participate in the furthering of this eschatological message requires a voluntary decision, as is evident from the invitational process by which Jesus gathers his followers around him and leads them to share in his message and work (1.16–20). There is no suggestion of intellectual, educational, or hereditary qualifications for the leadership roles to which the disciples were called. The word of Jesus carries its own authority, and to it they respond with a commitment that detaches them from home, family, tradition, and means of livelihood.

At the outset, the disciples' association with Jesus is as companion-observers, with Jesus as preacher (1.38) and agent (1.31–34). In 3.13–19, however, the circle of disciples is fixed in accord with Jesus' wishes (οὓς ἤθελεν, 3.13), and they are sent out with a commission to preach and to perform exorcisms. They do so on the basis of their having been with him in the course of his ministry (ἵνα ὦσιν μετ' αὐτοῦ 3.14).

The chief images of their role are those of fishers of men (1.16) and sowers of seed (4.3, 14). Unlike the metaphor of fishing, which is not interpreted within the tradition, that of the sower and the seed is provided with a full explication by the Markan tradition itself. What the sower spreads abroad is the word (ὁ λόγος), which is obviously not merely the initial message of the gospel but the instruction as well that is intended to nurture and strengthen the members of the community (4.20). However, we have already had occasion to observe how mixed are the results.

In the second, fuller account of the commissioning of the disciples

(6.6b–13) we learn that having received authority to preach and to perform exorcisms, they go about their work effectively. It includes preaching, exorcisms, anointing of the sick, and healings (6.13). The summary statement about their mission on the occasion of their return (6.30) indicates that in addition to preaching and exorcisms and healings, they also engaged in instruction. For the Markan community this factor was of great importance. No matter how urgent their eschatological expectation may have been, it was essential to instruct the members of the community, as the large amount of space in the Gospel of Mark devoted to interpretation of the Law and other didactic matters makes evident.

The evangelistic import of the healings and exorcisms is reflected in the Markan narratives, as well. This is evident from the report of the effects of the story of the cleansed leper (1.45) and the charge given to the cured demoniac from Gerasa (5.19). When Bartimaeus receives his sight, he becomes a follower of Jesus (10.52). Regularly the Markan editorial transitional passages assert that the crowds that flock to Jesus are attracted by the healings and exorcisms. His charismatic powers are an essential feature in the breadth of his appeal, although the healings and exorcisms are offered in the Markan narratives as events which must be grasped from the perspective of faith, rather than as events of self-evident significance. This is, of course, the whole point of the controversy in 3.22–30.

Consistently, Mark uses λόγος for the gospel,[40] the message about Jesus as the one who announces the coming of the kingdom, who liberates men and women from the powers that enslave them, who suffers and dies and is raised from the dead in obedience to God's will. That is more clearly the case from 8.32 on in Mark.[41] But although it is anachronistic in terms of Mark's own literary method, which withholds explicit mention of the message about Jesus' suffering and death until 8.31, it is perhaps unintentionally implicit in 1.45; 2.2; 4.14, 15, 16, 17–20; 4.33 as well. Obviously by the time Mark is writing his gospel, the λόγος includes the fuller Christian message of both kingdom and passion.

The plural, λόγοι, appears in three contexts, in each of which the reference is to the sayings of Jesus: 8.38; 10.24; 13.31. In the first and last instances, the words of Jesus are to receive eschatological confirmation. Their function is like that of the eschatological pronouncements discussed earlier.[42]

In the thirteen occurrences of ἀμήν in Mark, all appear as part of solemn asseverations. A single instance (12.43) refers to the unrecognized value of the pious act of the woman whose two λέπτα represented the entirety of her possessions. But all the other passages are either predictions (14.9, 18, 30), or eschatological pronouncements (3.28; 8.12; 9.1; 9.41; 10.15; 10.29; 11.23; 13.30; 14.25). They treat of such fundamental issues as the time of the consummation, the judgment on unbelief, admission to the community of the kingdom, eschatological rewards, the power of prayer, the bodily absence of Jesus from among the community until the eschatological fulfilment occurs.

In spite of recent attempts to show that ἀμήν is a special term employed by charismatics in apocalyptically inclined circles of Hellenistic-Jewish Christianity, there is good reason to regard the word as a confirmatory expression, employed in Semitic language areas to lend assurance as to the truth of what is being asserted.[43] We are here dealing, not with a formula unique to Jesus or even to the Markan tradition,[44] but with a venerable locution invoked to lend added weight to the predictive and judgmental pronouncements of Christian prophets speaking in the name of Jesus. It is with the authority of an eschatological message, supported by the prophetic speech of charismatics and by the healings and exorcisms that they performed on the authority of Jesus, that the evangelistic activity of the Markan community is carried out.

(ii) *Esoteric nurture within the Markan community*

But Mark's community is esoteric as well as evangelistic. How are these two dimensions of its life correlated? Paralleling the emphasis on preaching by Jesus and the disciples and his summons to certain persons to 'follow'[45] is the pervasive motif of 'calling aside'[46] the disciples for instruction, most frequently for private clarification. The word appears in the formulaic passages where secret explanations are provided for public teaching. In 3.13 and 6.7 it is used of summoning the disciples before despatching them on their mission. In 3.23; 8.1; 10.42; 12.43 special information is imparted to the disciples. More puzzling is 8.34, where the crowd as well as the disciples are told what is implied for his present or would-be followers to affirm his suffering messianic role. Significantly, this declaration of taking up the cross is in a context of eschatological pronouncements[47] (8.35, 38) and prediction (9.1). Thus we are not dealing here with a set of general principles of human behaviour, but with esoteric instructions, intended for those who are committed to Jesus and his words (8.38). For those who make this commitment and persevere through suffering, there is a promise of eschatological vindication, both personal (finding life) and corporate (seeing the kingdom having come with power).

The pattern of public teaching and private explanation is evident in yet another context where the term προσκαλεσάμενος is used (7.14ff.). At first glance it seems that this quasi-technical Markan word is to be employed in connection with instruction for a general audience, but closer reading shows that the teaching is considered by Mark to be a parable (= enigma; 7.17), for which an explanation is later provided privately for the disciples (7.18–23).

The question whether all members of the Markan community had access to all the secrets or whether there was an inner leadership core to whom alone they were confided is impossible to resolve on the basis of the evidence we have. The several indications in Mark of an in-group among the disciples, however, suggests that the latter may have been the situation. The first of these is the puzzling remark in 4.10 that those who hear Jesus' private (κατὰ μόνας) explanation of the parables are 'those around him with the Twelve'.

The first part of the designation, οἱ περὶ αὐτόν, could be interpreted as a wider term, referring to an unspecifically large group of followers and the curious,[48] but it is more likely to imply a distinction between the Twelve as the basic group and an inner circle of intimates to whom special experience and information are imparted. This may be the import in a similar passage (3.34) where the redefinition of the family is confirmed by an eschatological pronouncement (3.34b), though there the private (κατὰ μόνας) feature is not present as it is in 4.10.

The special disclosure to the inner core of the disciples is depicted in explicit terms at four crucial points in the Markan narrative. The first of these is that Peter, James and John, 'the brother of James' (5.37), are taken by Jesus into Jairus' house, where they observe him as he restores the little girl to life. The second is the story of the Transfiguration according to which the same persons accompany Jesus to the exceedingly high mountain (9.2). The privacy of the revelation is made doubly emphatic by κατ' ἰδίαν and μόνους. The third is the Synoptic Apocalypse, with its prediction of the fall of Jerusalem and the end of the age. Here also the witnesses are Peter, James, and John, although this time Andrew is added to the favoured circle (13.3). This experience, like the others, is κατ' ἰδίαν.

Finally, the inner circle of three are the only witnesses to the prayer and struggle in Gethsemane (14.33), although this time all of the disciples, including Peter (14.37), fall asleep during Jesus' time of struggle and commitment to the divine will (14.37, 41). Although Peter does not appear in the narrative following the discovery of the empty tomb, he is told once directly (14.28) and once by a messenger (16.7) that Jesus will precede[49] them to Galilee. The appearance of

Jesus risen from the dead, to which this instruction points, will be the signal for making known that facet of the gospel message, as 9.9 explicitly declares.[50]

But how does this dimension of secrecy – and there are others in Mark as well – comport with the obviously public nature of the ministry of Jesus and, by extension, of the Markan narrative, beginning with the indications of the huge response to John the Baptist: 'the entire Judean region and all the Jerusalemites' (1.5)? Crowds throng about Jesus in order to see his works or to benefit from his healing powers or to hear his teachings (1.32ff.; 1.37; 2.1ff.; 2.20, 32; 4.1; 5.21; 6.53; 9.14; 11.8). In spite of injunctions to the contrary, those who are healed spread the word openly about him (1.45), just as later the Gerasene is specifically ordered not to tell his story publicly (5.19f.) and yet does so. His activity attracts the attention of both religious (2.1ff.; 3.22; 7.1ff.) and governmental (6.14) authorities. Healings are performed in synagogues (3.1), which are frequented by Jesus and his disciples (1.39).[51]

The followers of Jesus later on would have visited Jewish congregations for evangelistic purposes, as we see Paul portrayed as doing in Acts.[52] Mark gives the reader the impression that the size of the crowds and the attendant public interest mounts as Jesus moves towards Jerusalem (10.1). Accordingly, he represents the preaching, teaching, exorcistic, and healing activity of Jesus and his followers (6.12f., 30) as public acts, with the observers at liberty to draw their own conclusions about the meaning of these events and this teaching.

The most vivid description of the public response to Jesus is in 6.53–56, a Markan transitional passage, which tells us that everywhere Jesus went throngs surrounded him, the ill sought him out, and the helpless were brought to him for healing. Public recognition of the authority that characterized the ministry of Jesus is indicated by Mark in editorial passages from the early part of the narrative (1.27). The rhetorical questions place the responsibility on the reader to decide the identity of the one who performs such deeds (4.41). Those disposed to be hostile, however, still demand proof of the source of his authority (8.11). Nothing is hidden in Mark's account concerning the fact, the extent, or the specifics of Jesus' powers. The issue is, What is the source of his authority and wisdom (6.2)?

In William Wrede's *The Messianic Secret*,[53] an understanding of the secrecy motif is rightly presented as essential to an understanding of Mark.[54] According to Wrede, the tension between secrecy and disclosure of Jesus' messiahship is not a matter of historical recollection, but represents a theological necessity: to show why one claimed as the Jewish Messiah died, and why his messianic role was not recognized during his lifetime.[55] The essence of the secret is the necessity of suffering,[56] which differentiates it from the normal Jewish expectation[57] with which otherwise Jesus accepted identification, as his acknowledgment before Pilate indicates.[58] Although the narrative contains a mass of unhistorical material, such as the exorcisms and healing stories,[59] the gospel as a whole is a mixture of historical recollections and dogmatically determined claims.[60] Wrede sees Mark as providing an apologetic explanation of the failure of friend and foe to perceive during his lifetime that Jesus was the messiah by a literary-dogmatic strategy of writing the account of Jesus' career in such a way as to demonstrate that he insisted on keeping his messianic identity as secret. These injunctions to secrecy are found throughout the gospel, are stereotyped in form, and convey the same basic significance.[61]

Although the long-term effects of Wrede's hypothesis have been constructive, by pointing to Mark's work as a document developed to serve the social, political needs of his own time,[62] rather than an objective report of historical recollections, Wrede's detailed analysis of the Markan text is of little value, precisely because the secrecy theme is treated by him as though it were a unity, which it is not.

In a penetrating critique of Wrede, H. J. Ebeling has shown that his error lay in the assumption that the early church required factual support from the life of Jesus for its dogmatic claims. The certainty of faith rested, as Ebeling correctly asserts, not on biographical information – whether authentic or alleged – but on the claim of an encounter with the Risen Christ. The church could afford a free-wheeling attitude towards the Jesus tradition because he was a living reality for its faith, not a dead figure from the past.[63]

Ebeling's work is itself marred by his assumption that the controlling factor in Mark is the kerygma of the cross with its theme of humiliation/exaltation.[64] But this weakness is more than compensated for by his recognition that the gospel serves on the one hand as detailed demonstration of the power of God who is accomplishing redemption through Jesus,[65] and on the other hand as the means by which the charismatic leadership of the church sought to ground the validity of its words and acts in the ministry of Jesus (Mark 2.1ff.; 2.18ff.; 4.35ff.; 5.1ff.; 10.17ff. – all of doubtful historicity, according to Ebeling). The needs of the church called forth traditions which were not simply alterations, no longer recognizable, of historical material but which comprised the erection of a structure in support of and for the elaboration of the church's confession of Jesus as Lord and Judge.[66]

Even more than Ebeling allowed for, however, stress must be laid not merely on the church's confession, but on its work as well. As we have had occasion to observe repeatedly, it is the spirit of Christian prophecy, appealing to the precedent and precept of Jesus, which provides the norms of faith and action in the Markan community.

Ebeling's criticism is more useful, however, as a corrective to Wrede than as a tool for analysing the secrecy elements in Mark. This can begin only when the distinctions between aspects of that theme have been made – an undertaking that Wrede ignored from the outset. A parallel distinction must be made in Mark between genuine elements of secrecy and features of the Markan narrative that have mistakenly been linked with secrecy. It may be useful to begin our examination with the second of these aspects of Mark.

Among those elements of Markan tradition that have nothing to do with secrecy about the kingdom or about Jesus' messiahship are the exorcism stories of 1.23–26; 9.14–29 and the stilling of the storm in 4.36–41. In each of these three cases, the command (a form of ἐπιτιμᾶν) is a technical term by which Jewish and early Christian exorcists brought demons under control and expelled them from the person or object in which they had set up operations.[67] What is at stake is a struggle for dominance, not a leak of secret information. The same term, ἐπετίμησεν, appears in Mark 8.33, but there it is not a matter of gaining control over a demon, but of challenging Peter for having rejected the idea of the necessity of Jesus' suffering – an idea which for all its human appeal is of Satanic origin. Again, the issue is not secrecy but gross misunderstanding. Peter is chastised, not for having spoken at all, but for having expressed diabolical thoughts.

Another set of sayings that have at times been taken as related to the secrecy theme includes 6.31; 7.24; 9.30. In each of these Jesus is portrayed as withdrawing from the crowds, usually without success. Here the central idea is not secrecy but prophetic vocation, which calls for periods of retreat and renewal, as in the classic case of Elijah (I Kings 19) or Jesus' own preparation for his public ministry (Mark 1.12f.). The secrecy of the locale is to avoid the pressure of the throngs seeking to be healed.

There is, of course, an extensive set of sayings and narratives in which the theme of secrecy does figure importantly, even centrally. These may be classified in five groups: 1. *Private disclosures to Jesus*. The baptism of Jesus, at which time the voice of God addresses him alone according to Mark (1.10), and the temptation, during which he is cared for by angels, are offered by Mark as purely private disclosures of divine support for his mission. The Transfiguration story, while witnessed by the inner circle of disciples, is described by Mark (9.6) as beyond their understanding at the time, although Jesus is addressed as Son of God in the third, rather than the first, person (9.7), indicating an attestation to witnesses rather than a private disclosure, as is the case in the account of the baptism. Although Mark then adds (9.9) that the disciples are not to disclose what they have seen until the Son of Man shall have arisen from the dead – a feature of the tradition which we shall consider under category 5 below – 9.10 indicates that they did not yet understand the event after which they could disclose the information, just as they had not understood the event while they were taking part in it (9.6). The proleptic vision of Jesus' eschatological vindication and exaltation, therefore, is depicted by Mark as primarily a disclosure to him.

2. The second category of secrecy elements has nothing to do with messiahship, but seems to be part of Mark's intention *to portray the followers of Jesus as an esoteric group*. The secret signs and arrangements for the ass on which Jesus rode into Jerusalem (11.1ff.) and the clandestine nature of the meeting in the upper room with the disciples (14.13ff.) are of this sort. Why secrecy was required, or how advance negotiations were carried on in order to provide the facilities is not indicated. All that comes through is the impression of a secret society laying and carrying out its plans. It is highly likely that Mark is reading the tactics of his own community back into the time of Jesus.

3. The third group of traditions concerned *the prohibition of the demons from disclosing Jesus' true identity*. In the Markan transitional passage, 1.34, the demons are forbidden to speak, lest they reveal their knowledge of who Jesus is. The same point is made at the conclusion of another Markan transitional section (3.11f.). In this case, both the prostration before Jesus and the specific outcry, 'You are the Son of God,' are unambiguous indicators of the authority of Jesus and of his true identity. The technical commanding word, ἐπιτιμᾶν, is employed by Mark in his depiction of Jesus as determined that his relationship to God should not be publicly disclosed. This dimension of secrecy is closely allied with 4. those *passages in which Jesus forbids his actions to be disclosed*, although these manifest a strange progress in the course of Mark's gospel. In the first instance (1.44), the leper is told that 'he should not say anything to anyone', but at the same time, that he is to show himself to the priest. That is to say, the incident is not to be kept absolutely secret, but is to be made known where its

impact will be the greatest: as a witness to the officials who had responsibility to declare persons clean or unclean in keeping with the regulations of Lev. 13. In 5.43, the astonished onlookers – apparently including both the family of the little girl and the inner circle of disciples – on seeing her brought back to life are instructed emphatically (διεστείλατο . . . πολλά) not to let this be known to anyone.

As indicated earlier, this may link up with the injunction in 9.9 against telling anyone about Jesus' exaltation until after his resurrection. The point in these incidents seems to be more general, however. The benefits of Jesus' healing powers are available to all who come with faith (2.5; 5.36; 9.24; 10.52) in his power to cure them, regardless of their understanding of his mission or lack of it. Indeed, the appropriateness of Bartimaeus' calling Jesus 'Son of David' is not at all clear (10.47f.),[68] and his request is met. When in 7.32–36 Jesus is described again as having taken aside κατ' ἰδίαν the deaf and dumb man in order to heal him, neither the withdrawal nor the specific instruction to the witnesses (unspecified as to number or identity) prevents the word from getting out. 'The more he restrained them, the more abundantly they were preaching '(7.36).

It is significant that this incident, like that of the cure of the Gerasene demoniac, takes place on Gentile soil (7.31). In both cases, the word about Jesus is widely proclaimed as a consequence of Jesus' miracles. Mark has in mind the contrast between the hostility of the Jewish leadership and the response in faith of the Gentiles. Both stories in their Markan form are, therefore, prototypes of the Gentile mission and its effectiveness. Significantly, the story of the Feeding of Four Thousand which follows immediately (8.1–10) and which likewise occurs among Gentiles leads directly to the sceptical request of the Pharisees for a 'sign from heaven': for proof that Jesus is indeed the agent of God (8.11ff.).

Mark presents Jesus as one who avoids crowds and shuns publicity. The throngs that crowd around him and the spread of reports about him are the unsolicited consequence of his work (1.28), not the product of a promotional campaign. The instructions not to noise abroad what Jesus has done is for Mark not linked with secrecy about his messiahship, but with the unsuccessful search for rest (6.31). Yet when the crowds do gather, Jesus is depicted by Mark as filled with compassion for them (6.34; 8.2), since they are a leaderless, uncared-for flock – a term often used of the old covenant people in their times of need,[69] from the Mosaic tradition on through the prophets. Yet Mark wants to avoid representing Jesus as a stunt-performer, using his extraordinary powers merely to attract people.[70] The miracles are

indeed performed, but to meet human needs. The faith of the beneficiaries as Mark portrays them is able to see in his miracles the health
and wholeness that Jesus provides; the reader can see in them the signs
of the gospel, both the defeat of the demonic powers and the healing
of mankind in preparation for the coming of God's kingdom. Mark's
point is not that Jesus' miracles are secret, but that only in the light
of the gospel can their full meaning be discerned.

That meaning is apparent in the final group of secrecy sayings:
5. those in which *insight is imparted privately to the disciples* about the
mystery of the kingdom, about the secret of Jesus' suffering, death,
and resurrection. The link between the coming of the kingdom and
the gospel of passion and resurrection lies in the conviction that only
through suffering and death can new life in the new age become a
reality. This is true both for Jesus and for the Markan community, as
Mark presents his account. That insight is not a matter of general
knowledge.

The secret about the kingdom (4.11), whose triumphant coming is
being proclaimed, is that in this period when its messengers and those
who aspire to enter it announce its coming, they must be prepared
for a life of deprivation and patient waiting, during which they will
be subject to attack and in danger of apostasy (4.13–20). Yet to them
has been granted the insight to understand both the goal and the
present process of service and expectation, while outsiders find the
message of the kingdom an enigma (4.12). They endure in confidence
of eventually spectacular results, in spite of the present modest, even
unlikely beginnings (4.30). The import of this perspective on the
coming of God's kingdom is granted in gradations, commensurate with
what the hearer is able to receive (4.33). Only the members of the
community have a full grasp of what God's eschatological purpose is
(4.34).

Analogously, the disciples are represented by Mark as having been
told of both the suffering and death through which Jesus was to pass
in fulfilment of his mission and the eschatological glory that God had
in store for him. So contrary were these ideas to the traditional Jewish
messianic expectations and to the power-hungry aspirations of the
disciples themselves, that the import of the message did not get
through to its original hearers (8.32). Jesus enjoins them against
speaking to anyone of him as messiah.[71]

No prohibition is, however, indicated in Mark in connection with
any of the three predictions of the suffering, death, and resurrection
of the Son of Man (8.31; 9.31; 10.33ff.). What seems to stand in the
way of their proclaiming this message about Jesus is that Peter rejects

the idea (8.33), the disciples as a whole do not understand it and are afraid to inquire further (9.32). But the sons of Zebedee continue to speculate about their favoured positions in the age of glory that they think is about to come (10.35–37), an attitude which elicits from Jesus the observation that they do not know what they are asking for (10.38a). Before Pilate, Jesus is reported by Mark as accepting the designation messiah (15.2),[72] while in the earlier hearing before the Sanhedrin Jesus' acceptance of the title messiah is unequivocal (14.62).

There is, therefore, no secrecy in Mark about a link between Jesus and messiahship. The esoteric factors lie in the specific nature of Jesus' messianic role. That is indicated in the response of Jesus to the High Priest's question, when in addition to acknowledging his claim to be messiah, or in the very moment of that acknowledgment, Jesus is reported as defining that role in terms of a blend of the traditional kingly role ('seated at the right hand of power', Ps.110.1) and the triumphant Son of Man figure (Dan.7.13).[73]

The 'secret' for Mark and his community lies in the insight that, contrary to appearances, there is not a hopeless incongruity between this claim of Jesus made before the seats of religious and political power that are about to put him to death and the death he did in fact shortly experience. Mark's theme is that the Jesus whose powers conquered demons, healed the sick, stilled storms, enabled him to walk on the sea and to feed multitudes miraculously, who redefined covenant community and its responsibilities, who could foresee the future, and who knew himself to have a central role in the outworking of God's purpose for his creation, that this man *must* die as a victim of those who saw in him a threat to their own authority. Similarly, they saw themselves as those commissioned by God through him and in his name to carry forward the work that he had begun, to continue to perform healings and exorcisms, to interpret his words for the new situations of his people, to live in obedience to the will of God as he interpreted it, to persevere in the face of the hatred and suffering that the members of the community were experiencing as they carried on in his name.

Mark presents his account to show his community that, just as Jesus had forewarned his disciples that he would suffer and die, although they did not comprehend the solemn prediction, so he had told them before the crucifixion that God would soon judge unfaith and vindicate both Jesus and his followers (13.1ff.; 8.38). His followers' abandonment of him on the night of his arrest showed that they really believed in neither his suffering nor his triumph, though

he had confided to them information about both aspects of his redemptive role. Even the vision of his eschatological glorification
(9.2–8) had not carried conviction for them.

In keeping with Mark's understanding of faith as a matter of insight, not merely of information, he includes in his gospel – in addition
to the three uncomprehended predictions in 8.31; 9.31; 10.33 – a
simple pair of promises to Peter (14.27f., 16.7) that the fellowship
shattered by Jesus' death will be restored when they 'see' him again
in Galilee, risen from the dead. In characteristic Markan fashion, that
event is merely pointed to in his narrative rather than being described,
as it is in various forms in the other gospels. By his account of their
flight in terror, Mark lets his readers know that the resurrection, in
spite of the predictions, was not expected, nor did the disciples even
understand what it involved (9.10) until after it had taken place. 9.9
reports Jesus' instruction that the vision of the glorified Jesus was not
to be recounted until after the resurrection; by giving the report,
Mark is telling us not only that that event has occurred, but how it
sheds light on all the preceding events, the meaning of which the
disciples previously could not comprehend.

Unlike all the other activities of Jesus and the redemptive events –
the sufferings and death, the eschatological vindication – the resurrection, though explicitly predicted (Mark 8.31; 9.9; 9.31; 10.34;
14.28), is not described in Mark. He offers us vivid details of Jesus'
wrestling with the will of God before the arrest, of the hearings, of the
execution and burial. We have in Mark visions of the exalted Jesus,
of the human and cosmic woes of the end time, of the final triumph
of the Son of Man. All these are offered as public events. Even the
story of the Transfiguration can now be told. But the resurrection is
a private event: ἐκεῖ αὐτὸν ὄψεσθε. By implication, you alone, as his
once faithful, recently scattered flock, will see him risen from the dead.
That is explicit in 14.28: μετὰ τὸ ἐγερθῆναί με the flock will be recon-
stituted by the once smitten shepherd. They *have* seen him risen from
the dead, Mark is telling his reader. Not only is that their secret
experience, but it is the secret solution to all the enigmas with which
they were confronted by his life and death. To change the figure, the
event to which Mark only points but which he does not depict is the
key to the meaning of his entire account.

Like the christological terminology of Mark, the 'secret' in Mark
points to both Jesus and the community, to the present and the
future. The one whose words, wisdom, and works precipitated his
suffering and death is soon to be vindicated by God, exalted as Lord
and Judge. The community is already living in a proleptic way the

life of the kingdom of God, and through its message, its witness of life, and its charismatic powers, it is calling the world to join it in obedient, joyful anticipation of the kingdom's consummation. It lives in confidence that the God who gave assurance of the eschatological vindication of Jesus by raising him from the dead will vindicate his covenant community as well and at the same time. It is well aware that not everyone puts the same construction on the career of Jesus and the progress of the community that it does. It has no guaranteed proofs that its claims are true or that its hopes will be fulfilled. But in the midst of suffering and potential martyrdom, it rejoices that God has vouchsafed to it the secret of his purpose through Jesus and his new covenant people. It seeks to live obediently, fruitfully, responsibly, faithfully in the corporate role for which God has chosen it and to which he called it through the one soon to be revealed as Son of Man, to whom God has assigned the rule in the kingdom of God.

AFTERWORD

The historical results of our study should be readily apparent: Mark was produced by an apocalyptic community, probably in the years just prior to the fall of Jerusalem. Writing in Greek for a community whose Bible was the LXX, the author has shaped the Jesus tradition in such a way as to demonstrate that Jesus' activity, interpretation of the scriptures, rejection and death were all part of the plan of God foretold in scripture. He was the agent of God to summon the community of the new covenant, which was to comprise all who discerned in his words and work the inbreaking of God's kingdom and who therefore sought to live in obedience to his will, to nurture and support one another within the community, and to urge all who would hear to join the expectant group awaiting God's vindication of Jesus as triumphant Son of Man.

The work was probably written in southern Syria, and served as a challenge and guidebook for the community whose members travelled as itinerant charismatics, carrying forward the tasks of preaching and healing inaugurated by Jesus, ready to follow him to death, if God willed. The whole of Mark was important and relevant for them, since the Jesus tradition was appropriated in this gospel in such a manner as to bear directly on the needs, responsibilities, self-understanding, anxieties, conflicts and weaknesses that characterized their community in their time.

The methodological results will have shown, I hope, the fruitfulness of employing both historical and sociological models, not only for purposes of identity and contrast, but also to focus the issues and the powerful, though unacknowledged life-world structures embedded in ancient documents like the Gospel of Mark. It may also warn against the perils of what Samuel Sandmel once called *parallelomania*, which I understand to be the fallacy of assuming that because features of the New Testament resemble phenomena of the Graeco-Roman world in certain formal ways, identical functions are to be assumed in both cases. Parallelomania leads to the raising aloft of slogans and attractive banners, to which many may rally, but it contributes little if anything to the twin tasks of exegesis and historical reconstruction.

To change the figure radically, superficial identification of a parallel type or a paradigm may lead to the cookie-cutter approach, by which all that does not fit under the arbitrarily selected shape is lopped off. The sage words of E. D. Hirsch with which we began will serve us well as an enduring standard of method, even though no attempt at historical reconstruction may achieve the goal fully: It is of the utmost importance to determine the horizon which defines the author's intention as a whole, for it is only with reference to this horizon, or sense of the whole, that the interpreter (or historian) may distinguish those implications which are typical and proper components of the meaning from those which are not.[1] The present work represents both an essay in the use of a holistic approach to Mark and an appeal to others to explore the possibilities of a similar method in the historical analysis of primitive Christianity.

NOTES

CHAPTER 1

1. W. G. Kümmel, *Introduction to the New Testament*, revised edition, Nashville and London 1975, 92f.

2. Kümmel, *Introduction*, 92.

3. E. D. Hirsch, *Validity in Interpretation*, New Haven 1967, 222f.

4. Alfred Schutz and Thomas Luckmann, *The Structures of the Life-World*, Evanston 1973, 7, 243, 256; Peter Berger, *The Sacred Canopy*, New York 1967, 22, 28, 178.

5. Papias, in Eusebius, HE 3, 39, 14.

6. Augustine, *De Consensu Evangelistarum* 1, 2.

7. H. J. Holtzmann, *Die synoptischen Evangelien. Ihr Ursprung und ihr geschichtlicher Charakter*, Leipzig 1863. See on this W. G. Kümmel, *The New Testament: The History of the Investigation of its Problems*, Nashville 1972 and London 1973, 151–5.

8. Johannes Weiss, *Die Predigt Jesu vom Reiche Gottes*, Göttingen 1892, 1900, ³1964 (ed. F. Hahn). There is an analysis with crucial excerpts on the eschatological message of Jesus in Kümmel, *History*, 226–30. ET of the first edition with introduction and notes by R. Hiers and D. L. Holland, *Jesus' Proclamation of the Kingdom of God*, Philadelphia and London 1971.

9. Albert Schweitzer, *The Quest of the Historical Jesus*, London 1910, esp. 328–75. See analysis and excerpts in Kümmel, *History*, 235–42.

10. William Wrede, *Das Messiasgeheimnis in den Evangelien*, Göttingen 1901; ET *The Messianic Secret*, Cambridge and Greenwood, South Carolina 1971. See H. J. Ebeling, *Das Messiasgeheimnis und die Botschaft des Markusevangeliums*, Berlin 1939, and discussion below, 167ff.

11. Kümmel, *History*, 327–41; also E. V. McKnight, *What is Form Criticism?*, Philadelphia 1969.

12. See Kümmel, *History*, for the influence of Gunkel on M. Dibelius with respect to both the growing awareness of the Hellenistic background of early Christianity (263ff.) and the development of the method which seeks the *Sitz im Leben* of the oral tradition (330f.). Kümmel also notes the influence on Dibelius of F. Overbeck and Eduard Norden, especially the latter's *Agnostos Theos*, Berlin 1913, in *History*, n. 406.

13. M. Dibelius, *Die Urchristliche Überlieferung von Johannes dem Täufer untersucht*, Göttingen 1911, 2, 4–6. Excerpts in Kümmel, 256–66.

14. M. Dibelius, *Die Formgeschichte des Evangeliums*, Tübingen 1919, ²1933; ET of second edition, *From Tradition to Gospel*, London and New York 1935.

15. K. L. Schmidt, *Der Rahmen der Geschichte Jesu, Literarkritische Untersuchungen zur ältesten Jesusüberlieferung*, Berlin 1919.

16. Schmidt, *Rahmen*, 317.

17. Dibelius, *Tradition*, 2f.

18. Dibelius, *Tradition*, 3.

19. Dibelius, *Tradition*, 223 n.1; he acknowledges that this is a variant of Wrede's theory of the messianic secret.

20. Dibelius, *Tradition*, 7.

21. Ibid.

22. Dibelius, *Tradition*, 29.

23. Dibelius, *Tradition*, 68.

24. Dibelius, *Tradition*, 28.

25. R. Bultmann, *Die Geschichte der synoptischen Tradition*, Göttingen 1921, ²1931; ET of second edition, *The History of the Synoptic Tradition*, Oxford and New York 1963, ²1968.

26. Bultmann, *History*, 5.

27. Ibid.

28. R. Bultmann, *Primitive Christianity in its Contemporary Setting*, London and New York 1965. Although it is highly readable and subtly informed by existentialist theological orientation, it does not break new ground, nor does it move beyond the neat, overworked, imprecise categories of Palestinian and Hellenistic Judaism. Oscar Cullmann wrote in 1925 about the need for 'a special branch of sociology, devoted to the study of the laws which govern the growth of popular traditions'. He went on to predict that 'form criticism will only be able to function profitably if conclusive results can be established in this area. In fact, the most serious defect in studies in the form-critical mode which have appeared thus far is the absence of any sociological basis.' (Quoted and translated by John Gager in his important new work, *Kingdom and Community: The Social World of Early Christianity*, Englewood Cliffs 1975, 7, from Cullmann's review of the early works on form criticism, 'Les récentes études sur la formation de la tradition évangélique', *RHPR* 5, 1925, 73.)

29. Bultmann, *History*, 347f.

30. H. W. Kuhn, *Ältere Sammlungen im Markusevangelium*, SUNT 8, Göttingen 1971, passim.

31. Schmidt, *Rahmen*, 317.

32. Schmidt, *Rahmen*, 303–9.

33. Schmidt, *Rahmen*, 317.

34. Ibid.

35. E. Lohmeyer, *Galiläa und Jerusalem*, FRLANT NS 34 (52), Göttingen 1936.

36. R. H. Lightfoot, *Locality and Doctrine in the Gospels*, London 1938.

37. Lightfoot, *Locality*, 125.

38. Lightfoot rejected the ancient tradition that our present Mark was produced in consultation with Peter (p. 21).

39. Lightfoot, *Locality*, 65, 73–7.

40. Lightfoot, *Locality*, 123.

41. F. J. Foakes-Jackson, K. Lake, H. J. Cadbury, *The Beginnings of Christianity*, Part 1, 5 vols., London 1920–33.

42. E. D. Hirsch, *Validity in Interpretation*, New Haven 1967.

43. H. Conzelmann, *The Theology of St Luke*, London and New York 1960; E. E. Ellis, *The Gospel of Luke*, NCB, London 1966; H. Flender, *St Luke, Theologian of Redemptive History*, London and Philadelphia 1967; E. Haenchen, *The Acts of the Apostles*, Oxford and Philadelphia 1971.

44. H. Strack and Paul Billerbeck, *Kommentar zum Neuen Testament aus Talmud und Midrasch*, 4 vols., Munich 1922–28; W. D. Davies, *The Setting of the Sermon on the Mount*, Cambridge 1964.

45. Solemn warnings and horrible examples of the misuse of rabbinic material are set forth by Jacob Neusner in the 'Bibliographical Reflections' as well as in the summary of 'Rabbinic Traditions about the Pharisees before 70', in his impressive three-part work, *The Rabbinic Traditions about the Pharisees before 70*, Leiden 1971, Part 3, 300–68.

46. Vincent Taylor, *The Gospel according to St Mark*, London 1953; William L. Lane, *The Gospel of Mark*, NICC, Grand Rapids 1975.

47. ET W. Marxsen, *Mark the Evangelist*, Nashville 1969.

48. J. Rohde, *Rediscovering the Teaching of the Evangelists*, London and Philadelphia 1968. Selected bibliography and perceptive analysis in W. G. Kümmel, *Introduction*, 84–95. See also J. M. Robinson, 'On the *Gattung* of Mark (and John)', in *Jesus and Man's Hope*, Pittsburgh 1970.

49. This has been identified as the 'divine man' (by Morton Smith), or as opposition to the 'divine man' (T. J. Weeden), or the kingdom of God (W. Kelber), or the cycle of the church year (P. Carrington), etc.

50. E. Haenchen, *Der Weg Jesu*, Berlin 1966, 35f. Haenchen offers penetrating comment that illuminates many details of Mark. His criticisms of others are discerning and his discussion of the ways in which Luke and Matthew have used Markan material are often brilliant, but he offers no new insights into the special aims or methods of Mark.

51. See J. M. Robinson (n. 48 above). Also M. Smith, 'The Aretalogy used by Mark', *Protocol 6 of the Center for Hermeneutical Studies*, ed. W. Wuellner, Berkeley 1973.

52. Thus K. L. Schmidt; also affirmed by H. J. Rose, 'Herakles and the Gospels', *HTR* 31, 1938, 141.

53. So W. L. Knox, *The Sources of the Synoptic Gospels*, Cambridge 1953. Also Pierson Parker, *The Gospel before Mark*, Chicago 1953.

54. W. R. Farmer, *The Synoptic Problem*, New York 1964; D. L. Dungan, 'Mark – The Abridgement of Matthew and Luke', in *Jesus and Man's Hope*, Pittsburgh 1970, 51–97.

55. Martin Kähler, *The So-called Historical Jesus and the Historic, Biblical Christ*, Philadelphia 1964, 80 n. 11; cf. Bultmann, *History*, 275.

56. P. J. Achtemeier, 'Pre-Markan Catenae', *JBL* 89, 1970, 270ff.

57. See n. 55 above.

58. Much of the current redactional study of the gospel tradition operates on the dubious pair of suppositions that 1. the traditions in their final edited form can be assigned to a *Sitz im Leben*, but that 2. the authentic teaching of Jesus can be identified only when it can be shown that a tradition is not in continuity with either Judaism of the period or the primitive church. The objectivity aimed at in this methodological proposal is commendable (as in E. Käsemann's 'The Problem of the Historical Jesus', in *Essays on New Testament Themes*, SBT 41, London and Naperville, Ill. 1964, 15–47; also Norman Perrin, *Rediscovering the Teaching of Jesus*, London and New York 1967, 39–43), but the result is to detach Jesus from any recognizable life-situation capable of being reconstructed historically. This approach is a kind of historical-methodological docetism. Our concern in the present work is not with the historicity of Jesus or with the authenticity of any version of his teachings (see on this, H. C. Kee, *Jesus in History*, New York 1970, esp. 263ff.). Rather, we are here concerned with the ways in which Mark has appropriated and/or transformed the traditions that were alive and potent in his own situation. A responsible historian cannot assume in advance that there was a

radical disjunction between a figure of the ancient past on the one hand and the conceptual-cultural antecedents shared by his contemporaries on the other. The assumption of cultural continuity holds true whether the subject under investigation is Jesus or Mark.

59. H. J. Schonfield, *The Passover Plot*, London 1965, 112, 167–9.

60. An illuminating survey of the resurgence of this method, as well as of its antecedents in the history of biblical studies, has been offered by L. E. Keck in 'On the Ethos of Early Christians', *JAAR* 42, 1974, 435–52. The most explicit and challenging methodological proposal and exemplars are now presented by John Gager in *Kingdom and Community* (see n.28 above). Gager undertakes a depiction of early Christianity as a millennarian phenomenon, with fruitful and convincing results (19–65).

CHAPTER II

1. There is a bibliography and survey of the problem of priority in the gospels in Kümmel, *Introduction*, 38–80. For an analysis of the leading synopses of the gospels, see R. Morgenthaler, *Statische Synopse*, Zurich/Stuttgart 1971, 7–29.

2. W. R. Farmer, *The Synoptic Problem*, New York 1964.

3. H. C. Kee, *Jesus in History*, 64, where Mark 2.1–4 is analysed with this problem in view.

4. 'Jesus *could not* do a mighty work in his own country' (Mark 6.5), as compared with Matt. 13.58: 'He *did not* do *many* mighty works there.'

5. In the Feeding of Five Thousand, Matt. 14.19 reports simply that the crowds were ordered to sit on the grass to be fed, while Mark 6.39f. states that they were ordered to be seated *(συμπόσια συμπόσια)* on the green grass and that they did so by companies *(πρασιαί πρασιαί)*. One can imagine a writer adding vivid details to his souıce, but the introduction of the awkward, un-Greek, repetitive phrases is inexplicable on the basis of the theory that Mark was copying Matthew.

6. 'You are the Christ, the Son of the living God' (Matt. 16.16) is in Mark 8.29 simply, 'You are the Christ'.

7. Cf. the two animals of Matt. 21.2 (and Zech. 9.9) with Mark 11.2.

8. Evidently sensing the gravity of this problem for Matthean priority, Farmer has written a short monograph on *The Last Twelve Verses of Mark*, Cambridge 1974, in which he tries to make a case for Mark 16.9–20 as clearly akin to the rest of Mark (83–103). But, in fact, the Pauline language *(πάσῃ τῇ κτίσει, ὁ κύριος, μορφή)* and the link with II Peter 1.19 *(τὸν λόγον βεβαιοῦντος)* show that Farmer's proposed solution 4 is by far the most plausible: that Mark 16.9–20 was written by a later writer who consciously imitated Mark's vocabulary and syntax, but his importation of terminology and perspectives from elsewhere in the New Testament betrayed his attempt to provide Mark with a more rounded conclusion.

9. W. R. Farmer, 'A Response to Robert Morgenthaler's *Statistische Synopse*', *Biblica* 54, 1973, 425–30: 'This kind of evidence suggests that Luke used Matthew in the composition of his gospel', i.e. rather than merely at the final stage of editing (p.430).

10. On the probable existence of Q, its contents and intent, see H. C. Kee *Jesus in History*, 62–103.

11. Farmer attempts to discredit the hypothesis of Markan priority by showing

that it has been used by New Testament scholars to support liberal Protestant prejudices (see his 'The Two Document Hypothesis as a Methodological Criterion in Synoptic Research', *ATR* 48, 1966, 380–96). But against this it may be argued that 1. the hypothesis has in fact been employed by interpreters as theologically diverse as Bultmann and Harnack, or V. Taylor and E. Fuchs; and 2. unwarranted exploitation of a hypothesis does not disprove its basic validity.

12. R. Morgenthaler, *Synopse*, 300–5. Morgenthaler allows for the possibility that the history of the tradition may be even more complicated than this, but does not regard that as undermining his basic conclusion about the priority of Mark (p. 305).

13. E. R. Sanders, *Tendencies of the Synoptic Tradition*, Cambridge 1967.

14. B. H. Streeter, *The Four Gospels*, London and New York 1925.

15. Kümmel, *Introduction*, 63–80; while affirming unequivocally the priority of Mark and the existence of a written sayings source utilized independently by Matthew and Luke, Kümmel acknowledges that the exact limits of the so-called Q source cannot be determined.

16. Morgenthaler, *Synopse*, 162.

17. Morgenthaler, *Synopse*, 189.

18. Morgenthaler, *Synopse*, 189f.

19. Morgenthaler, *Synopse*, 278f.

20. Where Mark reports miracles in simple, vivid narrative style (Mark 5.1–20; 5.21–43), Matthew has compressed, stylized accounts, even though his gospel as a whole is far longer than Mark's.

21. The curious, illogical detail in Mark 11.13b, 'it was not the season for figs', is missing in Matt. 21.19. The explicit identification of Jesus as Son of David in Matt. 21.9 is matched only roughly in Mark 11.10, where the greeting is addressed to the one 'who comes in the name of the Lord', and the further hope is for David's kingdom that is coming – scarcely a direct messianic title for Jesus.

22. Morgenthaler, *Synopse*, 189.

23. Morgenthaler, *Synopse*, 190.

24. The most serious and fruitful computerized attempt to identify substantive features of the gospels, especially on the issue of those to whom various traditions were addressed, is that of J. A. Baird, *Audience Criticism and the Historical Jesus*, Philadelphia 1969. The procedure could perhaps lay claim to complete objectivity, but the seemingly neutral categories by which the classification of the material has been carried out inform us only about the audience to which the evangelist has *represented* the tradition as addressed in the final edited form. And the resulting failure to distinguish between the evidence embedded in the tradition and that which derives from the editorial process renders dubious any historical judgments by this method about either the history of the tradition or the intention of the evangelists. These inherent problems, coupled with the regrettable reluctance of many biblical scholars to subject themselves (as Baird did) to the discipline required to master the computer technique, have meant that there has been a minimal impact from Baird's work on gospel studies. If – as is assumed in the present study – Markan editorial influence not only is evident in the connective tissue but has also permeated the narrative and sayings tradition as well, then Baird's identification of pattern words would have to be recast quite differently. Otherwise the analysis will gloss over distinctions rather than putting in focus the Markan features; and it cannot serve to point behind the present form of the tradition to the historical Jesus.

25. The theory that the Greek gospels were translated from Aramaic was advanced by C. C. Torrey, *Our Translated Gospels*, London 1937. An Ur–Markus theory was offered by H. J. Holtzmann, *Die synoptischen Evangelien. Ihr Ursprung und geschichtlicher Charakter*, Leipzig 1863; later he abandoned the hypothesis. Proposals for a primitive Matthew were made by X. Léon-Dufour, '*Redaktionsgeschichte* of Mark and Literary Criticism', in *Jesus and Man's Hope*, Pittsburgh 1970, 9–35; he calls the source of the triple tradition 'C'; by L. Vaganay, *Le Problème Synoptique. Une Hypothèse de Travail*, Tournai 1954; and by Pierson Parker, *The Gospel Before Mark*, Chicago 1953, 141–235. For comprehensive bibliography on the priority of the gospels see Kümmel, *Introduction*, 52–80.

26. Moses Hadas and Morton Smith, *Heroes and Gods: Spiritual Biographies in Antiquity*, New York 1965; Helmut Koester, 'One Jesus and Four Gospels', *HTR* 61, 1968, 230–6; T. Weeden, *Mark – Traditions in Conflict*, Philadelphia 1971.

27. Older studies of aretalogy include those of Salomon Reinach, 'Les aretalogues dans l'antiquité', *Bulletin de correspondance hellénique* 9, 1885, 257; A. Deissmann, *Bible Studies*, Edinburgh 1901, 95; Wolf Aly in Pauly-Wissowa, *Supplement* 6, 1935, 13–16. A recently published aretalogical text is R. Merkelbach, 'Zwei Texte aus dem Sarapeum zu Thessalonike', *ZPE* 10, 1973, 45–54. On aretalogy in LXX see Sir. 36.13; *aretalogia* is used in parallel with *doxa*, where the writer is hymning the praise of God for his mighty acts on behalf of his people (see pp. 25ff. above).

28. Moses Hadas in *Heroes and Gods*, 3.

29. E.g. M. Smith in *JBL* 90, 1971, 176f.

30. M. Hadas, *Heroes and Gods*, 7.

31. Thus K. L. Schmidt, 'Die Stellung der Evangelien in den allgemeinen Literaturgeschichte', 82f.

32. Thus Fritz Tager (in *Charisma: Studien zur Geschichte des antiken Herrscherkultes* II, Stuttgart 1960), followed by M. Smith, *JBL* 90, 1971, 179, denies that writings like those of Philostratus' *Life of Apollonius* can be considered as authentic witnesses for the earlier period about which they purport to tell; rather, they are the echo of an admired but irretrievable past (603–5). John Ferguson thinks that the ancient source, Damis, is probably a fraud, and remarks that such discoveries are a 'stock in trade of historical romances' (in *The Religions of the Roman Empire*, Ithaca, New York 1965, 180ff.). Similar estimates of 'Damis' are expressed by M. Hengel, *Nachfolge und Charisma*, BZNW 34, Berlin 1968, 30, and E. R. Dodds, *Pagan and Christian in an Age of Anxiety*, Cambridge 1965, 59: 'a fictitious romance'.

33. Detailed analysis of the evidence adduced for aretalogy as the paradigm for gospel and a case for rejection of the hypothesis are offered in my 'Aretalogy and Gospel', *JBL* 92, 1973, 402–22, and in *Protocol 8 of the Center for Hermeneutical Studies*, Berkeley 1975.

34. E. W. Burch, 'Tragic Action in the Second Gospel', *JR* 11, 1931, 346; also H. B. Carre, *Studies of Early Christianity*, New York 1928, 105–26; Curtis Beach, *The Gospel of Mark*, New York 1959. I owe these references to Vernon Robbins, in his unpublished University of Chicago dissertation, *The Christological Structure of Mark*, 1973.

35. David L. Barr, unpublished Florida State University dissertation, *Toward a Definition of the Gospel Genre*, 1974.

36. Vernon Robbins, *Christological Structure*.

37. Robbins, *Christological Structure*, 15.

38. Martin Braun, *History and Romance in Graeco-Roman Literature*, Oxford 1938, 23.

39. Braun, *Romance*, 26.
40. Braun, *Romance*, 32.
41. Dan O. Via Jr, *Kerygma and Comedy in the New Testament*, Philadelphia 1975.
42. Via, *Comedy*, 11. An approach similar in intention but different in detail is presented by Norman Petersen's forthcoming *Structural Aspects of Mark's Narrative*.
43. A technical structuralist term for texts that have actually been written, as contrasted with competence texts, which lie unrealized within the writer's repertoire of possibilities.
44. Via, *Comedy*, 93.
45. Via, *Comedy*, 113–59.
46. Via, *Comedy*, 99.
47. Via, *Comedy*, 98.
48. Via, *Comedy*, 11.
49. Via, *Comedy*, 84.
50. Via, *Comedy*, 4.
51. Via, *Comedy*, 23.
52. Via, *Comedy*, 25, 94, 162.
53. Via, *Comedy*, 11.
54. Via, *Comedy*, 93.
55. Via, *Comedy*, 7.
56. Via, *Comedy*, 95. Closer scrutiny of texts from the first two centuries before Mark would show that Via's description of apocalyptic (80f.) is at best selective and at worst a caricature. The societal dimensions of the apocalyptic movement are wholly missing from his investigation, or at least from his generalizations. But since he denies the significance of social context for the interpretative task, perhaps that omission is not surprising.
57. H. A. Musurillo, *Acts of the Pagan Martyrs: Acta Alexandrinorum*, Oxford 1954.
58. Musurillo, *Acts*, 239.
59. There is an interesting chronological parallel between the development of the so-called aretalogy and the martyr traditions. Musurillo thinks that 1. the martyr literature did not and could not have come into public view until after the assassination of Domitian, who together with his predecessors had been a tyrant who put to death the pagan martyrs; and 2. Philostratus' *Life of Apollonius*, which he considers a parody on the martyr literature, appeared at precisely the time that brought to a close the period that produced the pagan martyrologies. It was, of course, Domitian who harrassed Apollonius, and it was in the reign of the former's successor that Damis wrote down his memoirs of Apollonius. If Philostratus took a dim view of martyrs, this would account for his parodying the martyrology even though his 'hero' was never represented as a martyr.
60. Musurillo, *Acts*, Appendix III, 247–58.
61. Musurillo, *Acts*, 243–6.
62. Henry Fischel, 'Story and History: Observations on Graeco-Roman Rhetoric and Pharisaism', *American Oriental Society, Middle West Branch, Semi-Centennial Volume* (ed. Denis Sinor, Asian Studies Research Institute, Oriental Series, 3, Bloomington, Indiana 1969), 59–88; also 'Studies in Cynicism and the Ancient Near East: the Transformation of a Chria', *Religions in Antiquity*, ed. Jacob A. Neusner, Leiden 1968, 372–411; an article by him on 'Cynicism' is promised in *Cynicism and the Ancient Near East*, New York and Jerusalem, American Academy for Jewish Research.
63. Fischel, 'Story', 62. It is worth noting that Socrates is claimed by various

scholars as the model for aretalogy (Hadas), for martyrology (Musurillo), and for the sage around whom the anecdotes develop (Fischel). The implication of this is that rhetorical forms can serve a variety of ends. The least appropriate role for Socrates seems to be that of the subject of an 'aretalogy', since he performs no miracles.

64. Fischel, 'Story', 77. Fischel notes that this cautionary factor must be in the forefront of the consciousness of the historian, whether the focus of his research is the historical Thales, the historical Hillel or the historical Jesus.

65. Fischel, 'Story', 79.

66. Fischel, 'Story', 74 n.80, 78f.

67. Fischel, 'Story', 85.

68. Ibid.

69. Paul Fiebig, *Jüdische Wundergeschichten im Zeitalter Jesu*, Tübingen 1911, esp. 96ff.

70. See the critical remarks on Fiebig's work in M. Smith, *JBL* 90, 1971, 190 and n. 107.

71. H. Köster, 'One Jesus', in H. Köster and J. M. Robinson, *Trajectories through the New Testament*, Philadelphia 1971, 162–4. According to Köster, this source presents Jesus as a divine man – an interpretation of him which is corrected in Mark by appeal to the picture of the crucified Jesus (232): 'The true mystery of the Messiah is not visible in his performance of glorious acts and miracles. It is present in his suffering, and the disciples are asked to follow him in the road to Calvary' (233).

72. In his Cambridge University dissertation, *Theios Aner in Hellenistic Judaism*, Cambridge 1974, C. R. Holladay has subjected to painstaking analysis the key works of Josephus, Philo and Artapanus bearing on their use of *theos*, *theios* and *theios anēr*, with the aim of determining what the term *theios anēr* means for these writers. Among his well-documented conclusions are: 1. that none of these writers depicts Moses or any other Old Testament hero as deified (109, 114, 175, 210, 311, 332, 341); rather, in their apologetics the gap between God and man is widened; 2. the propagandizing efforts of Hellenistic Jews did not lead them to stress thaumaturgic or miracle tradition (336), and the real agent of the miracles is always God (32), never a *theios anēr* (334, 340); and 3. in both pagan and Hellenistic-Jewish sources the term *theios anēr* has such a fluid meaning (335) that it must be considered an 'ill-defined, if not indefinable category' (336). Accordingly, the practice which has become common among New Testament scholars of speaking of a *theios anēr* christology (335) and of assuming that the miracle tradition was of special utility in Gentile evangelism (333) is wholly unwarranted. The miracle tradition of Hellenistic Judaism is rather in continuity with the salvation history of the Old Testament.

73. P. D. Hanson, *The Dawn of Apocalyptic*, Philadelphia 1975, 369–88.

74. The regrettably fragmentary work *The Assumption of Moses*, which may well have been a Testament of Moses in its original complete form (as R. H. Charles suggested), moves from the deliverance of Israel in the Exodus to the final deliverance in the end time.

75. R. H. Fuller, *The Foundations of New Testament Christology*, London and New York 1965, 50–3; Wayne Meeks, *The Prophet-King, Moses Traditions and the Johannine Christology*, New York 1967.

76. A. N. Wilder, *The Language of the Gospel: Early Christian Rhetoric* (British title *Early Christian Rhetoric*), New York and London 1964, 36.

77. M. Kähler, *The So-called Historical Jesus and the Historic, Biblical Christ,* Philadelphia 1964, 80 n. 11.

78. Dibelius, *Tradition,* 22.

79. Bultmann, *History,* 275.

80. In Köster and Robinson, *Trajectories,* 612–4.

81. Dibelius' concern is not with historicity, but with the exposition and illumination of the Christian kerygma (170). The narratives are reported in the light of the soteriological meaning of Jesus (198).

82. Bultmann, *History,* 262–74.

83. Bultmann, *History,* 175.

84. Bultmann, *History,* 279.

85. Bultmann, *History,* 277. Eta Linnemann, *Studien zur Passionsgeschichte,* Göttingen 1970, 128f., thinks that she can demonstrate from 14.55–65 that there were two charges brought against Jesus: the destruction of the Temple, to which he responded in silence, and the messianic charge, to which he responded affirmatively. To achieve this neat division, Miss Linnemann must divide up verses and rearrange extensively in a manner which is not impossible, but arbitrary and – to this reader – unconvincing.

86. See below, 93.

87. It is assumed here that the word carried for Mark the same insurrectionist connotations that it does in Josephus, *Jewish Wars.*

88. J. C. Hawkins, *Horae Synopticae,* 106. Of 27 'harsh constructions', 6 occur in 14–15. Of 109 'pleonasms', 17 appear in Mark 14–16.

89. The proportion of those found in Mark 1–13 as compared with Mark 14–16 is as follows:

multiplication of participles: 2/2

double negatives: 11/6

ἤρξατο as an auxiliary verb: 19/7.

90. So H. D. Knigge, 'The Meaning of Mark', *Interpretation* 22, 1968, 68.

91. For a convenient summary with bibliography see Kümmel, *Introduction,* 44–50.

92. W. L. Knox, *Sources of the Synoptic Gospels,* Vol. I, *St Mark,* Cambridge 1953.

93. B. P. W. Stather-Hunt, *Primitive Gospel Sources,* London and New York 1951, esp. 74ff.

94. Pierson Parker, *The Gospel Before Mark,* Chicago 1953, 87–171.

95. Above all by W. R. Farmer, *The Synoptic Problem,* New York 1964. See above, 14–16.

96. H. Köster, 'One Jesus', *Trajectories,* 164.

97. H. W. Kuhn, *Ältere Sammlungen im Markusevangelium,* SUNT 8, Göttingen 1971, although by intention the apocalyptic and passion sections are not analysed here.

98. P. J. Achtemeier, 'Pre-Markan Miracle Catenae', *JBL* 89, 1970, 265–91. See the discussion in V. Taylor, *Commentary on Mark,* Additional Note C, 628–32, who infers from the duplicated accounts that they 'offer some assurance that the reconstruction is not without objectivity' (632).

99. Achtemeier, see under n. 61.

100. The existence of pre-Markan cycles is rejected by Kuhn, *Ältere Sammlungen,* who wants to give Mark credit for the parallel accounts (31). Since Kuhn's view of Markan structure requires him to posit a major division in the gospel, marked by a summary, at 6.53–56, he is unwilling to grant the existence of cycles which

Mark would have used partly before, partly after this supposed major division. The function of the so-called summaries is discussed below (36f.), but the presence of a summary at any point in Mark has no bearing on the question of sources. Kuhn finds himself unable to account for the occurrence of miracle stories in juxtaposition with controversies with Jewish authorities on any basis other than the weak theory that these stories represent 'typical Markan contrast' (220).

101. P. J. Achtemeier, 'Catenae', avoids using the term 'aretalogy' to refer to the cycles of miracle stories on the ground that in much of the current discussion the term is poorly defined or inappropriately used, or both together (226 n. 2).

102. Josephus, *Antt.* 18, 21.

103. B. W. Anderson, 'The Waters of Chaos', *IDB*, IV, 806–10.

104. The term here is the technical one employed in connection with exorcisms: גַּעַר/ἐπιτιμάω. See H. C. Kee, 'The Terminology of Mark's Exorcism Stories', *NTS* 14, 1967–68, 232–46.

105. In the Jewish setting the bread is blessed *(εὐχαριστήσας)*, while in the Gentile setting the word used is εὐλόγησε.

106. The Markan explanation for these two feeding stories is discussed below, 95.

107. Dibelius classifies it as a 'less pure paradigm' *(Tradition,* 43); Bultmann places it as the first of his 'miracle stories' *(History,* 109ff.). I have designated it an anecdote *(Jesus in History,* 274).

108. See n. 105 above.

109. See E. Haenchen, *Der Weg Jesu,* Berlin ²1968, 87.

110. See my discussion in *JBL* 92, 1973, 418 n. 123.

111. See below, 167–70.

112. Anacolouthon; a participle with an impersonal verb. Cf. V. Taylor, *Commentary,* ad loc.

113. πάλιν 28 times in Mark!

114. With εὐθέως, 41 times in Mark.

115. Whether Aramaic or Greek as spoken among people of Semitic heritage will be considered below, 149.

116. Contra Bultmann, *History,* 12, who regards this story as 'an organically complete apophthegm'.

117. See ch. III below.

118. See ch. III below, 51–53.

119. Bultmann, *History,* 13, esp. n. 2. Bultmann also notes the similarity of the mode of argument employed here to that of Jewish scribal debate.

120. See below.

121. For the background of this motif in the Old Testament prophetic tradition, see P. D. Hanson, *The Dawn of Apocalyptic,* Philadelphia 1975, 369ff. See below, 70–71.

122. The term here includes narratives concerning explicit controversies with scribes/Pharisees etc., sayings which reflect a controversy background, disputes over legal or interpretational issues and pronouncements against Jesus' opponents.

123. Bultmann, *History,* 51; also 145–50.

124. Cf. 3.14; 5.18. See also 3.21, οἱ παρ'αὐτοῦ; 4.10, οἱ περὶ αὐτόν.

125. Where responsibility lies for the support of Christian missioners is considered below, 152ff.

126. ἤρξαντο; multiple participles; πάλιν, εἰς τὸ πέραν.

127. 12.26–28 shifts the sense and may well be a later addition. V. Taylor, *Commentary,* ad loc., defends the integrity of the passage. W. J. Lane, *Commentary,*

428ff., discusses the theological basis of the argument, building his case on an analysis of the text by F. Dreyfus, 'L'argument scripturaire de Jésus en faveur de la resurrection des morts', *RB* 66, 1959, 213–24.

128. Bultmann, *History*, 22, considers this to be an 'organic unity', with only 12.28a and 34b as editorial additions.

129. The christological import of this puzzling passage is discussed below, 124ff.

130. See chs. V and VI below.

131. See chs. V and VI below.

132. N. A. Dahl's defence of linking 4.11f. with 'the parables of growth' is misleading. Dahl is correct in assuming that 'the secret presence of the kingdom' in Jesus' preaching and actions manifests 'that the powers of the new aeon are at work', and that it does so only for those to whom it has been revealed. But the merely verbal link with the parables distorts rather than clarifies the function of the parables as teaching devices. The fact that this explanation is located by Mark in the editorial setting of private instruction (4.10) shows that Mark is not transmitting a tradition unchanged but rather is turning it to serve his own special purposes.

133. The similarities between this material and the Q tradition are remarkable, as to both form and function. Whether Q was a document or not continues to be hotly debated, but the statistical evidence compiled by R. Morgenthaler (in his *Statistische Synopse*) points in the direction of a written source.

134. *JBL* 84, 1965, 341ff. More dubious is his differentiation of two christological strands: the 'strong man' and the θεῖος ἀνήρ. That the miracle-story tradition of the period has influenced these narratives is beyond question, but the point about the effects of physical contact with a holy man is by no means a peculiarity of the Hellenistic period: cf. II Kings 13.21 with 3.10; 5.28; 6.56; 8.22.

135. See the analysis of the structure of Mark in ch. 4 below.

136. Reading μου with D, Θ, and the corrector of ℵ in 9.41.

137. The ὡς ἄν clauses in the first part of Mark serve the same end: 3.29; 3.35; 6.11.

138. V. Taylor, *Commentary*, 498–500, sketches the history of interpretation of the discourse (down to 1953) and in note E (636–644) traces the development of the discourse, assigning verses to various groups (for example, signs preceding the parousia, consisting of 5–8, 24–27; sayings on persecution, 9–13; abomination of desolation, 14f.; sayings on watchfulness, 28–37). Taylor concludes that Mark has assembled these with slight editorial modifications.

139. Bultmann, *History*, 125.

140. E. Haenchen, *Weg*, 437. E. Schweizer takes much the same view in *Good News according to Mark*, London and Atlanta, Georgia, 1970, 266.

141. E. Lohmeyer, *Das Evangelium des Markus*, KEK, Göttingen 1937, 269–75.

142. Lohmeyer, *Commentary*, 275.

143. Lohmeyer, *Commentary*, 285.

144. Discussed at length with critical assessment of various theories by Jan Lamprecht, *Die Redaktion der Markus-Apokalypse*, Analecta Biblica 28, Rome 1967.

145. Lamprecht, *Redaktion*, 256.

146. Lamprecht, *Redaktion*, 257.

147. Lamprecht, *Redaktion*, 258.

148. Lamprecht, *Redaktion*, 112 n. 1. Lamprecht calls the theory of Lohmeyer 'phantasievoll'.

149. See Lamprecht's impressive and illuminating fold-out appendix on the structure of the text of Mark 13 (inside the back cover).

150. Lamprecht, *Redaktion*, 259.

151. Highly dubious, however, is the attempt to show the dependence of Mark 13 on Q. For example, 13.5f., with its mention of false claimants to messiahship, which is linked with 13.21 (where the issue is the location of Christ), is traced back by some scholars to Luke 17.23, where the text reads: καὶ ἐροῦσιν ὑμῖν, ᾿Ιδοὺ ἐκεῖ. ᾿Ιδοὺ ὧδε. The weakness of the evidence for attributing this tradition to Q is apparent, however, on several grounds: 1. The title used in Luke is Son of Man (17.22, 24), while in Matthew it is Christos. 2. The omission of the crucial terms ἐκεῖ / ὧδε in Matthew, added to the fact that there the subject of the verbs is simply the pronominal 'he', suggests that Matthew has here preserved a more original form of Q than has Luke, who has possibly been influenced by Mark 13. Or what is more likely, we have here – as elsewhere in Mark (cf. Mark 6.8–11 with Matt. 10.9–14/Luke 10.4–11) traditional material preserved in Mark and Q in different forms.

152. L. Hartmann, *Prophecy Interpreted: The Formation of Some Jewish Apocalyptic Texts and of the Eschatological Discourse Mark 13 par.* (Coniectanea Biblica, NT Series 1), Lund 1966.

153. Hartmann, *Prophecy*, 172–4.

154. Hartmann, *Prophecy*, 177.

155. Hartmann, *Prophecy*, 242.

156. C. H. Dodd, *According to the Scriptures*, London and New York 1952. More attuned to the dynamics of the process of scriptural interpretation is Barnabas Lindars, *New Testament Apologetic*, London 1961.

157. H. C. Kee, 'The Function of Scriptural Quotations and Allusions in Mark 11–16', *Festschrift for W. G. Kümmel*, ed. E. Grasser and E. E. Ellis, Göttingen 1975, 165–88, where documentation is offered for the following analysis. Mark's use of scripture has been widely discussed over the past fifteen years. S. Schulz's article, 'Markus und das alte Testament', *ZTK* 58, 1961, 184–97, assumes that the basis of Mark's theology and therefore of his exposition of scripture is the pre-Pauline kerygmatic tradition of Gentile Christianity which is taken to comprise a scheme of pre-existence, epiphany and enthronement (185f.). Schulz would like to see as corresponding to these themes the Markan motifs of 1. Son of God, 2. messianic secret, and 3. enthronement. The flaws in this interpretative approach are patent: there is no real evidence in Mark for the pre-existence of Jesus; the messianic secret – which is in itself by no means a unified motif as Wrede supposed (see below 167ff. – can fit into this scheme only by Schulz's inappropriate equating of the 'mystery of the kingdom' with the passion; the enthronement is promised (Mark 13) and envisioned (Mark 9), but never described. The chief value of Schulz's article is his having drawn attention to Mark's redefinition of the covenant community (191ff.). Schulz asserts that the major achievement of Mark is to have shown by appeal to scripture how Jesus' death was in obedience to the Old Testament, and therefore to the will of God (196).

A. Suhl's treatment of the subject (in *Die Funktion der alttestamentlichen Zitate und Anspielungen im Markusevangelium*, Gütersloh 1965) is limited to explicit quotations of known texts, and his conclusions are quite general: he rejects the notion of promise/fulfilment (Maurer; Kümmel), and prefers instead to think of Mark as using Old Testament expressions in portraying New Testament facts (65). Of value in Suhl's monograph is his insight that Mark is not interested so much in the history of Jesus as in the significance of that story for the church of his own time (95), both in the reinterpretation of the Law and in the use of the Old Testament to illuminate the church's present understanding of Jesus (159).

158. From Old Testament texts in a known context.
159. A. C. Sundberg, 'On Testimonies', *NovT* 3, 1959, 272.
160. Sundberg, 'On Testimonies', 274.
161. H. C. Kee, 'Transfiguration', in *Understanding the Sacred Text*, ed. J. Reumann, Valley Forge, Philadelphia 1972.
162. H. C. Kee, 'Function', 171–4.
163. E. E. Ellis, *Paul's Use of the Old Testament*, London 1957, 141.
164. J. A. Fitzmyer, 'The Use of Explicit Old Testament Quotation', *NTS* 7, 1960–61, 319–21. Fitzmyer observes that the פשרים are commentaries on sequential portions of the biblical texts unlike the pointed, sometimes atomistic quotations in Mark. But the underlying assumptions and methods of Mark and the פשרים are very nearly identical, even though the form varies. In the case of Mark 13, however, even the reliance on a sequential text is the same as at Qumran.
165. A. Dupont-Sommer, *The Essene Writings from Qumran*, Oxford and Cleveland, Ohio 1972, 255.
166. Here, correctly, J. Jeremias, *The Parables of Jesus*, 1955, 13–15.
167. F. F. Bruce, *Biblical Exegesis in the Qumran Texts*, The Hague and Grand Rapids 1959, 8f.
168. On this see V. Taylor, *Commentary*, 156–8, and W. L. Lane, *Commentary*, 158f.
169. So Rudolf Otto, *The Kingdom of God and the Son of Man*, London 1951, 249ff. Also V. Taylor, 'Detached Note on Mark 10.45', in *Commentary*, 445f.; W. L. Lane, *Commentary*, 383–5. R. H. Fuller, *Foundations of New Testament Christology*, London and New York 1965, 115–19, acknowledges a change of mind on the subject and offers a short summary of the evidence.
170. Quoted from the translations of A. Dupont-Sommer, in *Essene Writings*, 216–18.

CHAPTER III

1. In the Westcott-Hort text.
2. Lists of these 'harsh' expressions appear in J. C. Hawkins, *Horae Synopticae*, 106–8.
3. V. Taylor, *Commentary*, 45.
4. J. C. Hawkins, *Horae*, 12f. Of the 35 listed ,the following are noted by him as most important (number of occurrences in parentheses):

$$\dot{\epsilon}\kappa\theta\alpha\mu\beta\dot{\epsilon}o\mu\alpha\iota \ (4)$$
$$\ddot{\epsilon}\rho\chi\epsilon\tau\alpha\iota \ (-o\nu\tau\alpha\iota) \ (24) \text{ as historical presents}$$
$$\dot{\epsilon}\nu\theta\dot{\upsilon}\varsigma, \ \epsilon\dot{\upsilon}\theta\dot{\epsilon}\omega\varsigma \ (41)$$
$$\kappa\alpha\tau\dot{\alpha}\kappa\epsilon\iota\mu\alpha\iota \ (4)$$
$$\dot{o} \ \dot{\epsilon}\sigma\tau\dot{\iota}\nu \ (6)$$
$$\pi\epsilon\rho\iota\beta\lambda\dot{\epsilon}\pi o\mu\alpha\iota \ (6)$$
$$\pi o\lambda\lambda\dot{\alpha} \ (\text{adverb}) \ (5)$$
$$\sigma\upsilon\zeta\eta\tau\dot{\epsilon}\omega \ (6).$$

5. V. Taylor, *Commentary*, 45.
6. There are transliterations of Aramaic words:

ἀμην *amen*
βοανηργές *Boanerges*

'αββα *abba*
Γόλγοθα *Golgotha*
'Ελωί, 'Ελωί, λαμὰ σαβαχθάνι *Eloi, eloi, lama sabachthani*

Semitic locutions: συμπόσια συμπόσια= חברות חברות
That this is a semiticism is questioned by J. H. Moulton, *Grammar of the Greek New Testament*, Edinburgh 1906, 97, as well as in *The Vocabulary of the Greek Testament*, with G. Milligan, London 1928, 599. It remains a possibility, however: see V. Taylor, *Commentary*, 60f., 303. More certainly a semiticism, however, is εἰ δοθήσεται . . . (8.12) with its dangling protasis. Behind some of the Markan language there can be presupposed Semitic words or phrases, as is the case with the exorcistic terminology, but this evidence does not point to a pre-Markan Semitic document used by Mark as a source.

7. See above, 46f.

8. J. C. Hawkins lists 73, to which M. J. Lagrange, *L'Evangile selon saint Marc*, Paris ⁴1929, LXIV–LXXVII, adds even more.

9. Discussed by J. Jeremias, *The Parables of Jesus*, rev. ed. London and New York 1962, 14. V. Taylor's suggestion that the phrase may be a 'formula of citation' is not supported by a close examination of all the occurrences.

10. P. J. Achtemeier, 'Catenae', 197 n. 6, suggests that the phrase is used by Mark as a literary device to link a sentence to a context with which it was not joined in the tradition.

11. Bultmann, *History*, 31.

12. Less explicitly, Bultmann, *History*, 331f.

13. See below, 53f.

14. At 14.48 there is a variant addressed to opponents: καὶ ἀποκριθεὶς ὁ 'Ιησοῦς εἶπεν αὐτοῖς.

15. Διδάσκαλος occurs eleven times in Mark: once on the lips of Jesus' opponents (12.14), five times spoken by his disciples (4.38; 9.38; 10.35; 13.1; 14.1), and an equal number of times uttered by earnest inquirers seeking healing (5.35; 9.17) or requesting an interpretation of the Law (10.17, 20; 12.32).

16. Although the possibility cannot be excluded that Mark has intentionally linked this verb and the noun with which the gospel begins, the logical connection is not evident. It may be implied that history is divided up into periods: the beginning of creation (10.6; 13.19); the beginning of the gospel (1.1); the beginning of the eschatological woes (13.8). See on this Vernon Robbins, *The Christological Structure of Mark*, ch. 6, 10ff.

17. Noted by E. Klostermann, *Das Markusevangelium*, Tübingen 1907, 36, 50; also V. Taylor, *Commentary*, 191f.; Bultmann, *History*, 15f., 331; referred to briefly in ch. II, 37–39.

18. E. Auerbach, 'Odysseus' Scar', in *Mimesis*, Princeton 1953, 3ff.

19. V. Taylor, *Commentary*, 310.

20. See details in E. Lohmeyer, *Commentary*, 117f. Unique to this passage are συντηρεῖν, ἐξαυτῆς, ἀνὴρ δίκαιος καὶ ἅγιος, εὔκαιρος (adj.), ὀρκῆσθαι, πίναξ, σπεκουλάτωρ (here only in the NT), ἀποκεφαλίζειν Taylor, *Commentary*, 315, notes the influence of the Book of Esther (LXX) on this story.

21. Schmidt, *Rahmen*.

22. Schmidt, *Rahmen*, 160ff.

23. Schmidt, *Rahmen*, 301–5.

24. V. Taylor, who regarded Schmidt's major conclusions as unduly radical, has a far longer list of summary passages, which include in addition to Schmidt's

proposals 1.28; 1.45; 2.1f.; 3.6; 4.1f.; 4.33f.; 6.1; 6.7, 53, 56; 11.1, 11, 12, 15, 19, 20, 21; 13.1, 3; 14.1, 3, 12, 26, 32, 53; 15.1.

25. See below, 62ff., for proposed outlines based on the identification of these pivotal passages.

26. Bultmann, *History*, 155.

27. For christological implications of the 'I'-words, see below, 112, 156f.

28. The only occurrences of the words for prayer which do not fit in either group are 12.40, where the hypocrisy of long-winded prayers is exposed, and 11.17, where the Temple is called the house of prayer.

29. Bauer-Arndt-Gingrich gives only this reference with this meaning in the New Testament, although the term occurs frequently in the papyri and is found in Josephus, *Antt.* 6, and in LXX, I Esdr. 4.12.

30. θλίβειν, προσκαρτερεῖν and ἐπιπίπτειν appear in 3.7–12 and nowhere else in Mark; the diminutive for boat, πλοιάριον, is used here. περιφέρειν, κράσπεδον, Γεννήσαρετ, appear in 6.53ff. as does the Markanism ἤρξαντο + the infinitive, κράββατος (changed in the other synoptics to κλίνη, κλινίδιον) and the use of impersonal plurals (6.54f.).

31. L. E. Keck, 'Mark 3.7–12 and Mark's Christology', *JBL* 84, 1965, 341–58. The delineation of the sections, consisting of double clusters of wonder stories framed by summaries, is offered by Keck on 348f. He observes that this document is free of 'conflicts with Judaism' (349), and then goes on to infer that it presupposes a divine-man christology (350).

32. Keck, 'Mark 3.7–12', 349.

33. Lohmeyer, *Commentary*, 29, 356.

34. Lohmeyer, *Commentary*, 355ff.

35. The same theory about Galilee as the place of revelation was developed by R. H. Lightfoot in *Locality and Doctrine in the Gospels*, London 1938, 1–78. Lightfoot, however, proposed that Mark may originally have ended at 16.8 with the expectation that 'the appearance or manifestation [of the Risen Lord in Galilee] was to be the consummation itself' (65).

36. See V. Taylor, *Commentary*, 331ff.

37. Taylor, *Commentary*, 148f.: 'In sum we may say that in Mark we have an authority of first rank for our knowledge of the story of Jesus.' While acknowledging that there are gaps in the outline of the main events, Taylor declares Mark to be 'a writing of first rate historical importance'. A similar outline, developed geographically and embodying the conviction that Mark's account is based on knowledge of historical facts, leads W. L. Lane to conclude that Mark is to be regarded as a 'historian and theologian in his own right' (*Commentary*, 7,12).

38. N. Perrin, *The New Testament: An Introduction*, New York 1974, 147.

39. Although the pattern of transitional and introductory passages is different from the one adopted above, 56, the two schemes overlap at 3.7–12 and in the treatment of the two healing of the blind stories: both serve transitional roles in Mark, although this view of these pericopes is developed differently by Perrin from the present work.

40. See above, 32f.

41. Several recent studies have revived this approach to Mark. See the remarks of L. E. Keck, 'Mark 3.7–12', n. 15; also the unpublished dissertation by David L. Barr, *Toward a Definition of the Gospel Genre*, mentioned above, 18.

42. *Poetics*, 7–8. Aristotle's assertion that the end should have nothing following it is not congruent with Mark, where the last of the document cries out for completion (7.31f.). Paradoxically, the genre tragedy as defined by Aristotle cannot

provide the central unity he calls for, but rather leaves dangling certain features 'whose presence or absence makes no visible difference' and thus fails to account for the whole (8.34–36).

43. Erich Auerbach, *Mimesis*, Princeton 1953, 42f.

44. Auerbach, *Mimesis*, 45.

45. The influence of Daniel on Mark has been considered above, 45ff., with special reference to the reworking of scriptural tradition and the literary pattern of the apocalypse (Mark 13).

46. In spite of linguistic differences between 2–7 and 1 + 8–12, the book represents a uniform outlook, correlating eschatological vision and present covenantal obligations.

47. Quoted from Dan. 9.27; cf. also Dan. 11.31; 12.11. I Macc. 1.54 emerges from a crisis precipitated by efforts to enforce the Hellenizing of Jews in Palestine – in direct historical analogy to the situation of Mark's time and circumstances.

48. So H. H. Rowley, *The Relevance of Apocalyptic*, rev. ed. London 1963, esp. 39ff.

49. See my discussion in the Introduction to *Testaments of the Twelve Patriarchs* in the forthcoming Duke-Doubleday edition of the Pseudepigrapha, and n. 66 below.

50. These differences probably reflect the bifurcation in the hasidic movement, which developed in one direction along apocalyptic lines and in the other towards mysticism. See below, 79ff.

51. Rowley summarized the aims as divine judgment on the nations, deliverance and vindication of the righteous remnant, a golden age of justice and peace in which creation is transformed and human life greatly extended (24). These phenomena are present in most apocalypses, but they are secondary rather than primary, constitutive features of apocalyptic. Klaus Koch, *The Rediscovery of Apocalyptic*, SBT II, 22, London and Naperville 1970, distinguishes between form-critical features (24–27) and historical features (28–32). In what follows, we draw attention to some of Koch's important insights as they shed light on Mark and his community.

52. The literature on the kingdom of God is enormous. The classic study, only recently made available in English, is Johannes Weiss, *Jesus' Proclamation of the Kingdom of God*, Philadelphia and London 1971. Two able studies of recent critical work on this theme are N. Perrin, *The Kingdom of God in the Teaching of Jesus*, London and Philadelphia 1963, and R. Schnackenburg, *God's Rule and Kingdom*, New York 1963. See also W. Kelber, *The Kingdom in Mark*, Philadelphia 1973.

53. Rowley, *Relevance*, 43.

54. A familiar but significant bit of evidence is offered by the contrast between the pre-exilic account of David's sinful census in II Sam. 24.1 (where God incites David to commit his proud misdeed) and the post-exilic report in I Chron. 21.1, where Satan is held responsible for leading David astray.

55. Cf. Ex. 3, where God appears visibly to Moses, or Ex. 33.18–23, where Moses sees God's back.

56. Martin Hengel, *Judaism and Hellenism* I, London and Philadelphia 1974, 210–12.

57. These chapters are from the Parables of Enoch, which are regarded by some scholars as of Christian origin (e.g., J. T. Milik, *Ten Years of Discovery in the Wilderness of Judaea*, SBT 26, London and Naperville, Ill. 1959, 33f.). But there is nothing distinctively Christian in this passage, nor is there any direct, literary evidence of interpolations. See on the date of the Enoch material, including the Parables, H. H. Rowley, *Relevance*, 57ff.

58. The mingling of historical enemies and cosmic/demonic forces informs Ps. 77.16–20; 114.1–8. See B. W. Anderson, 'The Waters of Chaos', *IDB* IV, 806–10.

59. Lines 17b, c, and 18a here probably are intended to set forth a contrast between the obedient response to the waters (the Law) on the part of the elect community and the self-serving reaction of the official leaders who exploit their position for their personal advantage: 'This is ours!' Or the passage may represent a confession on the part of the community that initially it had responded sinfully to the proffered revelation, a reaction for which it has now sought and received forgiveness.

60. Note the similarity in the view of time in Mark 13.19 and in Dan. 12.1. In both instances, however, the uniqueness of the eschatological moment lies in the severity of suffering that the elect are called upon to endure, rather than in the gloriousness of their deliverance.

61. Apparently this is a reference to Ps.8.5ff., interpreted eschatologically as the assignation to faithful human beings of responsibility for ruling over God's realm. This is explicitly stated in IQS 3.16–18, and is reflected elsewhere in the Hellenistic period (Sir. 17.1–11; Wisd. 9.1–13).

62. Although IQS does not mention tablets, it does refer to the engraved decrees which determine the movement of the seasons and the time of God's visitation (IQS 10.1–8; also CD 2.9–13).

63. In addition to the introduction and translation of the Assumption of Moses in R. H. Charles, *Apocrypha and Pseudepigrapha* II, 407–412, see now on the Moses apocalypses A. M. Denis, *Introduction aux pseudepigraphes grecs d'Ancien Testament*, Leiden 1970, 3–14.

64. See on this, together with translations of the commentaries, A. Dupont-Sommer, *Essene Writings*, 255–78.

65. As is widely recognized, the Chaldeans of Hab.1.5 are identified by the Essenes as the *kittim* = Romans in the Habbakuk Commentary 2.12. IQ Hab. 1.13, the Wicked (One) = the Wicked Priest = one of the Hasmonean priests, probably Hyrcanus II.

66. There is no reason to date these documents in the first century AD or later, nor is their attribution to a Christian author plausible. The Qumran materials show that it was in an Essene environment that the concept of the Testaments of the Twelve Patriarchs flourished, and closely kindred writing developed, of which the Aramaic fragment of a Testament of Levi from Qumran (4 QTLevi[ar]) and other testaments of the patriarchs preserved elsewhere in Hebrew and Aramaic represent traditions similar in design and style elsewhere but different in detail from the Greek testaments.

67. The Testament of Job is not an apocalypse, if by that is meant a document depicting the eschatological destiny of the nation or of the faithful remnant from within the chosen nation. Rather, the Testament of Job treats of personal eschatology: the vindication of the righteous, faithful individual through the suffering that has been endured in this life. See my study, 'Satan, Magic, and Salvation in the Testament of Job', *SBL Seminar Papers I*, Missoula, Mont. 1974, 53–76.

68. This is clearly the case in the Testament of Job, although only his personal vindication is in view.

69. Probably the Teacher of Righteousness (or One who Teaches Rightly) himself.

70. 4.24; 5.31; 8.15; 12.38; 13.5, 9, 23, 33.

CHAPTER IV

1 Koch, *Rediscovery*, 10.

2. Thus Hans Dieter Betz, in 'On the Problem of the Religio-Historical Understanding of Apocalypticism', *JTC* 6, New York 1969, 134–56. Betz differentiates literary from conceptual features of apocalyptic, but leaves out of consideration the nature of the community that produces apocalyptic documents, and takes no account of the socio-religious dynamics of such a group nor of its understanding of its life structure.

3. Thus Rowley, *Relevance*, esp. 150–78. Similarly, P. Vielhauer's essay on Apocalypses in *New Testament Apocrypha* II, London and Philadelphia 1965, 579ff., concentrates largely on literary questions, with some attention to ideological issues.

4. Max Weber, *Sociology of Religion*, Introduction by Talcott Parsons, London and Boston 1964 (ET from 4th German ed., 1956), 60ff.

5. Weber, *Sociology*, xxxix, xliv, xlvii.

6. Weber, *Sociology*, 59, 139.

7. Weber, *Sociology*, 46, 55.

8. Weber, *Sociology*, 47.

9. Weber, *Sociology*, 53.

10. Weber, *Sociology*, xliv.

11. Weber, *Sociology*, 139.

12. Quoted (by K. O. L. Burridge; see n. 13 below) from A. C. Haddon, in E. W. P. Chinnery and A. C. Haddon, 'Five New Religious Cults in British Guinea', *Hibbert Journal*, XV, 1917, 448–63.

13. K. O. L. Burridge, *New Heaven, New Earth: A Study of Millennarian Activities*, New York 1964.

14. Burridge, *New Heaven*, 97–9.

15. Burridge, *New Heaven*, 164f.

16. Martin Hengel, *Judaism and Hellenism*, London and Philadelphia 1974; Otto Plöger, *Theocracy and Eschatology*, Oxford 1968.

17. Hengel, *Judaism* I, 56.

18. Hengel, *Judaism* I, 57.

19. Plöger, *Theocracy*, 42.

20. Plöger, *Theocracy*, 30–42. Also, Hengel, *Judaism* I, 191f., where the effects of Chaldean astrology and Stoic eschatology on Jewish apocalypticism are discussed.

21. D. S. Russell, *The Jews from Alexander to Herod*, London 1967, 213.

22. See on this P. D. Hanson, *The Dawn of Apocalyptic*, Philadelphia 1974, 26–8.

23. Especially in I Enoch 90.22ff. Although R. H. Charles in his introduction to this text insists that the 'great horn' in I Enoch 90.9 could well be the founder of Hasidism, either the Teacher of Righteousness or his predecessor is a more likely candidate.

24. J. A. Sanders, DJD IV, Ps. 154; also in *The Dead Sea Psalms Scroll*, Ithaca 1966, 104ff.

25. Sanders, *Psalms Scroll*, ll. 3f. See the discussion in Hengel, *Judaism* I, 176–8.

26. Sanders, *Psalms Scroll*, 121 = 11 Q Ps. – col. XIX, ll. 4–14.

27. Sanders, 11 Ps. – col. XIX, ll. 14–17. Also Hengel, *Judaism* I, 177.

28. Dupont-Sommer, *Essene Writings*, 320f. 4QpsDan (in Aramaic) represents an Essene expansion on the Daniel tradition; cf. J. T. Milik, *RB* 63, 1956, 407–15.

29. Cf. Mark 13, which builds directly on Daniel. See above, 44.

30. So Hengel, *Judaism* I, 224. Dupont-Sommer, *Essene Writings*, 119, however,

thinks the Teacher of Righteousness began his work during the reign of Alexander Jannaeus, and broke with the Hasmoneans at the time of Hyracanus II after 76 B.C. The longer period for the development of the community, as proposed by Hengel, is more likely. The 'little help' of Dan. 11.34 is probably a polite nod in the direction of the Maccabees after disillusionment with the Hasmoneans had set in but before the final break with them came.

31. Assuming that Hasidim = Hasideans of I Macc. 2.42 (cf. Plöger, *Theocracy*, 7–9, 51) and that the Essenes were a separatist wing of the Hasidim who took the name Essenes, from Osioi (= 'saints'; cf. Russell, *The Jews*, 166) or from Ezaioi (= 'men of the Council'; cf. A. Dupont-Sommer, *Essene Writings*, 24, 41, 43). See also M. Hengel, *Judaism* I, 175ff.

32. Discussed by D. S. Russell, *The Jews*, 235. The term is regularly used thus in Enoch: I Enoch 9.3; 12.2; 14.23; 39.5; 47.2; 57.2; 60.4; 61.8, 10, 12; 65.12; 71.8; 87.5; 106.19.

33. The figure of the community as God's planting is elaborated in 1QH 8.4–13. The metaphor of the planting to represent eschatological Israel is developed in Isa. 60.21f., where emphasis is placed on the reversal of status in the new age, and in Isa. 61.3, where the promises are to the afflicted, the broken-hearted, the alienated (61.1f.).

34. Since he is reluctant to attribute the forgiveness of sin to anyone but God, R. Meyer renders *gzr* as seer. But A. Dupont-Sommer correctly identifies the role as that of an exorcist, whose control over the demons is linked with his pronouncing the forgiveness of sins (in *Essene Writings*, 322, esp. n.3; similarly G. Vermes, *The Dead Sea Scrolls in English*, London and Baltimore 1962, 221). Dupont-Sommer draws attention to CD 13.10 where the promise is offered of loosing all bonds, apparently with reference to Isa. 58.6, where liberation of those bound by evil is promised. A striking coincidence is evident in the juxtaposition in the Prayer of Nabonidus and in Mark 2.1–5 of words of forgiveness with instructions to the afflicted persons to show themselves to the priest (as in Mark 1.40–44).

35. See now Joseph Fitzmyer, *The Genesis Apocryphon*, Rome 1971, 138. A. A. MacIntosh has shown (*VT* 19, 1969, 471–9) that גָּעַר cannot be adequately translated as 'rebuke', but is used rather to convey 'the threat of effective anger of God and the extermination of wickedness' (476).

36. I Enoch 1.5; 10.3; 10.13f.; 15; 88.1; Similitudes of Enoch 69.27, where the wicked angels are defeated in the last days.

37. In the Oxford Congress Volume, John Strugnell, 'The Angelic Liturgy at Qumran', SVT 7 (Congress Volume Oxford 1959), Leiden 1960, 318–45. G. Vermes rightly recognizes in this literature evidence for esoteric Merkebah mysticism, participation in which was explicitly prohibited by the rabbis. See Vermes, *Dead Sea Scrolls*, 210.

38. 4Q Nabᵖ 2.12–14.

39. 4Q Pesh Ps. 37, 3.15, 19; Pesh. Hab. 2.

40. In John Allegro, 'Qumran Cave 4, 4Q 158–186', *DJDJ* V, Oxford 1968, 15ff.

41. J. A. Sanders, *DJDJ* IV, Oxford 1965, 68ff., lines 1, 2, 3, 12, 16, 18. In 11Q Psᵃ Plea, lines 7f., they are also called the *hasidim*.

42. *DJDJ* IV, 69.

43. Designated the 'annexe' by Dupont-Sommer, the document was called 'The Rule of the Community' by its original editor, and has more recently been labelled 'The Messianic Rule' by G. Vermes in his *The Dead Sea Scrolls in English*. It is

clearly a description of the procedures for entering the community 'in the last days', and therefore the sense of eschatological expectancy is heightened; even so, it makes provision for the ongoing life of the community and lays down regulations for it.

44. The date suggested by G. Vermes, *The Dead Sea Scrolls*, 118.

45. C. H. Kraeling, *John the Baptist*, New York 1951, 123–57.

46. Wilhelm Wuellner, *The Meaning of "Fishers of Men"*, Philadelphia 1967.

47. Especially as it is presented in the Q tradition (Matt.3.7–10; Luke 10–14), where stress is placed on the imminence of the catastrophic judgment: the axe, the fire.

48. All the occurrences of ἀκολουθεῖν relate to 'following' Jesus, with the exception of 14.13, where instruction is given to follow the man who will show the way to the guest room to be used for the supper, and 14.54, where Peter follows Jesus at a distance – although even in these two cases symbolic instruction for discipleship may be implied. Cf. 1.18; 2.14. 15; 5.24; 6.1; 8.34; 9.38; 10.21; 10.28; 10.32; 10.52; 11.9; 15.41. For ὀπίσω, cf. 1.17; 1.20; 8.34. There are two other occurrences (1.7; 13.16) that are non-technical.

49. Martin Hengel, *Nachfolge und Charisma*, BZNW 34, Berlin 1968. Hengel builds his case for the charismatic aspect of discipleship more by appeal to the Q tradition than to Mark('I have not come to bring peace but a sword . . . a man's foes will be those of his own household . . . He who loves father and mother more than me is not worthy of me . . .'). Especially significant are the complete break with the legal tradition (Matt.8.22; Luke 9.60) and the abandonment of household ties and obligations (Matt.8.19f.).

50. V. Taylor, *Commentary*, 156.

51. In connection with the rupture of family relationships, Hengel points to Mic.7.6; Zech.13.3; I Enoch 99.5; 100.1f.; Jub.23.16; Syr. Bar.70.6.

52. Of 22 occurrences of διδαχή, διδάσκω, all but two (7.7 and 14.49) are in editorial contexts. The title διδάσκαλος is used 11 times: once in an editorial passage, 5 times attributed to interrogators, and 5 times to the disciples.

53. This theme is developed in Ch. VI.

54. J. Jeremias, 'Der Ursprung der Johannestaufe.', *ZNW* 38, 1939, 312–20.

55. C. H. Kraeling, *John the Baptist*, 59–63.

56. Josephus, *Wars*, describes these revolutionary prophets who appear in the desert (2, 261–63). In Book 6, the cosmic portents – the star over the city like a sword (289), the light at midnight around the altar (290), the cow that gave birth to a lamb (292), the self-opening gate (293), and the celestial armies (299) – reach their climax in the prophetic oracles of Jesus, son of Ananias, who announced the doom of Jerusalem over a period of seven years and five months. The eschatological imagery of the desert has been explored by R. W. Funk, 'The Wilderness', *JBL* 78, 1959, where ἔρημος is correctly seen as a conceptual rather than a geographical term, and by U. Mauser, *Christ in the Wilderness*, SBT 39, London and Naperville, Ill. 1963, who shows that in the Pentateuchal account, the 'desert' is the place of deliverance, of revelation, of election, of promise, of parenetic appeal (20–26).

57. See Ch.V, below, 111f.

58. See the discussion above, 56–62.

59. M. Hengel, *Nachfolge*, 110, rightly regards the master-disciple relationship of John the Baptist to his followers as providing the closest analogy to the link between Jesus and his disciples. There may have been a tradition of John's resurrection, as Mark 6.14, 16; 8.28 suggest. The argument of 9.9–13 is puzzling, in which are linked the resurrection of the dead, the Son of Man and Elijah, but the conclusion

drawn by Vernon Robbins (in *The Christology of Mark*) that Jesus was regarded as John the Baptist *redivivus* is unfounded and unconvincing.

60. Building on their own tradition, as well as on Mark and Q material, both Matthew and Luke have modified and formalized these instructions. Matthew has created one of his great discourses (9.35–11.1) which is introduced by a typical Matthaean Summary (9.35) and concluded by characteristic Matthaean terminology, 'When Jesus had finished . . .' (11.1). On the other hand, Luke uses the material from Mark and Q in two different settings in his gospel (9.1ff.; 10.1ff.) and then again in Acts 1.

61. Thus Bauer-Arndt-Gingrich. See also M. Hengel, *Judaism* I, esp. 18–32, on the administration and taxation of Palestine as established by the Ptolemies and continued in subsequent centuries under the Seleucids and the Romans.

62. The city is viewed more positively, or references to the villages are omitted in such parallel passages in Matthew and Luke as Matt.8.33; 9.35; 16.13; 21.10; 24.3; Luke 9.18; 19.45; 21.7.

63. See discussion below (101–102) and n. 92; also in ch. V (109–110).

64. Saul Lieberman, *Greek in Jewish Palestine*, New York 1942, 89. See also below, ch. VI, 147ff.

65. The second of which is omitted by Matthew, and both of which are absent from Luke.

66. J. Jeremias, *The Parables of Jesus*, rev. ed., London and New York 1963, 16, esp. n. 22. Also E. Lohmeyer, *Commentary*, in loc.

67. The chapter is filled with characteristic Markan expressions: κατὰ μόνας, v. 10; καὶ ἔλεγεν αὐτοῖς, vv. 11, 21, 24; καὶ ἔλεγεν, vv. 26, 30; καὶ λέγει αὐτοῖς, v. 35; καὶ . . . ἐλάλει αὐτοῖς τὸν λόγον, v. 33, etc. Cf. the discussion of the Markan Jesus as offering private instruction in K. Reploh, *Markus – Lehrer der Gemeinde*, Stuttgart 1969, 214ff. The private nature of the instruction is omitted in the Lukan parallels to Mark 7.33; 9.2; 9.28; 10.10, 23, 42, and is modified or omitted by Matthew in all except 9.28 (if we follow the D-text in 9.2).

68. Matthew preserves and Luke omits the private nature of the apocalyptic discourse.

69. Q. Quesnell, *The Mind of Mark: Interpretation and Method through Exegesis of Mk 6:52*, Analecta Biblica 38, Rome 1969, 259.

70. Acts has ameliorated the conflict between the two wings by depicting the Seven as deacons whose assignment was to handle the administrative affairs (Acts 6.1–6), although even Acts shows that their actual role was that of Gentile evangelism. See H. C. Kee et al., *Understanding the New Testament*, Englewood Cliffs, NJ 1973, 386.

71. William Wrede, *The Messianic Secret*, ET. Cambridge and Greenwood, S. C., 1971, 1, 67, 131, 145. See below, 167ff. for a discussion of theological issues in connection with Wrede's theory.

72. H. C. Kee, 'The Terminology of Mark's Exorcism Stories', *NTS* 14, 1968, 232–46.

73. I Enoch 10.21; 18.1, 5, 14; 25.4f.; 33.1; 36.1f.; 39.1; Test. Levi. 18.9; Test. Simeon 5.7; among canonical texts, Isa. 60.3–16; 42.5–13; Zech. 14.9, 16–19.

74. Detailed in Josephus, *Wars* 1, 401–429, where we learn of Herod's building public colonnades, temples consecrated to Caesar Augustus (Sebaste), and of course founding Caesarea itself on the Mediterranean coast as an elaborate example of the complete Hellenistic *polis*, built with amphitheatres and stadia, and even a statue of Olympian Zeus (414). The relation of the Herodians to the Sadducees

remains a riddle, since Josephus (*Wars* 2, 164–66) tells us nothing of substance about the Sadducees. Apart from the tradition that they were aristocratic fundamentalists who recognized only the Pentateuch as authoritative scripture, we can infer about them only that they were Jewish aristocrats who collaborated with Rome and who probably dominated the γερουσία. The hypothesis of T. W. Manson that Sadducees = σύνδικοι is plausible but not demonstrable. Herod's partisans approved his harsh treatment of those who had removed the golden eagle that he had placed over the gate of the temple. To both pious and nationalistic Jews – who might indeed be the same persons in many instances – the eagle was an offence as both an idolatrous object and a symbol of pagan Rome (*Wars* 2, 648–55).

75. The suggestion by Vernon Robbins (see n. 59 above) that 'the leaven of the Herodians' is to be interpreted by means of Herod Antipas' notion that Jesus was John the Baptist raised from the dead (Mark 6.14) is fanciful, and it is based on contradictory evidence. Can John the Baptist have been beheaded (6.15) and also have ascended bodily into heaven, as Robbins wants to read Mark 9.1? Is John the Baptist also among the θεῖοι ἄνδρες?

76. On Essene origins, see above, 83f. Josephus' full and sympathetic account of this sect is given in *Wars* 2, 119–61. For excerpts from and an analysis of the ancient literature on the subject, see Dupont-Sommer, *Essene Writings*, 21–38.

77. In addition, Philo's *Apologia pro Judaeis* mentions that members chose a simple tunic from the common store, as they had need (cf. Mark 6.9).

78. IQS 5.7–11; 6.14–23.

79. IQS 6.24–7.25. Cf. Josephus *Wars* 2, 143.

80. IQM. Text, notes, translation in Y. Yadin, *The Scroll of the War*, Oxford 1962.

81. Josephus *Wars* 2, 457.

82. Josephus *Wars* 2, 458f.

83. Josephus *Wars* 2, 463.

84. Josephus *Wars* 2, 466ff.

85. Josephus *Wars* 2, 482.

86. Josephus *Wars* 2, 559.

87. Josephus *Wars* 2, 479.

88. See the discussion of the literary structure of Mark 13 in ch. III above, 44f. Two full-scale studies of Mark 13 are: 1. Lars Hartmann, *Prophecy Reinterpreted: The Formation of Some Jewish Apocalyptic Texts and of the Eschatological Discourse Mk 13 par.*, Lund 1966, and 2. Lloyd Gaston, *No Stone on Another: Studies in the Significance of the Fall of Jerusalem in the Synoptic Gospels*, Leiden 1970. Hartmann is more concerned with the reinterpretation of Danielic material and the adaptation of its motifs to the new situation of Mark, while Gaston seeks to show not only the literary development of Mark 13, but also the ways in which the crucifixion of Jesus as an insurrectionist and the rising tide of Jewish nationalism in the 60s required the Christians to specify the nature of their hope and to declare unequivocally their attitude toward the threatening of the temple and of the city of Jerusalem. Gaston emphasizes the 'prophetic school' (61ff.) that carried forward the process of interpreting the changing scene in the light of the changing circumstances. He sees in the term 'Son of Man' an ambiguous phrase by which Jesus designated the community, but by which they defined his role of the suffering/vindicated one, and thereby understood their own destiny as the elect (391–5). In the tradition of Daniel, the Markan community's prophets employ the scriptures and the Jesus tradition to do as Daniel did: to interpret the political crisis and to exhort the

faithful to endure (457). Gaston's interpretation of Mark is in general persuasive. P. Vielhauer's argument that Mark 13 must be from a time after the fall of Jerusalem (in 'Apocalypses', *NT Apocrypha* II, 619) is fallacious, since it is based on an artificial differentiation between historical and supernatural units, in the latter of which the eschaton is no longer historical (here he is following Conzelmann), and on the assumption that the discourse must be composite because the predictions are interpersed with hortatory passages. But it is precisely this mingling of prediction and parenesis that is characteristic of apocalyptic literature and typical of the outlook of the communities that produce such works, as Vielhauer himself notes on p. 587 of the same article!

89. See ch. III n. 6 above.

90. ʼΑββα (14.36) and ταλιθα κουμ (5.41) and 5 of the 13 occurrences of ἀμήν are omitted by both Matthew and Luke, while Luke drops 4 more of them independently.

91. There has been a modest resurgence of interest in the background of 'Amen', stimulated in part by the discovery of a seventh-century BC ostracon containing a letter in which ἀμην appears in a formulaic affirmation of the writer's integrity (edited by J. Naveh, 'A Hebrew Letter from the Seventh Century BC', *IEJ* 10, 1960, 129–39). John Strugnell has conveniently summarized and critically analysed the discussion (in '"Amen, I say unto you" in the Sayings of Jesus and in Early Christian Literature', *HTR* 67, 1974, 177–90), including critical observations concerning two recent monographs on the subject: Victor Hasler, *Amen. Redaktionsgeschichtliche Untersuchung zur Einführungsformel der Herrenworte 'Wahrlich, ich sage euch'*, Zurich/Stuttgart 1969; and Klaus Berger, *Die Amen-Worte Jesu. Eine Untersuchung zum Problem der Legitimation in apocalyptischer Rede*, BZNW 39, Berlin 1970. Strugnell is justified in rejecting Berger's hypothesis that the *amen* arose in apocalyptically oriented Hellenistic Judaism as a replacement for lengthier oath formulations in prophetic pronouncements (177) and draws attention to evidence assembled by S. Talmon (in *Textus* VII, Jerusalem 1969, 124–9) for the use in later biblical texts, including the textual tradition lying behind LXX, of what Strugnell calls 'the affirmatory pre-positive *amen*' (180 n.6). He remarks, however, that although the term cannot be shown to have originated as a bilingual pun in Hellenistic Jewish Christianity, as Berger had claimed, it may very likely have been used by Jesus in solemn asseverations and then 'spread later to new sayings in the Synoptic tradition' (181 n.8). Wherever and whenever the term originated as a prepositive formula of affirmation, it was used by Mark in the pronouncements of Holy Law which he attributed to Jesus and which provide the eschatological sanctions for regulating the life of his community.

92. E. Käsemann, in *NT Questions of Today*, London and Philadelphia 1969, 66–81. The English translation renders Käsemann's phrase as 'sentences of holy law'.

93. Summarized and affirmed by V. Taylor, largely on the basis of patristic evidence, *Commentary*, 32, although he also offers the evidence for Antioch. W. L. Lane, *Commentary*, 24f., argues for Rome as well, based on the use of Latinisms and Roman time reckoning.

94. W. Marxsen, *Mark the Evangelist*, Nashville 1969, 54–95.

95. Mark 4.2–8, 26f. Jeremias, *Parables*, 149ff.

96. Mark 2.4, a detail omitted by Matthew and modified by Luke (5.19) to the kind of roofing (tiles) with which he was familiar. Similarly, Mark represents a single lamp as sufficient to light a house, presumably of one room (4.21), while Luke

thinks of a single lamp as adequate only for a light in the vestibule, where it shows the way into the house proper for those who enter. Again, the passage is omitted in Matthew.

97. C. H. Dodd, *Parables of the Kingdom*, London and New York 1938, 95.

98. Mark 12.1–9. The basic pattern of tenant-farmer/absentee-owner is preserved in Matt. 21.33–40 and Luke 20.9–16. See on this Jeremias, *Parables*, 74ff., and Hengel, *Judaism* I, 18–29.

99. For Dalmanutha (A, B with variant spellings, c, K, etc.) other MSS have Μαγεδά (syrᶜ), Μελεγαδά (D), Μαγδαλα (אּ). For χώρα τῶν Γερασηνῶν (א*, B, D, etc.), other MSS offer Γαδαρηνῶν (A, C, K, etc.), Γεργεσηνῶν (אᶜ, L, Δ, Θ), or Γεργυστήνων (W).

100. See 97 above.

101. See ch. III, 51.

102. See 98 above.

103. Gerd Theissen, 'Wanderradikalismus: Literatursoziologische Aspekte der Überlieferung von Worten Jesu im Urchristentum', *ZTK* 70, 1973, 245–71: ET in *Radical Religion* 2, nos. 2 and 3, Berkeley 1975, 84–93. Theissen's work is of great importance methodologically as well as substantively. His insistence on examining the socio-economic conditions which lie behind and are filtered through ancient texts like the New Testament – rather than focussing on the religious ideas alone and in the abstract – is a salutary move of the kind called for in our introductory chapter. Theissen anticipates sceptical reaction to his approach, expressed in proverbial form: 'Man hier nichts wissen könne, weil man im Grunde nichts wissen möchte' (258).

104. Especially close to the Cynics is the Lukan form of the instruction in 9.3 ('Wanderradikalismus', 259).

105. Theissen, 'Wanderradikalismus', 260.

106. Theissen, 'Wanderradikalismus', 251.

107. Theissen, 'Wanderradikalismus', 268, esp. n. 68, in criticism of J. M. Robinson, '*Logoi Sophon*', in Köster and Robinson, *Trajectories*, Philadelphia 1971, 71–113. See also my criticism in '"Becoming as a Child" in the Gospel of Thomas', *JBL* 82, 1963, 307–14.

108. Theissen, 'Wanderradikalismus', 252.

109. Theissen, 'Wanderradikalismus', 265.

110. Theissen draws attention (266) to the famous Letter 96 of Pliny to Trajan. Theissen is interested primarily in the Q tradition, which he seeks to trace back to Palestine, because of its concern for relations with rabbis and synagogues.

111. Theissen, 'Wanderradikslismus', 267 n. 41.

112. Hengel, *Judaism* I, 83–8.

113. Or is the textual tradition correct which locates the story in Gadara (A, C, K, syrᵖ, Diatessaron)? See the unpublished Graduate Theological Union (Berkeley) Dissertation of Darryl Schmidt, *Transformational Grammar of Mark*, on this. Also Yj Baarda, 'Gadarenes, Garasenes, Gergesenes and the "Diatessaron" Headings', in *Neotestamentica et Semitica*, Festschrift for M. Black, Edinburgh 1964, 181–97.

114. E. R. Dodds, *Pagan and Christian in an Age of Anxiety*, 53–68. Also David L. Tiede, *The Charismatic Figure as Miracle Worker*, SBL Dissertation Series 1, Missoula, Mont. 1972, where the picture of the itinerant wonder-workers is specified.

115. As H.-D. Betz has sought to do in *Lukian of Samosata*, Berlin 1961. It is an

understatement when Betz acknowledges that 'the concept of Divine Man is open to considerable variation' (in 'Jesus as Divine Man', in *Jesus and the Historian, Festschrift* for E. C. Colwell, ed. F. T. Trotter, Philadelphia 1968, 116.

CHAPTER V

1. A succinct assessment of the eschatological-redemptive figures in the Dead Sea Scrolls is offered by Geza Vermes in *The Dead Sea Scrolls in English*, London and Baltimore 1962, 47–52. Somewhat differently analysed by Matthew Black, 'The Qumran Messiah and Related Beliefs', in *The Scrolls and Christian Origins*, London and New York 1961, 145–63.

2. As in Dan Via's discussion of apocalyptic as a genre in *Kerygma and Comedy*, 78–84. Via also discusses apocalyptic in conceptual terms, however, concentrating on what he calls a negative evaluation of history (87).

3. As in R. W. Funk's characterization of apocalyptic largely in terms of a view of time, in 'Apocalyptic as an Historical and Theological Problem in Current New Testament Scholarship', *JTC* 6, New York 1969, 275–92.

4. The personal laments in the Hodayoth and the regulations in CD and IQS do not qualify as apocalyptic by merely literary or conceptual definitions, yet they are clearly essential features of the community movement which also produced the eschatological commentaries and the War Scroll, which are apocalyptic in the more limited literary-conceptual sense.

5. I Enoch 25.4f.; 90.19; Sim. Enoch 48.7; CD 2.11–13, 14–16.

6. IQM 1.124; I Enoch 1.5; 10.3; 15; 88.1; 102.2; Test. Naphtali 8.4; Test. Asher 7.3; Test. Benj 3.3; Test. Levi (arm β) 18.12.

7. I Enoch 1.8; 90.19; Sim. Enoch 38.2.

8. I Enoch 88.1; Sim. Enoch 39.6; 39.10; 46.1; 51.3; CD 7.18f.; Test. Levi 5.10; Test. Iss. 7.7; probably also IQSa 2.11–17; Comm. on Isa.; Frag d 1–8; Patr. Blessings 1–6.

9. IQM 11, 15, 16, 18.

10. For a recent comprehensive treatment of this theme in Mark, see Werner Kelber, *The Kingdom in Mark*, Philadelphia 1974. Although the book devotes an inappropriate degree of attention to christological and geographical factors (notably, Galilee) to the neglect of other aspects of the kingdom, Kelber's study rightly draws attention to Mark's fundamental thesis that the new beginning which Jesus brings (1.1) terminates the old order and inaugurates not only a new era but also a new people (23).

11. Johannes Weiss, *Jesus' Proclamation of the Kingdom of God*, ET Philadelphia and London 1971. The original German edition was first published in 1892.

12. A full discussion of ἐγγίζειν in this passage by W. G. Kümmel, *Promise and Fulfilment*, SBT 23, London and Naperville, Ill. 1957, esp. 19–25.

13. Cf. N. A. Dahl, 'Parables of Growth', *Studia Theologica* 5, 1951, 132–66.

14. The Beelzebul section has itself been inserted into the story of the opposition of Jesus' family toward him (3.20f., 30–34). See the discussion of Mark's interpolation technique above.

15. Assuming that αὐτούς (v.23) refers to the disciples, as it does in the comparable passages with προσκαλεσάμενος.

16. See 89f.

17. See below, 140, and n. 120.

18. The imperative of Matthew and LXX has been changed by the Markan tradition into the first person singular indicative, stressing thereby that the death of the shepherd is God's own action, not merely a tragic event that God must deal with after the fact.

19. Taylor, *Commentary*, 549, correctly observes that the text moves smoothly from 14.27–29, and that 14.28 is intrusive here. It is essential for Mark to have included it at this point, however, since he wants to show the divinely ordained establishment of the community following the death and resurrection. A recent study of the composite nature of the passion narrative is that of Eta Linnemann, *Studien zur Passionsgeschichte*. Unfortunately, Miss Linnemann does not take into account sufficiently the fact that later conflicts among segments of early Christianity as well as between primitive Christianity and the political and religious authorities are reflected in the details of the passion story as it is preserved in Mark.

20. The incident also recalls Gen. 49.11, where the rising of a king from Judah is predicted; in I Kings 1.38f. Solomon enters Jerusalem – and hence is recognized as David's royal successor – by riding in on David's mule. See below, 127f.

21. The elaborate Markan introduction has been abbreviated by Matthew and Luke independently of each other; both omit the reference to Zechariah, although Matthew reproduces it elsewhere (9.36).

22. Ps. 78.67–72 presents David as shepherd-leader of Israel, although Ps. 80 addresses Yahweh himself as 'Shepherd of Israel'.

23. Cf. Paul's version of the eucharistic word in I Cor. 11.23–25, where the element of ἀνάμνησις (v. 25b) is made explicit.

24. See references in Josephus above, p. 88 and ch. IV n. 56.

25. Isa. 40.3–11; 42.10–17; 43.1–13; 51.1–11; 62.10–12.

26. These verses, which follow those quoted in Mark 12.10f. (=Ps. 118.22f.), are quoted in Mark 11.9, with import discussed below in connection with Son of David.

27. There is extensive – though not highly trustworthy – manuscript tradition for the reading τῆς καινῆς διαθήκης in 14.24, as well as strong support in the ancient versions: it, vg, syr, cop, arm, eth, and the Diatessaron.

28. The quotation from scripture is attached to the narrative by a typical Markan seam: καὶ ἐδίδασκεν καὶ ἔλεγεν αὐτοῖς. See further on this L. Gaston, *No Stone on Another*, Leiden 1970, 88.

29. See above, 92.

30. Setting aside the sabbath law is one of the authoritative functions of the Son of Man according to Mark 2.28. See below, 138.

31. P. Volz, *Jüdische Eschatologie von Akiba bis Daniel*, Tübingen 1903, 196.

32. Josephus' regular term in *Wars* and *Antiquities* for referring to insurrectionists.

33. See above, 53.

34. R. E. Brown has noted the close resemblances between Jesus and Elijah as miracle workers in his article, 'Jesus and Elisha', *Perspective* 12, Pittsburgh 1971, 85–99. See further n. 49 below.

35. So Kähler, Bultmann, Köster et al.

36. This might be inferred from considering Mark as essentially a debate on christology, as proposed by T. Weeden, *Mark: Traditions in Conflict*, Philadelphia 1971.

37. T. H. Gaster, *The Dead Sea Scriptures*, rev. ed., New York 1964, 6.

38. IQHab 2.8f., translation from Vermes, *Dead Sea Scrolls*, 136.

39. IQH 18.10–12, *Dead Sea Scrolls*, 199.

40. E.g., the Commentary on Nahum, which apparently refers to 'Demetrius of Greece', by which is probably meant either the third or the first Ptolemy of that name to dominate Palestine. Other biblical figures from the past are given a new historical identity in the time of the commentator, or shortly before his time. In each case, the denouement of the historical conflict is awaited in the near future.

41. 4Q Ps. Josh. 5. This text then goes on to depict the coming of the two other end-time figures: the anointed prince (Star) and the anointed priest (Levi).

42. See below, 121.

43. O. Bauernfeind, *Die Dämonenworte im Markusevangelium*, Stuttgart 1927, presents useful parallel material, but he was unduly influenced by the urge to conform the miracle stories to the Hellenistic tradition.

44. As was supposed by W. Wrede in *The Messianic Secret*.

45. See my 'Terminology of Mark's Exorcism Stories', 232–46. O. Bauernfeind, *Dämonenworte*, 6.

46. Less convincing is the alleged parallel with Philo, *On the Immutability of God* (138).

47. See discussion of aretalogy and θεῖος ἀνήρ, above, 17ff.

48. Noted by E. Schweizer in the Festschrift for J. Jeremias, *Judentum, Urchristentum, Kirche*, ed. W. Eltester, Berlin 1960, 90–2. Schweizer's theory about Ναζαρηνός as a variant for Ναζιραῖος is untenable, and the anarthrous form of both nouns functions more like an adjectival phrase, 'sanctified by God' than a title in Mark 1.24. The address to God as 'the Holy One' in Isa. 40.25 and 57.15 is of no interpretative help here. The only other individual spoken of as ἅγιος in Mark is John the Baptist (6.20).

49. In addition to the article by R. E. Brown (n. 34 above), the analogies between the miracle-working activity of Jesus and Elisha have been discussed by Barnabas Lindars, 'Elijah, Elisha and the Gospel Miracles', in *Miracles*, ed. C. F. D. Moule, London 1965. Brown proposes that in the older tradition John the Baptist = Elijah, and Jesus = Elisha, who receives a double portion of the Spirit (II Kings 2.9–12). His warning about drawing theological inferences from miracle cycles is salutary.

50. The best mss that include υἱὸς θεοῦ offer it anarthrously, just as it appears in the testimony of the centurion at Mark 15.39.

51. LXX at Ps. 2.7 reads Υἱός μου εἶ σύ.

52. The second half of Ps. 2.7 is quoted in the 'Western' text of Mark 1.11; some commentators argue for it as the original reading (for example, J. Weiss, *History of Primitive Christianity*, London and New York 1937, 133).

53. So Dupont-Sommer, *Essene Writings*, 108 n. 1.

54. On the Servant as individual and community representative, see the critical survey of the literature and the judicious conclusions of C. R. North, *The Suffering Servant in Deutero-Isaiah*, Oxford 1963: 'we ought not to confine ourselves to "either-or" categories' (215) – i.e., either individuals or corporate figure, either the prophet or his circle, either historical or eschatological.

55. See above, 118.

56. Bauernfeind, *Dämonenworte*, 21–3.

57. Bauernfeind, *Dämonenworte*, 6.

58. That the heavenly host is silenced by God is in keeping with the injunctions to silence in Mark.

59. Test. Simeon 6.6; Test. Levi. 18.11f. (also 3.3 in arm. text); Test. Issachar 7.7; Test. Dan 5.6; 6.1–4; Test. Naphtali 8.4; Test. Asher 7.3; Test. Benj. 3.3.

60. R. H. Fuller, *Foundations*, 33f.

61. As in Frag D of the DSS Isaiah Commentary; cf. Isa. 11.1, where 'shoot' and 'branch' are combined.

62. As in 4Q Florilegium 1.10–14. Cf. Zech. 3.8; Ps. 132.17; Isa. 4.2; Jer. 23.5; 33.15.

63. B. Lindars, *NT Apologetic*, London 1961, 169–75. See fuller discussion in Taylor, *Commentary*, 456f.

64. Lindars, *Apologetic*, 169.

65. S. Mowinckel uses this phrase as an inclusive term for messianic-eschatological expectations in Judaism in *He That Cometh*, Oxford and Nashville 1956.

66. See above, 46f.

67. It is possible, but unlikely, that Mark means that God (= Lord) has a purpose in fulfilment of which this ass is essential.

68. Probably no single theme in synoptic studies has received more attention in recent decades than that of the Son of Man. The basic classification of the Son of Man sayings in the synoptic tradition was developed by Bultmann (in *The History of the Synoptic Tradition*): 1. the present Son of Man words, which rest on a misunderstanding of the Aramaic (15, 152 n.1); 2. the suffering Son of Man words, which are 'secondary constructions of the church' (152, 331); 3. the coming Son of Man words, in which Jesus refers to someone other than himself (122). On the mythological background, F. W. Borsch, *Son of Man in Myth and History*, London and Philadelphia 1967; Borsch has made a strong case for the pervasive, variegated and enduring presence in Judaism of the concept of primordial man. Entering the Jewish tradition under the influence of the widespread ancient Near Eastern view of the king and his enthronement as divine son and agent, the concept affects the liturgy of ancient Israel (Ps. 2; 110), the speculation about Adam, Moses, Melchizedek, Enoch, and surfaces in Jewish apocalypticism, especially in Daniel, Test. Levi, and IV Ezra. Similarly, S. Mowinckel, *He that Cometh*, 21–96. From a somewhat different perspective, R. G. Hamerton-Kelly, *Pre-existence, Wisdom, and the Son of Man*. Cambridge 1973, esp. 15–102. Among the most useful surveys of the Son of Man discussion are those of H. E. Tödt, *Son of Man in the Synoptic Tradition*, London and Philadelphia, 1965, and A. J. B. Higgins, 'Is the Son of Man Problem Insoluble?' in *Neotestamentica et Semitica*, ed. E. E. Ellis and M. Wilcox, Edinburgh 1969. Both come to the conclusion that the future Son of Man words are primary and authentic.

69. The sixth vision.

70. For example, in N. Perrin, *Rediscovering*, 170, although Perrin acknowledges that I Enoch and IV Ezra have a common base in Dan. 7 (1965).

71. As N. Perrin has noted, *Rediscovering*, 170.

72. For example, R. H. Fuller, *Foundations*, 34ff.

73. H. E. Tödt, *Son of Man*, while noting that there are superficial differences among the portraits of the Son of Man in Similitudes of Enoch, Dan. 7, IV Ezra, sees in them all the transfer of the sovereignty of the Most High to the Son of Man, which results in the exaltation of a transcendent Perfecter to a place above all earthly sufferings (23–31). That the apocalypse remains within Judaism and is not of Christian origin is evident in 14.44–48, where the basic scriptures number 24 and consist entirely of the Hebrew canon.

74. The basic myth is epitomized by Borsch, *Son of Man*, 92–96.

75. Developed by S. Mowinckel, *He that Cometh*, 59–75.

76. Mowinckel, *He that Cometh*, 32–51.

77. C. Colpe, art. υἰὸς τοῦ ἀνθρώπου, *TDNT* VIII, 400–77.

78. On the influence of the Primal Man concept on the enthronement ritual and the prophetic tradition, see Baruch 108–11. The cultic influence is evident in Pss. 2; 89; 110.

79. Borsch, *Son of Man*, 113–15. Note especially the quotation from E. Herzfeld, *Zoroaster and His World* II, Princeton 1947, 840: 'Grant of sovereignty to the Son of Man means his investiture as heir to the throne.'

80. Borsch, *Son of Man*, 117–21. There is probably a geographical link to this prophecy in the founding of the Essene community at the site known as Qumran, which is beside a wadi that receives the run-off from the Jerusalem area. See W. R. Farmer, 'Ezekiel's River of Life', *BA* XIX, 1956, 17–22.

81. Borsch, *Son of Man*, 143.

82. Ibid.

83. In *IB* VI, 'Daniel', 387. Noted by Borsch, *Son of Man*, 143.

84. T. W. Manson, in *The Teachings of Jesus*, London 1951, 24–36, argued that Son of Man was originally a corporate figure for the elect community, which Jesus came to see as embodied in his own person and expanding through his followers to include ever larger numbers. His position has not been widely accepted, but see now John Collins, 'The Son of Man and the Saints of the Most High', *JBL* 93, 1974, 50–66, who regards Michael as Son of Man, leader of the angelic hosts as well as of the righteous from on earth (56f.). Like the cosmic battles of Canaanite and other literatures, the apocalyptic battle takes place on two levels. This is evident in IQM 17.6–8, and in the Similitudes of Enoch (40.9). In IQM 17.7 (cf. Ps. 82.10f.), a similar role is assigned to Melchizedek. And in Rev. 12, the defeat of the angelic hosts by Michael leads to the awarding of the kingdom to Christ. Thus Collins regards 'one like the Son of Man' in Dan. 7 as symbolizing both the angelic host (together with its leader) and the faithful Jews who are associated with the heavenly host in the eschatological era (66). Whatever may have been the origins and development of this imagery and terminology, there can be no mistaking that for Mark Jesus is the once-suffering, soon-to-be-triumphant Son of Man who will deliver his own community from oppression, if they remain faithful in the midst of trials.

85. Wrede, *The Messianic Secret*, 67f.

86. See my study of 'Satan, Magic and Salvation in the Testament of Job', in *SBL Seminar Papers I*, 1974, Missoula, Mont., 53–76.

87. See on this 'The Function of Scriptural Quotations and Allusions in Mark 11–16', in *Jesus und Paulus*, Festschrift for W. G. Kümmel, ed. E. Grässer and E. E. Ellis, Göttingen 1975, 165–88.

88. For a detailed analysis of Mark 13.24–27 see J. Lamprecht, *Die Redaktion der Markus-Apokalypse*, Rome 1967 (Analecta Biblica 28), 173–93. Lamprecht shows that the literary structure in Mark 13 involves duplication: 13.4–6 and 21–23 parallels 13.24–26. He summarized the evidence, which points to Mark as the author of this chapter, including the presence in this passage of such Markan characteristics as his dependence on LXX, typical vocabulary and stylistic features (especially in 8.38–9.1 and 14.62), and the familiar linking terms.

89. Bultmann, *History*, 152, remarks that Mark 8.38 could have come from Jesus, but he then goes on to note that in this saying Jesus seemingly makes a distinction between himself and the coming Son of Man, who will confirm men's

response to him, i.e., to Jesus. H. E. Tödt thinks that the coming Son of Man words include at least one genuine word of Jesus: Mark 8.38 (*Son of Man*, 40), even though in its present form he regards it as having been reworked in the tradition. P. Vielhauer ('Gottesreich und Menschensohn', *Festschrift for G. Dehn*, Neukirchen 1957, 329–45), followed by N. Perrin, considers all the future Son of Man words to be the creation of the church, but as K. Koch has accurately observed, the motivation behind this radical handling of the Son of Man tradition is to preserve Jesus from apocalypticism (*Rediscovery of Apocalyptic*, SBT II 22, London and Naperville, Ill. 1971). Tödt concludes, against Vielhauer, that Son of Man and kingdom of God are integrally related in the Jesus tradition (*Son of Man*, 329–45). Even scholars such as E. Käsemann, who rightly recognizes the central importance of apocalypticism for primitive Christianity, try to tone down that dimension of Jesus' message, preferring rather to stress the 'nearness of the Kingdom' (*New Testament Questions*, 122–4). These unacknowledged prejudices are mentioned here because they affect the outcome of analysis of the gospel tradition, although ˙n the present work our concern is for what Mark has done with the tradition rather than with the extent to which it may be traced back to Jesus.

90. In *On Language, Culture and Religion: Essays in Honor of Eugene A. Nida*, ed. Matthew Black, The Hague 1974, 133–47.

91. Examples are Job 6.20, where the travellers look in vain for water in the desert, or Joel 1.10–12, where wine and vine fail; or Prov. 10.5; 14.35; 17.2; 19.26, where the issue is whether life will be fruitless or productive and rewarding.

92. Here characteristic texts include Pss. 25.3; 71.4; 119.116. Especially clear is Ps. 35.23f., where vindication in the face of opponents is the psalmist's expectation.

93. Jer. 1.17; 17.18; 46.24; 48.1, 20; 50.2f.; Isa. 41.10. At Qumran, IQM 15.8.

94. As we shall note below, the prophetic teaching carried on in the name of Jesus has its own authority and is uttered in its own distinctive forms.

95. E. Haenchen, *Der Weg Jesu*, 511 n.4, properly rejects the notion that this phrase is a 'theophany formula' to be understood in connection with Ex. 3.14. It is actually both a way of accepting the designation, Messiah, and a definition of that appelation.

96. Thus C. Colpe, *TDNT* VIII, 435, 453.

97. H. E. Tödt, *Son of Man*, 39; also E. Haenchen, *Weg*, 515f.

98. C. Colpe, *TDNT* VIII, 419f. Even if it could be proved that the Similitudes of Enoch are post-Christian, as E. Longenecker argues in *The Christology of Early Jewish Christianity*, SBT II, 17, London and Naperville, Ill. 1970, 82–5 – based largely on G. Vermes' appendix to M. Black, *An Aramaic Approach to the Gospels and Acts*, Oxford 1967, 310–28 – the very fact that the term is employed as a title in IV Ezra, where there is no evidence of Christian doctrinal influence and the term is used for a Jewish nationalistic leader, shows that the title was extant and in use in the first century of our era, and that it lent itself to a range of uses and interpretations. Jonas Greenfield sides with E. Sjöberg in *Der Menschensohn im äthiopischen Henochbuch*, Lund 1946, in concluding that there is no Christian element in the Similitudes of Enoch. He finds two historical references: the Parthian invasion in 40 BC (57.5–7) and Herod's unsuccessful attempt at achieving a cure in 4 BC (67.7–9), so that the work could have gained its present form by the turn of the eras. Greenfield draws attention to evidence of kinship with the earlier Enoch literature, as well as with Qumran documents (e.g., Lord of Spirits; cf. IQH 10.8), and suggests that the Similitudes are very close to the Merkebah tradition, as well (in

Prolegomenon to the reprint of H. Odeberg, *3 Enoch, or the Hebrew Book of Enoch*. New York, 1973, xviif.). M. Hengel dates the Similitudes to the first century BC on the basis of the allusion to the Parthian invasion (in *Judaism and Hellenism* II, 117 n.460).

99. For other texts, see below, 137f.

100. Classic statements of this position in Rudolf Otto, *Kingdom of God and Son of Man*, London 1938, 244–61; O. Cullmann, *Christology of the New Testament*, London and Philadelphia 1959, 51–82; R. H. Fuller, *Mission and Achievement of Jesus*, SBT 12, London and Naperville, Ill. 1954, 86–95; Fuller has subsequently abandoned this position: *Foundations of New Testament Christology*, London and New York 1965, 115, 135 n.43.

101. Colpe thinks that the argument from scripture was not part of the earliest passion predictions (*TDNT* VIII, 444), but that it has been inserted in the process of the development of the suffering Son of Man sayings in 10.45 (448, also n.343).

102. H. E. Tödt, *Son of Man*, 205–11.

103. J. Jeremias, *Servant of God*, SBT 20, London and Naperville, Ill. 1957, 90 (= *TDNT* V, 654–717).

104. F. H. Borsch, *Son of Man*, 94f., 122f. Ps. 118, which Borsch adduces as evidence, does not use Man or Son of Man, and while it describes the speaker (a king?) as in distress (118.5), it explicitly excludes his death (118.18) and therefore cannot be employed as support for the concept of the atoning death of the Son of Man.

105. C. Colpe has conveniently summarized the range of triumphant achievements of the Son of Man in the Similitudes of Enoch (*TDNT* VIII, 424f.).

106. R. Longenecker, *Christology*, 87, and bibliography in Ps. 110. Perhaps passages other than Ps. 22, which is quoted in Mark 15.34, and Zech. 13.7 (= Mark 14.27) were of indirect help in shaping this view; among these oblique influences may have been Isa. 53 and Zech. 12.10ff., with its moving portrait of the rejected, pierced agent of God.

107. C. Colpe, *TDNT* VIII, 444.

108. Noted by Lohmeyer, *Commentary*, 161; affirmed by Tödt, *Son of Man*, 145. But perhaps more important for Mark is his having positioned in conjunction with each of these predictions an account of the disciples' inability to penetrate the mystery of suffering and a miracle of restoration of sight to the blind. See above, 34.

109. As Colpe seems to imply, *TDNT* VIII, 444.

110. As Borsch asserts, *Son of Man*, 333 n.2, 337, largely on the basis that baptism as performed among the Jewish baptizing sects (with which Jesus was earlier affiliated) was understood as a water rite in continuity with the humiliation/exaltation pattern derived from the ritual of divine kingship in the ancient Near East (218f.).

111. So Bultmann, *History*, 29, 152, where he states that בר נשא (which really means simply 'man') has wrongly been translated as ὁ υἱὸς τοῦ ἀνθρώπου.

112. G. Vermes, in Appendix E to M. Black's *Aramaic Approach*[3], 310–28, claims that בר נשא was used by the rabbis 1. to mean 'a man' or 'man' generically; 2. as a circumlocution for 'I' to avoid undue or immodest emphasis on the speaker; and 3. that the term lacked messianic import. C. Colpe, *TDNT* VIII, while acknowledging that the Aramaic phrase can mean 'the man' generically in the sense of 'someone', asserts that it can also mean 'the Man' messianically, but he denies that it is used as a substitute for 'I'. The colloquial locution for 'I', according to Colpe, was 'that man' (גברא ההוא), although בר נשא could be used to refer to men

in general, including the speaker, as in the impersonal English 'one'. The term would not automatically be a title, but 'undoubtedly became normative for 'the Man" in the messianic sense' (401–5).

113. Correctly, Bultmann, *History*, 17.

114. See above, 119.

115. E. Haenchen, *Weg*, 149.

116. On the background and connotations of βλασφημία see Taylor, *Commentary*, 242f.

117. The Spirit as God's agent is familiar in apocalyptic literature: Sim. Enoch 49.3; Test. Levi 18.7; Test. Judah 24.2.

118. Käsemann, *New Testament Questions of Today*, 66–81.

119. See n. 90 above.

120. Closely related in both form and content are other sayings where ἄν and the subjunctive are missing (as in 9.39), or where a form of τις replaces ὃς ἄν (as in 9.1), or where εἰ + indicative are in the protasis and the future indicative is in the apodosis (as in 8.34).

121. See above, 91. Crucial here is the use of κωλύετε in 10.14.

122. For the relationship of Mark's view of divorce to those views prevailing in the two major wings of first-century Judaism, see Taylor, *Commentary*, ad loc.

123. Cf. Matt. 10.32–33/Luke 12.8f. (from Q), where the technical terms ὁμολογέω / ἀρνέομαι represent the language and outlook of a different segment of early Christianity – one that is more consciously ecclesiastical – from Mark, and where the distinctive Matthean language is employed (τοῦ πατρός μου ἐν τοῖς οὐρανοῖς).

124. The reading of ℵ, D, etc. (ἔσται) is to be preferred here, and it emphasizes the eschatological nature of the judgment. The present tense is readily accounted for as an accommodation at a time and in a situation where eschatological judgment has been replaced by ecclesiastical decisions, such as excommunication.

125. E.g. Tacitus, *Annals*, 15, 44.

126. E. Käsemann, 'Sentences', 90ff.

CHAPTER VI

1. See ch. V, n. 89. Perrin's adoption of Vielhauer's radical view of the inauthenticity of the future Son of Man words rests on curiously contradictory grounds (*Rediscovering*, 196–8): the main criterion for determining the authenticity of tradition attributed to Jesus is that it is dissimilar from the thought of Judaism of the Second Temple period and from that of the early church (39). But the major argument against Jesus' having referred to himself or anyone else as the coming Son of Man is that 'no such concept of a coming Son of Man existed (sc., in pre-Christian Judaism) to be referred to in this way' (197f.). As indicated above, 129ff. our own reading of the evidence concerning the image of the (Son of) Man in Judaism during the period from the Maccabees to Bar-Kochba is rather different from that of Vielhauer and Perrin. H. D. Betz, 'The Concept of Apocalyptic in the Pannenberg Group', *JTC* 6, New York 1969, 201; and R. W. Funk, 'Apocalyptic as an Historical and Theological Problem' in the same publication.

K. Koch, *Rediscovery of Apocalyptic* (67–9) – bearing in German the telling title *Ratlos vor der Apokalyptik* – shows that existentialist exegesis is reductionist as a way of avoiding problematical aspects of apocalyptic views and thus turns attention inward to the moment of truth. Perrin manifests that outlook when he asserts that the words attributed to Jesus concerning the future are to be regarded, not as 'temporal', but as 'experiential' (205). In this way the criterion of discontinuity has been employed as a means of reinforcing existentialist interpretation of both Jesus and the gospel tradition (Koch, 64). The dismissal of the so-called objectifying myth of apocalypticism as being not traceable to Jesus and the concomitant assignment of the inwardness of the kingdom to Jesus sounds remarkably like the older liberal Protestant solution of convenience advanced by Harnack and others: 'the kingdom of God is within you'.

2. W. G. Kümmel, *Promise and Fulfillment*, SBT 23, London and Naperville, Ill. 1957, 19–48.

3. Funk, 'Apocalyptic as Problem', 187.

4. N. A. Dahl argues persuasively that this is based on historical fact, in *The Crucified Messiah*, Minneapolis 1974, 23f.

5. Taylor, *Commentary*, 190, takes αὐτοῖς as a dative of advantage, thereby denying that any hostility is involved. E. Haenchen, *Weg*, 95, considers the instruction to go to the priest to be merely official confirmation that a healing has occurred. But the phrase εἰς μαρτύριον αὐτοῖς does indeed imply some kind of challenge or controversy: the identical phrase is used as an invocation of judgment on unbelief among the unresponsive villages in 6.11.

6. See above, 35ff.

7. Bultmann, *History*, 25, 47f., 56, shows the composite nature of this passage in 2.13–17. The awkward syntax confirms this judgment.

8. Bultmann, *History*, 12.

9. See above, 100.

10. Note the parenthetic nature of 7.3f., the typical Markan connective locutions in 7.9, 14, 18, the private explanations offered to the inner circle (7.17), the syntactical and logical break at 7.19.

11. At the very least, the procedure and interpretations are non-Palestinian in origin, as even so conservative a scholar as V. Taylor acknowledges (*Commentary*, 338f., the 'Detached Note on Ritual Cleansing'); he sides with the judgment of Montefiore that this story may be of non-Palestinian provenance.

12. Gentile territory is the setting for the story of Syro-Phoenician woman (7.24–30), the healing of the deaf and dumb man (7.31–37), and the Feeding of Four Thousand (8.1–10), since only at 8.11 does Jesus once more encounter Jews.

13. See above, 100.

14. IQS 2.19; 5.14–23; 8.1.

15. IQM 2.1–7; 6.1–7.3.

16. The maintenance of the number twelve as the circle of disciples, following the defection and death of Judas, plays no role in Mark as it does in Acts 1; thus the twelveness is significant only in a general way as pointing to the true Israel – a point which is made explicit in the Q tradition (Luke 22.30/Matt.19.28).

17. Thus J. Jeremias, 'Paarweise Sendung im NT', in *New Testament Essays*, Festschrift for T. W. Manson, ed. A. J. B. Higgins, Manchester 1959, 136–8.

18. Bultmann, *History*, 21f.

19. For a judicious assessment of attempts to ease the hyperbolic force of this image, see Taylor, *Commentary*, 431.

20. The rabbinic evidence on this is assembled in Strack-Billerbeck, *Kommentar* I, 312–20. Lohmeyer rightly notes that this passage in Mark is a controversy story

in which Jesus appears in a formal role as interpreter of Torah, carried out in conversation with colleagues (*Commentary*, 198f.).

21. As noted by Taylor, *Commentary*, 420, the Aramaic papyri from Elephantine show that as early as the fifth century BC the Jewish community there had already a freer view of divorce than was later to obtain among the rabbis.

22. Καὶ εἰς τὴν οἰκίαν πάλιν οἱ μαθηταὶ περὶ τούτου ἐπηρώτων αὐτόν. Καὶ λέγει αὐτοῖς ... David Daube (*Expository Times* 57, 1945/6, 175–7) notes certain similarities between Mark and the rabbinic tradition in that in each case the teacher gives a public explanation of a teaching, usually in response to a question, which is then followed by a private explanation to his disciples. He offers as an example an incident in which Johanan ben Zakkai discloses to his disciples a secret about the efficacy of a certain root that is used in exorcisms. But apart from the fact that Jesus does not reveal any thaumaturgical techniques to his followers in the Markan stories, Daube's note fails to account for the stylized connective material depicting these private disclosures, using language and style that are typically Markan, as the omission or modifications by Matthew and Luke attests.

23. A frequent theme in apocryphal and apocalyptic literature, however, is the notion derived from Gen. 6 that angels consorted with human females. Cf. Jub. 5.1ff; I Enoch 6.1ff.; 10.12.

24. Dan. 12.2f. is a late, notable exception.

25. Haenchen, *Weg*, 410f.

26. See especially IQS 6.24–7.25.

27. On rabbinic parallels, see Lane, *Commentary*, 431–3.

28. The *Shema* and the command to love God linked directly in Deut. 6.4–9 are offered in that setting as a kind of comment on the commandments proper, which have just been set forth in Deut. 5.7–21. But the love command is of a wholly different order from the laws proper, whether of the casuistic or apodictic type, since it rests on an existential ground (love) and appeals to the will (heart) rather than merely enjoining obedience, whether by direct decree or on threat of the consequences of disobedience. A law like the love command serves as an exhortation and an appealing reminder of obligation to another person rather than as a regulation demanding conformity.

29. Curiously, in agreement against Mark, Matthew and Luke omit the *shema*. In this, the combination of affirmation and obligation that is so powerful in Mark and so characteristic of his approach to ethics, is lost.

30. Cf. the profound discussion of this in the classic work of Martin Buber, *I and Thou*, Edinburgh 1937.

31. W. Kelber, *Kingdom*, 140, esp. n.31, develops the thesis that the inconclusive ending is intended to point towards the eschatological future.

32. ℵ and B omit νηστεία; P45, ℵ b, A, C, D, W, Θ, 33 and most of the versions include it, either following or preceding προσευχή.

33. καὶ ἔλεγεν αὐτοῖς (twice).

34. For the translation of the text, see H. C. Kee, *The Origins of Christianity: Sources and Documents*, Englewood Cliffs, N. J. 1973, 259 and note.

35. Comparison with Matt. 17.20/Luke 17.6 shows that here once more we have a Q form of a tradition found also in Mark – a genuine parable tradition, rather than the Markan use of Q.

36. Bryan R. Wilson, *Magic and Millennium: A Sociological Study of Religious Movements of Protest Among Tribal and Third-World Peoples*, London and New York 1973.

37. B. R. Wilson, *Millennium*, 19.

38. B. R. Wilson, *Millennium*, 20.

39. B. R. Wilson, *Millennium*, 21.

40. That is not to say that λόγος always means 'gospel'; non-technical uses of the term are to be found in 5.36; 7.29; 11.29; 12.13; 14.39. In 7.13 λόγος = scripture.

41. Including 9.10 and 9.32 (where τὸ ῥῆμα is used).

42. See above, 142f.

43. See above, 101ff, and ch. V, n. 92.

44. It is noteworthy, however, that in more than half of the Markan occurrences of ἀμήν Matthew and/or Luke have omitted the term, or have replaced it by ἀληθῶς, as in Luke 21.3. This tends to confirm our proposal (101) that Mark is writing to a Greek-speaking area with a strong Semitic cultural-linguistic background lingering on.

45. See above, 91.

46. By contrast, καλεῖν is used of calling the disciples only twice in Mark (1.20 and 2.17).

47. Although 8.34 has εἰ with the indicative rather than ὃς ἄν with the subjunctive, it reads like an eschatological pronouncement as well.

48. Thus Lane, *Commentary*, 156. Taylor, *Commentary*, 255, simply distinguishes between the disciples 'around him' and 'the Twelve', with an indication of the relative size of the two groups.

49. In 6.45 Jesus tells the disciples to precede him to the other side; the only plausible meaning for προάγειν in this case is to arrive before someone else. The same meaning is appropriate when the term appears in the account of the journey to Jerusalem (10.32), and the entrance into the city (11.9), as is confirmed in each case by the contrast in the narratives, 'go before' . . . 'follow after'. The effort to assign the significance 'head a procession' is unwarranted and unconvincing; rather, it announces that Jesus will arrive there before they do, as is asserted from different standpoints by both Lohmeyer, *Commentary*, 355, and Taylor, *Commentary*, 608. On 16.7 see below, 174.

50. The secrecy surrounding the raising of Jairus' daughter (5.43) is a direct parallel to the secrecy concerning the resurrection linked by Mark with the Transfiguration story (9.9). The former narrative prefigures the resurrection; the latter provides a proleptic vision of God's vindication and exaltation of Jesus. Both are to be kept secret until the appropriate time of disclosure.

51. The expression τὰς συναγώγας αὐτῶν may embody a contrast (noted above, 88) between the Jewish synagogue *(αὐτῶν)* and the Christian congregations in the Markan wing of primitive Christianity. These would have developed in Syria as local assemblies on the Jewish model, both with their own distinctive, evangelistics didactic, and liturgical practices.

52. Acts 13.14; 14.1; 17.1 *(κατὰ τὸ εἰωθὸς τῷ Παύλῳ)*; 18.4.

53. Wrede, *Secret*.

54. Wrede, *Secret*, 1.

55. Wrede, *Secret*, 49, 130f.

56. Wrede, *Secret*, 80.

57. Wrede, *Secret*, 47f.

58. Wrede, *Secret*, 45.

59. Wrede, *Secret*, 49.

60. Wrede, *Secret*, 130–31.

61. Wrede, *Secret*, 37–38.

62. Thus J. C. S. Reid in his introduction to Wrede, *Secret*, xxi.

63. H. J. Ebeling, *Das Messiasgeheimnis und die Botschaft des Markusevangeliums*, Berlin 1939.

64. Ebeling, *Messiasgeheimnis*, 109–111, 113, 200, 221, where he indicates his agreement with Kähler's regrettable, offhand dictum that the gospel is a passion narrative.

65. Ebeling, *Messiasgeheimnis*, 102.

66. Ebeling, *Messiasgeheimnis*, 100.

67. In 4.39 ἄνεμος is equivalent to πνεῦμα which can, of course, in Greek – or Hebrew – mean 'wind' or 'spirit'.

68. See above, 126f.

69. Num. 27.17; II Chron. 18.16; Ezek. 34.1–10; Isa. 40.11; Zech. 10.2.

70. This Markan theme is the closest Mark comes to manifesting the negative attitude towards miracles attributed to him by T. Weeden in *Mark: Traditions in Conflict*.

71. There is no hint of an absolute prohibition against the disciples' speaking of Jesus; rather, the verse implies that they are to be silent on the matter under discussion: Jesus as Messiah.

72. In contrast, to interpretations which regard Σὺ λέγεις as a non-committal statement ('That is what you say'), the absence of any denial can be regarded as implying 'What you are saying is true'. See on this, N. A. Dahl, *The Crucified Messiah*, Minneapolis 1974, 33 and n. 30.

73. See above, 134ff.

AFTERWORD

1. Hirsch, *Validity*, 222f.

INDEX OF BIBLICAL REFERENCES

OLD TESTAMENT

THE BOOKS OF THE APOCRYPHA

PSEUDEPIGRAPHA

DEAD SEA SCROLLS

NEW TESTAMENT

INDEX OF MODERN AUTHORS